Contents

Acknowledgements

There are many people who have helped, directly or indirectly, in the making of this book. I would like to thank Professor Neville Bennett, Clive Carre and Elisabeth Dunne from the Leverhulme Primary Project for their stimulation and support on the project and in my own research. In particular I owe Neville a great deal, for introducing me to the ideas of Shulman and giving me a research training second to none. It is thanks to Neville that I encountered some of the key ideas in this book and I am immensely grateful. Thanks go to the University of Exeter and the University of Hertfordshire for the small grants which have enabled me to continue my research. Dr Jon Nichol is a long-standing colleague and friend whose advice and criticism I value highly. Both Professor Robin Campbell and Rose Drury have commented on drafts of part of this book, and I greatly appreciated their advice. I would also like to thank Mary Macmullen for her high quality work as a research assistant, and Loraine Adams for much-needed practical support in the final stages. I would also like to thank the teachers who have welcomed me into their classrooms to observe, teach and experiment, and the many teachers who have contributed in some way to this book. Finally special thanks go to my daughters, Eleanor and Harriet, who have kept me writing.

Preface

This book has had a long slow genesis. Several different research projects have contributed to it over a period of about ten years; prior to that there were my own experiences of teaching, which have shaped my perceptions and interpretations. Doubtless there will be critics of this conception of teaching, but the notion of teaching as a knowledge-based profession has much to offer, not least as an antidote to the teaching as competence movement.

One feels nervous about presenting a book called *Expert Teaching*. It seems to be inviting criticism: that this is only one way of thinking about teaching, and not necessarily the best way. The book is also focused on the primary phase of education, rather than across all phases of education. The reasons for this are twofold. Firstly, to discuss all phases of education would have required several books. Secondly, the primary phase is a very specialised context for education, with its own history and peculiarities, such as the class teacher system. To be an expert teacher in the primary phase is not like being one in the secondary phase, for one has to teach many different subjects. Therefore the title is 'Expert Teaching' rather than 'Expert Teachers'. This reflects the difficulty of achieving expert teaching across all the subjects of the primary curriculum.

So, the book is both practical and theoretical. Thus readers will find plenty of theory, but this is related to practical examples which offer material for analysis and reflection on teaching. The case studies and brief examples are generally included to illustrate one particular knowledge base; however, they can be analysed for evidence of others. They are presented as stories, for stories are one way of making sense of experience: a profoundly human way. They can be read many times, and interpreted in different ways. It is for the reader to sample my interpretations and to make his or her own.

Thus, the book can be read in several different ways. One can of course, start at the beginning and work through to the end. Alternatively, it can be dipped into for particular teaching knowledge bases and illustrative material. Some of the case studies are revisited: the reader is recommended to do the same, to analyse the ones found most interesting or valuable, as a basis for reflection on one's own teaching. It is not a handbook or a 'how to' book: instead it offers material which is meant to spark reflection and which helps readers to take a pace back from their own teaching and look at it afresh.

Writing a book, like teaching, involves a huge investment of the self. Implicit in the book are my own passions and perceptions. I have tried to keep these in order, as it were, but inevitably readers will find some evidence of them. I hope you find much to enjoy, much to which you can relate, and much to inform your teaching.

Rosie Turner-Bisset
University of Hertfordshire
May 2001

Prologue

In the week following the Dunblane tragedy, I drove to a city in the south-west of England to visit a primary school and observe a teacher for a research project. The school was on a large council estate in a very deprived part of the city. It had electronically-controlled doors, a voice-entry system and visitors' passes. Such heavy security is now common-place, in the wake of that tragedy, but I was surprised, and realised that vandalism and theft must be rife in that area. I wondered, as I pressed the bell how it would be to teach there, and what the lesson I had come to observe would be like. I was privileged to watch one of the best and most exciting lessons I have ever seen or taught.

David taught a Year 4 class of 28 children. Many of the children had reading difficulties, and there were two classroom assistants working full time with the class on reading. As I entered the room, two children arrived carrying an overhead projector (OHP). All the children had their coats on, normally against school rules, but David explained that he would be taking them out into the playground later, and had given them permission. This change in routine, and my arrival caused some excitement. There was more bustle as a child brought in cartons of milk. While the children drank their milk, David placed an overhead transparency of a Roman galley on the projector. The children's attention was immediately focused on the image on the classroom wall, and there was a buzz of interest, followed by quiet.

In the lull, David reminded the children about classroom routines, such as putting hands up to answer questions. He introduced me briskly and moved on the lesson with the minimum of fuss. He started by asking two questions: 'What have Romans to do with Celts? What did Julius Caesar decide to do?' The children were still looking at the picture. David moved into role as a storyteller. He told the children it was 55 BC, and the picture was a clue. It was a picture of a Roman galley, a trireme, and the ship had one purpose only. One child put up his hand and exclaimed: 'A warship!' David explained concisely why they had coats on, linking it into the theme of the lesson: 'Later on we are going to draw the ship in the playground.' He asked the children what they thought the plank on the front of the ship would do. Another child suggested that it would be used to ram the opposing ship. David explained the idea of poles and ramming, acting out ramming with movement and gestures. There followed a question and answer session in which David asked questions about the picture and questions to make the children think, do simple sums, estimate measurements and apply existing knowledge. It seems impossible to do justice to this discourse without quoting some of it.

David: These ships were very fast. How is this ship powered? How does it move? These days ships have engines.
Child: Those things on the side.
Children: Oars!
David: It would take about two men to one oar. If you were bad, you'd work in the galley.
Children: Slave.
David: Yes, slaves. How many people rowing 24 oars?
Children: 48.
David: In that case. That's only one side. There'd be people just the same on the other side. How many altogether?
Children: 92.
David: No, more than that.
Children: 96.
David: Are all these going the same way?
Children: Yes.
David: They had to keep in time. What would happen if one side rowed faster?
Child: Go round to one side.
David: How would they row in time?
Child: Someone in charge to make them.
David: Could they escape from there?
Child: They'd be chained by the neck.
David: If the ship sank, who would die first?
Children: Slaves!
David: They had a way of keeping time.

At this point David got a large drum out of the cupboard and drummed a beat. The children's attention was immediately caught and held by the beat. David moved back into role as storyteller:

David: The slaves don't want to be there. There'd be two of us. I'd be drumming and one would be whipping.

He suddenly modelled a gesture of whipping with the drumstick which flew out of his hand and across the room. The children ducked. This was accidental. There was much laughter while a child retrieved the drumstick and returned it to David. Still almost in the mode of storyteller, through question and answer, he got the children to tell him how they would row on a calm day with a long way to go; then what they would do if they saw an enemy ship. The children showed that they understood the idea of varying the speed of rowing according to the circumstances. When he asked how they would row if he wanted them to ram the ship, they called out: 'Faster!' All the children were very involved with the imaginary scene. David beat faster and faster, then stopped.

He drew the outline of the ship on the board, telling them that the ships were designed to be long and fast. He asked them why the spike was long and thin. He reminded them about Julius Caesar setting sail from Gaul in 55 BC and asked them who was there on the shore. The children replied that the Celts were. He joked that they weren't taking notes! The children responded with ideas such as they were getting ready for battle, or making war sounds. He told them that they were going to make a noise: shout for one minute, and asked them what they would do if they saw the Romans coming. The children suggested shouting 'Help!' The whole class, with David then shouted: 'Help!' very loudly. There was much enjoyment. The children were smiling at each other and showing their engagement and excitement.

David pointed out that if one Roman left the ship with something, the rest would have had to follow him. A child suggested 'That pole thing,' obviously remembering the standard and its significance, if not the actual correct name. David explained about the standard and the idea of disgrace: how the soldiers would realise they would have to follow him. David then asked the children how long they thought the ship was, returning to earlier talk of measurement. In response to the question: 'How many metres,' one child offered five metres as an answer. David held up a metre stick and asked if it was longer than that. It was clear that he knew the children did not yet fully grasp the idea of the size of the ship, and he wanted to make it clearer before they went into the playground. There followed an episode of the lesson in which David, using well-behaved children as volunteers, measured out a one third section of the ship. He spaced 12 children down the side of the class, and measured the line using the metre rule. This was four metres. He asked them if that was one third, how long was the whole ship. The answer came back: 12 metres. He introduced another idea: that of each person needing a metre to row in comfort. The children worked out that 12 people would need 24 metres. He suggested that the measurement might be between these two, all the time using language like 'I think' or 'we think'. He said that he thought the length of one third of the ship would have been between 12 and 24 metres, perhaps about 20 metres. The next question was how wide was the ship. He used the diagram on the board to show there was a walkway in the centre, and suggested a walkway one metre wide with three metres on each side.

David told the children that they were going down to the playground to draw out the ship. He had to tell them two things. One was that Gaul was quite a warm country and that the Romans were shocked by the temperature. The second thing was that he didn't want anyone being silly. We all trooped down the stairs and out into the playground. One boy carried the drum and David gave it to a girl, Sadie, to beat during the role-play. The only other equipment was a large lump of chalk and several metre sticks. It was extremely cold. As we stood there, flakes of snow drifted down. This preparatory part of the lesson had taken 30 minutes in all.

David got the children to stand in a long line, reminded them about other classes working, and told them they would not be chosen if they were silly or moved out of the line. The children waited patiently. David drew out the length of the ship, which was about 65 metres, using the metre sticks as markers and the chalk for the outline. He made the ship seven metres wide and selected children to stand on chalk marks he had made on the outline. He placed them boy, girl, boy, girl, down each side, and drew the battering ram on the pointed bow end. Once all the children were in position, he asked them to all face the front, and look around them at the ship. He said seriously that it was freezing cold and they now knew how those Roman soldiers felt. The children were silent, gazing at the size of the ship, which stretched almost to the other end of the playground.

David then moved swifly into storyteller mode again. He said they were about to attack, and needed a fast beat. They had to row together. The children mimed rowing movements. David allocated the role of the man with the whip to Sean, who made whipping actions. Another girl he told to be Julius Caesar and had to shout: 'On to Britain!' Sadie continued to beat the drum. The story continued:

| David: | So we're approaching Britain. It's shallow water, so slow down and stop (the drummer slowed the beat as he spoke). Drift for a while. We can hear in front of us on the beaches a war-cry . . . (The children shouted loudly) . . . and now you're thinking: No way! Now, stop being slaves. Be soldiers now. Come together. (The children moved together on the imaginary walkway running the length of the boat.) |
| David: | Quiet! You're soldiers of Rome now, very disciplined. The slaves are now beneath you. You can hear the Celtic army and you are very afraid. You're waiting to fight. Robert is the standard bearer. He thinks if I go, they will go. Julius Caesar, tell him to go. |

The standard bearer jumped off the 'ship' into the 'water'. The children followed him and rushed to the 'beach'. They pretended to fight. The metre sticks had become swords in their imagination.

| David: | Back to the ship! Back to your oars! It's getting late now. Back for tea. Back to Gaul for a warm climate and some wine. Off you go, Sadie: a nice beat. |

The children returned to their places on the 'ship'. Sadie beat the drum slowly and steadily. After a few moments, David broke the spell and returned to the manager role. He asked a child to go round to the reception office and arrange for the side door to be electronically opened. David lined the children up and led them back in. The children were excited from the episode in the playground. One boy turned to me and said: 'Did you see, Miss? When we jumped in the water, I fell over and got wet! None of the others did though!'

On our return to the classroom, which was orderly despite the excitement, David put away the drum in the cupboard and rescued the lump of chalk from a child. He set them the task of writing a front-page of a newspaper about the invasion. He commented that they did not have newspapers in Roman time: it was just a bit of fun. He held up a prepared news-sheet to show them and suggested that they think of a good headline. His example of 'Crippled Celts!' was enjoyed by a child who countered with: 'Us Fighting Romans!' There was very little time left, but the children started on their headlines and pictures immediately, totally engaged with the writing task.

Comment

Why do I judge this to be such a good lesson? It was exciting, interesting, amusing, full of variety and well-paced. I was struck by the obvious respect in which these difficult children held their teacher. One or two quick reminders of class routines and norms of behaviour were all that were needed, in a lesson full of activity and movement, including traipsing down flights of stairs, out of and back into the building. From the beginning of the lesson there was an air of excitement and of purpose. It was clearly part of a sequence of lessons dealing with the Romans in Britain, and followed on from the previous lesson on the Celts. The lesson did not follow a standard format. He did not tell them where the lesson was going: instead, he put up the overhead transparency and attracted their interest. Once that was achieved, he questioned them about the picture; so that the children were thinking about: the boat; its purpose; how it was powered; how many oars and men were needed; and its size. In the question and answer session which generated this thinking, each question was short, simple and matched to the children's abilities. Measuring the section with 12 oars in the classroom, using children in a line to see how long one third of the ship would be, was very effective, as a visual representation of part of the ship.

The children's interest was sustained throughout. The lesson lasted an hour, during which the children were engaged in a variety of tasks: listening to the teacher storytelling; looking closely at the picture; thinking about the space needed to row; doing simple addition and multiplication, estimating the size of the ship; helping to 'draw' the outline of the boat by acting as physical markers; imagining themselves as Roman soldiers, slaves and Celts; participating in role-play of the invasion of Britain; helping with resources, and writing and drawing on the news-sheets. The depth of the children's engagement was demonstrated in the child's comment: of how he imagined he fell over in the water when he jumped overboard. For this child the role-play experience had been real. He had been there in the historical situation of the Roman soldiers jumping into shallow water to follow their standard. The invasion for him was not merely words on a page, but an imagined experience with its attendant physical discomforts. I had no direct oral evidence from the rest of the class, but their ideas for headlines and busy engagement with the writing task, indicated that their imaginations too had been engaged and they had plenty to write about. In any case, their immediate responses to David as play leader and storyteller in the playground, showed the total engagement with the historical situation.

Discussion

One of the ways in which we judge teaching, whether our own or that of others, is by the response of the children. We use our observations of the children to gauge the accuracy of the match of work to children's abilities, and the effectiveness of the teaching and organisational strategies employed. Other factors are also involved in judging teaching. Such judgements are always to an extent subjective, for they are coloured by the observer's own classroom experience, knowledge of teaching and learning, and subject knowledge. We all view classrooms, teachers and learners through our own lenses. Sets of criteria or lists of competences, can influence and help frame our judgements, but they are as much formed by our beliefs, values and attitudes, as by criteria alone. A further problem with competences, or standards as they are now termed, is that they describe merely a part of what it means to teach well or competently. Underpinning the act of teaching described above were a whole range of different kinds of knowledge, some in the particular domain of teachers and some which are shared by other professionals. In addition, the teacher's beliefs, attitudes and values played a part in that lesson, as they do in all lessons. To describe teaching, good or otherwise, in terms only of competences or skills, is to describe it inadequately, to deal merely with the observable, and to ignore the complexity of professional knowledge.

The purpose of this book is to grapple with that complexity: to map out the extent and nature of the knowledge bases needed for teaching, in relation to the skills or competences fundamental to the business of teaching. What can be observed about teaching can be likened to the tip of an iceberg. Under the surface of a seemingly effortless act of teaching is the other nine-tenths of the iceberg: a wealth of different kinds of knowledge on which the teacher has drawn for that particular teaching performance. In this book, I will describe and analyse each of these knowledge bases. The exposition of the knowledge bases will be illustrated by examples and case studies from beginning teachers and expert teachers. In each case it will be made clear: how the episode of planning, teaching or evaluation is underpinned by the knowledge bases; how in a novice performance these knowledge bases and skills are developing; and how in an expert performance, the knowledge bases mesh in different combinations to produce expert teaching.

The story of the lesson in this Prologue, 'Creating a Roman galley', has a number of functions in this book. It serves as an example of expert teaching. It sets the scene for what is to follow. It will be revisited several times during the course of this book, and analysed from the perspective of the different knowledge bases for teaching. It is the first of several case studies which offer examples of teaching and material for analysis and reflection. As mentioned earlier the case studies are from both beginning and experienced teachers. Critics of this approach might argue that only material from expert teachers should be presented in a book on expert teaching. This is understandable: however, I would argue that there is a great deal to be learnt from the struggles of beginning teachers. While much can be learnt from a case literature of excellent teaching, the study of those learning to teach can illuminate our understanding of the professional knowledge of teachers. Just as Piaget discovered that he could learn a great deal from systematic and careful observation of the very young, we can learn much from the mistakes, successes and refinements in practice made by beginning teachers. Shulman offers this argument for the study of beginning teachers:

Their development from students to teachers, from a state of expertise as learners through a novitiate as teachers exposes and highlights the complex bodies of knowledge and skill needed to function effectvely as a teacher.

(Shulman 1986b, p. 5)

Thus, in this book, there are case studies from both beginning and experienced teachers. There are several sources for case study material. The first source is a major three-year research project, the Leverhulme Primary Project, in particular the subject knowledge and teaching competence strand. The second project was funded by Exeter University: it investigated the impact of a 20-day subject knowledge course in history on the knowledge and classroom practice of primary teachers. Data was collected over two years: teachers were interviewed following the course and then observed and interviewed two years later to investigate the continuing influence of the course. The third source is a longitudinal study, funded by the University of Hertfordshire, of the beliefs and practice in teaching history of students on a four-year BEd course. Material presented here is from interviews at the end of the course. Two further sources were used. A sample of teachers identified by Hertfordshire Local Education Authority as expert teachers of maths were observed and interviewed. These teachers all worked regularly in other classrooms and schools, and gave demonstration lessons and in-service training as part of the LEA's training for the introduction of the National Numeracy Strategy. The final source for the case studies, was the author's own teaching in the process of curriculum development work in schools. If it seems immodest or hubristic to claim to be an expert teacher myself, I would counter this by arguing that anyone writing a book on expert teaching ought to be able to demonstrate that knowledge and expertise herself.

CHAPTER 1

What is expert teaching?

Introduction

The Prologue introduced the notion of 'expert teaching' and herein lies a problem. There is no agreement as yet as to what this might be. Several terms have been used to describe good or excellent teaching and teachers. There is 'good teaching' (Brown and McIntyre 1993); 'effective teaching' (Perrott 1982; Cullingford 1995; Cooper and McIntyre 1996; Kyriacou 1997); 'creative teaching' (Woods and Jeffrey 1996); 'veteran teachers' (Shulman 1987a); 'quality teaching' (Stones, 1992); and even 'good enough teachers' (Cullingford 1995). OFSTED use the term 'outstanding' in their criteria for both teachers and student-teachers in training, to denote the very highest levels of teaching performance. The most recent large-scale research into effective teaching, the *Hay McBer Report* (DfEE 2000), uses the terms: 'competent;' 'effective;' and 'outstanding' to describe different levels of quality in teaching. The problem with all these terms is twofold: such terms are sometimes used interchangeably, while logically there is reason to think that there might be differences between them; in addition, educators do not always agree as to how the very best teaching can be defined, or what criteria might be used to to describe it. This chapter is intended to do four things. It presents: a discussion of ways of conceptualising teaching; surveys some of the research into teaching of the last four decades; gives a brief overview of the kinds of knowledge considered necessary for teaching; and presents a new paradigm of teaching as a knowledge-based profession.

The paradigm problem

The problem of the mixture of terms to describe the best teaching perhaps lies with what Squires (1999) called 'the paradigm problem'. He argued that, following

Masterman (1972), there coexists a multiplicity of paradigms, which lay claim to being good ways of conceptualising teaching. These are: 'teaching as a common-sense activity; teaching as an art; teaching as a craft; teaching as an applied science; teaching as a system; teaching as reflective practice; and teaching as competence,' (Squires 1999, p. 3). These paradigms do not always manifest themselves in pure or discrete form, whether at the level of teachers' professional work, or at the level of national trends and policies. However, they can be detected in various writings about teaching, and indeed in some of the works on effective teaching.

A paradigm operates like a set of lenses or beliefs through which our perceptions of subjects, or of an activity such as teaching, are filtered. Thus if the guiding paradigm is that of teaching as a common-sense activity (Hargreaves 1993), good teaching is something of a pragmatic activity: accepting and working with what is there. It involves a certain view of the world, and being pragmatic, places limits on the usefulness of analysis or reflection on action. The teaching as an art paradigm has a long history (e.g. Highet 1963). Its most explicit formulation is that of Eisner, who argued that teaching could be seen as an art in four senses:

it is sometimes performed with such skill and grace that it can be described as an aesthetic experience; it involves qualitative judgements based on an unfolding course of action; it is contingent and unpredictable rather than routine; and that its outcomes are often created in the process.

(Eisner 1985, pp. 175–6)

The problem with this paradigm is that in its most extreme form, it carries the implication that teachers are born, not made, and that teaching is a gift. Teaching as a craft is a particularly prevalent paradigm at the moment. It has developed from early, not very successful attempts to codify teachers' craft knowledge, (e.g. Desforges and McNamara (1979) to the work of Tom (1984), Brown and McIntyre (1993) and Cooper and McIntyre (1996). This is not to say that teaching as a craft is the only paradigm in such research, but it is the dominant one for the aspects of teaching in which they are interested. I would argue that the craft paradigm in its focus on the particular and the concrete in teaching, concentrates only on one aspect of teacher's knowledge.

The applied science paradigm assumes that professional work involves the application of scientific principles and evidence to practical tasks. In its milder form it includes the 'foundation disciplines' of education: history, philosophy, sociology and psychology. It is the paradigm which underpinned much teacher training until recently, when increasing criticism about its inadequacies in the face of classroom realities, meant that it was sidelined in favour of other paradigms. The notion that teaching, or indeed any profession, can be seen simply as an applied science has become discredited, not least because the general principles gleaned from sociology or psychology have to be applied in concrete and particular teaching situations: they may not 'fit' or seem applicable.

The teaching as a system paradigm has enjoyed some interest: it is one form of a general rationalistic paradigm applicable to a number of fields, which has had a widespread influence on late twentieth-century thinking. Its main contribution to education and training has been in helping people to think about teaching as a complex whole. However, it tends to be decontextualised and does not take enough account of the contingencies of teaching. Teaching is often unpredictable, occurs in a wide range of contexts, and has to be adapted for particular contexts and groups of learners. It is also purely a process model, which can be applied equally well to running a small business as to teaching, and it says nothing about the content of teaching. Although a very different paradigm, the reflective practice approach is also a process model. It is associated with the work of Schon (1983; 1987) and can be seen as a reaction against technical rationality. Schon argued that the work of professionals is often messy and problematic: neither applied science nor rationality could resolve some of the problems professionals face in their practice. These problems require a continuing process of reflection on practice. Schon's ideas have had a widespread application, not only in teaching but in managerial work, architecture, nursing and social work. Their appeal is recognised in the amount of writing and thinking within this paradigm (e.g. Calderhead 1989). However, since it is purely a process paradigm, there are problems in applying it to teaching: it is only a part of what is involved in teaching. Other aspects must also be considered, such as substantive knowledge, skills and other processes.

The final paradigm outlined by Squires (1999) is that of teaching as competence. Its emphasis is on performance, on what the teacher can do. It does offer clear objectives for teachers and learners, but in breaking down teaching into a number of discrete competences or competencies (the terms seem to be used inter-changeably), via functional analysis of all the tasks involved in teaching, it generates somewhat unwieldy jargon and bureaucracy. In teacher education, there is the present reality of hundreds of 'standards' against which new 'trainees' are to be measured and evidence found for their having achieved them (DfEE 1998a). Critics of this approach argue that as well as being unmanageable, the competence approach fails to capture adequately the reality of teaching. It atomises what should be seen as a whole entity.

Squires' (1999) analysis is very useful in providing an overview of the different ways in which teaching has been characterised, and how the different paradigms underpin much research about efficient, good, or excellent teaching. It can be seen that all of these paradigms, or ways of conceptualising teaching, are inadequate in some way, or are only a partial model of teaching. They all have their limitations. It is the purpose of this book to offer a new paradigm of teaching, one based fundamentally on the kinds of knowledge needed for teaching: knowledge being interpreted in its widest possible sense. This paradigm encompasses all the knowledge, skills, processes, and dispositions essential to teaching of high quality, and contains elements of other paradigms. It can be characterised as teaching as a knowledge-based profession, and carries with it the notion that teachers work towards a state of expertise, of mastery over all the kinds of knowledge, skills and processes needed for expert teaching. Before presenting the new paradigm, it is useful to consider some of the literature on effective teaching since it can provide a historical context and overview of the ways in which educationists have conceptualised effective, excellent or expert teaching. The purposes of reviewing this research are to establish what is already known about effective teaching as a background to discussing expert teaching, and to set the context for the new paradigm.

Effective teaching (1) 1960–1990

There is much research on effective primary teaching from these three decades (see Gipps 1992 for a useful summary). This research has been informed by shifting theoretical perspectives which can be summarised briefly as those concerned with qualities of effective teachers, teaching style, opportunity to learn, and tasks (Bennett 1987). Early attempts to characterise effective teaching tend to be descriptive rather than analytical: more a list of qualities than analysis of action or thinking (e.g. Ryan 1960; Rosenshine and Furst 1973). Flanders' (1970) observational studies identified two contrasting teaching styles, direct and indirect, and suggested that both were needed for good teaching. Research into teaching styles developed from this early work: it began in the early 1970s and continued through that decade. Teaching styles tended to be characterised as 'traditional' and 'progressive', these terms being based on the prescriptive theory of teaching reflected in the Plowden Report (DES 1967). Other terms were also used, such as 'formal' and 'informal' (Bennett 1976); and 'didactic' and 'exploratory' (HMI 1978) which seem to be close in definition to 'traditional' and 'progressive'. Bennett's (1976) study identified three styles: informal, mixed and formal, but he found that most teachers adopted a mixed teaching style. HMI (1978) reported that three-quarters of the teachers employed mainly didactic styles. What is suggested by a review of these studies is that examples of the idealised traditional and progressive teachers used to inform the research were rare; these prescriptions of teachers were more in the nature of a caricature, and an example of the kinds of false polarities which have influenced thinking on primary teaching.

If classifying teachers into traditional and progressive was unhelpful in the search for characteristics of effective teaching, other research provided a more useful focus. The ORACLE (Observational Research and Classroom Learning Evaluation) studies (Galton *et al.* 1980; Galton and Simon 1980; Simon and Wilcocks 1981) used systematic classroom observation, based on a process–product paradigm, to study teacher and pupil behaviour in the classroom. The first studies (Galton *et al.* 1980) introduced a classification of six teaching styles. Of these, two groups of teachers were more successful than the other types: the infrequent changers who made conscious switches of strategy from class to individual teaching in order to maintain their desired pattern of teaching tactics; and the class enquirers. Children were also classified into groups in the ORACLE study. In the consistency studies when the same children were observed over a two-year period, many with different teachers, the majority of children, 80 per cent, adjusted their behaviour to fit in with the teaching style. None of the remaining 20 per cent of the sample of teachers changed their style over the two years. Although mediated by pupil behaviour, teaching style was the dominant influence. These are most significant findings in terms of investigating effective teaching. If the pattern of a child's behaviour and work is set by the teacher's style, then the teacher's performance and teaching strategies in lessons become major factors in effective teaching.

However, some educationists considered that research into teaching styles failed to inform improvements in practice. The attention of other researchers was on the amount of time which pupils spend on areas of the curriculum, the amount of time which they spent involved in tasks, and pupil mediation of tasks. Within this opportunity to learn paradigm, one of the most extensive studies was the ILEA Junior School Study, published as *School Matters* (Mortimore *et al.* 1988). This study looked at effective schools, rather than effective teachers, and identified a range of factors which contributed to some schools being more effective in terms of pupils' progress than others. However the ILEA study, like other studies, neglected the curriculum tasks on which children were engaged. The next research step was a shift in thinking to the quality of the work provided. Thus by 1984, the focus of research had shifted to the idea of 'match' of task to children's abilities: an important theme in the HMI surveys of 1978 and 1983. The main concern for HMI was the mismatch between task and pupil performance: this concern was justifed in the Bennett *et al.* (1984) study. Their findings confirmed that teachers tend to underestimate their higher attainers and overestimate the low attaining children.

Effective teaching (2) 1990–2000

Recent research studies into effective teaching tend to generate lists of different qualities, dispositions, attributes and behaviours of effective teachers. Several are quoted in Kyriacou (1997), with some items repeated. Rather than produce a chapter of lists, I have given only two examples of the kind of criteria of effective teaching found in such studies. An early study into effective teaching by the Organisation for Economic Co-operation and Development (OECD) collected data from 11 countries, including the UK, the United States, France, Japan and Australia (OECD 1994). This study was based on the view that teaching quality should be regarded as a holistic concept, made up of competencies across five key dimensions:

- knowledge of substantive curriculum areas and content;
- pedagogic skill, including the acquisition of and ability to use a a repertoire of teaching strategies;
- reflection and the ability to be self-critical, the hallmark of teacher professionalism;
- empathy and the commitment to the acknowledgement of the dignity of others;
- managerial competence, as teachers assume a range of managerial responsibilities within and beyond the classroom.

(OECD 1994)

This list is interesting because it is the first one to mention subject knowledge as a key quality. Subject mastery was often overlooked in studies of effective teaching, perhaps because its importance is so obvious, but more importantly, because researchers were looking for generic teaching qualities applicable across all subjects, age-phases and teaching contexts. This is a serious weakness of research into effective teaching. In addition, in the attempt to itemise the characteristics of effective teaching, studies tend to produce long checklists of these characteristics. There is a danger of losing the holistic quality of teaching referred to in the OECD study. It is the interplay between these different characteristics or qualities which is the crux of teaching, as the evidence in this book will show. A further problem is that many of the lists contain qualities of effective teaching, or behaviours which promote effective teaching and learning, but there is nothing to say what knowledge, understanding, beliefs or values underpin those qualities or behaviours. These lists or accounts of effective teaching are inadequate, for they give only a superfical understanding of how such teaching works. Nonetheless, the ideas of some studies are briefly mentioned here, to illustrate recent thinking about effective teaching.

The ideas of Cullingford (1995), as already noted, are an example of the teaching as an art paradigm. He offers five characteristics or qualities of an effective teacher: *integrity, learning, organisation, communication* and *humour*, and states that all these are central to effective teaching. Cullingford stressed that teachers can 'learn' these qualities. Cooper and McIntyre's (1996) study within the teaching as a craft paradigm offered a transactional theory of teaching and learning. They argued 'that learning opportunities are felt by pupils and teachers to be heightened when teaching strategies are transactional, in that they involve the integration of pupil concerns and interests with teachers' pedagogical goals' (Cooper and McIntyre 1996, p. 156). This study builds on earlier work by Brown and McIntyre (1993) also within the craft tradition of teaching, in which teacher ways of thinking about their teaching, the perceived impact on pupil reference groups, and the perceptions of the pupils themselves, were informative about effective teaching.

In Kyriacou (1997) are several lists of aspects of effective teaching; most of them include similar items. One typical example is given here, from reviews of process–product studies (e.g. Anderson 1991; Cruikshank 1990 – both cited in Kyriacou 1997), which identified these ten characteristics of effective teaching:

- clarity of the teachers' expectations and directions;
- establishing a task-oriented classroom climate;
- making use of a variety of learning activities;
- establishing and maintaining momentum and pace for the lesson;
- encouraging pupil participation and getting all pupils involved;
- monitoring pupils' progress and attending quickly to pupils' needs;
- delivering a well-structured and well-organised lesson;
- providing pupils with positive and constructive feedback;
- ensuring coverage of the learning objectives;
- making good use of questioning techniques.

(Kyriacou 1997, p. 120)

The most recent work on effective teaching was the *Hay McBer Report* (DfEE 2000). This 'blueprint for the perfect teacher' (TES 23.6.00) was a controversial document, not least because of its links with performance pay for teachers, and the fact that with the government's characteristic mistrust of educationalists and teachers, outside consultants were brought in to do the research. The key findings were that there were three main groups of factors within teachers' control which significantly influence pupil progress. These are *teaching skills, professional characteristics* and *classroom climate*. This means more lists of dispositions, qualities and behaviours, but the lists are at least hierarchical, with levels of performance. They vary in quality and understanding of teaching, but are an improvement on the DfEE standards, which as I have argued elsewhere, are deeply flawed (Turner-Bisset 1999a). However there are some oddities in the levels: for example, under passion for learning, level 1, 'Creates a learning environment' seems an odd criterion. It is attending to the external or peripheral detail of a teacher's practice rather than on the central core, which is about demonstrating that passion for learning.

The model has other weaknesses. One weakness is that some of the levels need reconsideration in the light of informed understanding about teaching and knowledge bases for teaching. One final weakness of the Hay McBer model is the lack of mention of all the various kinds of knowledge which underpin what effective and outstanding teachers do. It reflects much of the previous research on effective teaching in concentrating on the visible aspects of teaching, as for example in the passion for learning example quoted earlier. The emphasis is on qualities, aptitudes, dispositions, behaviours, processes, values, and attitudes, less so on knowledge. The model is a more fully delineated model of teaching than those reviewed previously, but lacks the dimension of knowledge for teaching. It is 'a tip of the iceberg' model. In this book it is argued that for expert teaching, a wide range of knowledge bases must be employed in the processes of teaching; not merely within the applied science paradigm, but using all the other knowledge bases essential for the very best teaching. Before presenting these knowledge bases, there follows a brief historical overview of the kinds of knowledge deemed necessary for teaching.

Knowledge for teaching: historical overview

What kinds of knowledge do teachers need for teaching? There have been in the past different schools of thought on this. In medieval times and from the sixteenth to the eighteenth century, the possession of subject knowledge was all, although there was some evidence that some textbook writers laid great emphasis on the method of teaching. However this applied to the public school and academic tradition of education, identified by Blyth (1965). Those who would argue that subject knowledge is all that is required for teaching, e.g. Lawlor (1990), reflect this academic tradition; indeed for many years it has been possible to teach in the university and private sector without training or qualified teacher status. For the second tradition of education, that of elementary education, there were different priorities. This was about a basic education in reading, writing and arithmetic, to prepare future workers for the industrial age, with a liberal dose of religious education for the moral improvement of the lower classes, and plentiful needle-work for the girls, who would need this skill in service and in the home. For the third, more recent developmental tradition (Blyth 1965), knowledge of children and their social, physical, emotional and cognitive development were deemed important.

Teacher education has thus reflected these three traditions: the curricula of teacher education institutions has mirrored both what is taught in school and the dominant tradition of the period. However, it has also reflected the flavour of the times, government priorities and class structures; thus teaching and teacher education have to be placed in the context of the wider society. Thus in the nineteenth century, the knowledge necessary for teaching was first and foremost craft knowledge, of how to manage large classes, learnt by demonstration, example and practice in the pupil-teachers' long apprenticeship; academic subject knowl-edge gained during the two-year college-based phase; and the correct moral attitudes of humility and self-sacrifice, instilled during the college training, to ensure a properly subservient and malleable teaching force. The last of these was important, because the majority of those undertaking elementary teaching were usually bright working-class youngsters. It was considered important to train them in a higher standard of morals, manners and habits; however at the same time, humility and altruism were necessary to prevent elementary teachers from indulging in inconvenient social aspiration and personal ambition. There were real dangers in their socially ambivalent position in society, yet it was necessary to distance them in some way from the pupils they would be teaching. Thus for these teachers, at the start of mass elementary education, the requisite kinds of knowledge were: practical craft knowledge; academic subject knowledge; knowledge of appropriate behaviour and attitudes for their status and occupation; and finally, the principles of the monitorial system. They came to the colleges to internalise a closely prescribed form of knowledge transmission and schoolroom organisation (Gardner 1993). This was an early notion of effective teaching, and a very powerful one, in which the phrase 'a good teacher' was used to express a teacher with a particular set of attributes and teaching methods.

With the movement towards a full secondary education for all in the late nineteenth and early twentieth centuries, and the personal academic education which this endowed to would-be teachers, the pupil-teacher system fell into disuse. At the same time, there was room on the college courses for more educational theory, since academic subjects were being taught in secondary education. The new non-residential training colleges associated with universities which began to appear in the 1890s, offered a more intellectually challenging course. There was a move away from school method towards giving attention to the underlying educational principles. In this new climate, it was considered that anything which contributed towards the intellectual development of the intending teacher, would ultimately benefit the child. The beginnings of the applied science paradigm are visible here, in the notion that through the broad and philosophic treatment of educational principles and method, the beginning teacher would be able to devise her or his own methods of teaching, rather than relying on the craft skills associated with a particular system. The move towards an all-graduate profession in the 1960s accentuated the dominance of the applied science paradigm. This has subsequently given way to the reflective practioner paradigm and the competence paradigm.

Alongside this change, the flowering of the child development tradition, exemplified in the teachings of Dewey, Froebbel and Montessori, among others, has transformed our views of children's learning and cognition, through the work of first the behaviourists and then the work of Piaget, Vygotsky and Bruner. The child has been seen at the centre of education, in literally child-centred approaches and ideologies. Knowledge of children, gained through close proximity to a class of children for a year, is still seen as an essential part of the primary teacher system, though it is merely a vestige of the old elementary system, imposed as a cheap and efficient way of managing mass education. Alexander pointed out how in primary teacher education, knowledge of child development was seen as the most important part of the college/university-based courses for primary teachers, for they did not claim the subject mastery of secondary teachers. Their claim to professionalism lay in specialist knowledge of child development (Alexander 1984). In primary teaching, the science to be applied was above all child psychology. Thus for intending primary teachers, the forms of knowledge deemed important or essential now came to include knowledge of the four 'foundation disciplines' of philosophy, sociology, psychology and history, and in particular, knowledge of child development.

From the above account it can be seen that historically speaking, a number of different kinds of knowledge have been required for teaching. The relative importance of each of these waxes and wanes in accordance with the fashions of the time and the dominant political and educational ideologies. These kinds of knowledge are shown in Figure 1.1.

Kinds of knowledge for teaching

- academic subject knowledge
- craft knowledge
- knowledge of a particular moral code
- curriculum knowledge (what is to be taught)
- knowledge of educational theory informed by the four foundation disciplines
- knowledge of child development

Figure 1.1 Knowledge for teaching from historical overview

In recent years, however, the emphasis in effective teaching and in teacher education has moved away from the knowledge needed, to the skills and processes of teaching. In this book I shall argue that to conceptualise teaching in terms of either knowledge, or skill, or processes is inadequate. The whole professional knowledge base of teaching comprises knowledge, processes, skills, beliefs, values and attitudes. This statement is underpinned by a particular view of the knowledge in any field or discipline. Schwab (1964; 1978) suggested that academic disciplines could usefully be described as having substantive and syntactic structures, a distinction similar to Ryles' 'knowing that' and 'knowing how' (Ryle 1949). The substantive structures of a discipline are both the facts and concepts contained within it, and the organising frameworks or paradigms used to marshall its ideas and information. Syntactic knowledge is the ways and means by which the propositional knowledge or the substantive knowledge has been generated and established. These ideas will be explored in greater depth in Chapter 2, but it is possible to describe the discipline of education in these terms, despite the fact that it is a composite and recent discipline, bringing together elements of other subjects and forms of knowledge to make its own peculiar identity. Other disciplines such as geography, for example, have been forged from history, economics and science: their relative newness does not detract from their present acceptance in academic communities.

Beliefs about a subject are informed by one's knowledge of the substantive and syntactic structures of that subject. The same is true of education and teaching. If one believes education to be training, this belief shapes one's thinking, discourse and actions within education. If one believes teaching and learning to be a simple matter of transmission of knowledge, this belief too will shape one's thinking, discourse and actions in the classroom. In the case of policy-makers, that particular belief will shape educational provision at whatever level.

Thus, in regarding education as a discipline, and teaching as a knowledge-based profession, one can begin to sketch out some kind of map of all the knowledge, in the broadest sense of the term necessary for teaching. A preliminary sketch might look something like Figure 1.2.

Substantive knowledge	Syntactic knowledge	Beliefs
Varieties of knowledge	Skills and processes	Beliefs/attitudes/values

Figure 1.2 The professional knowledge base of teaching

The substantive knowledge underpins and informs the syntactic knowledge and both of these inform beliefs. To give a simple example: knowledge of the historical concepts of primary and secondary evidence would underpin a lesson in which a teacher gave examples of primary and secondary evidence to her pupils to sort, justifying their categorisation. The variety of forms of evidence presented could challenge the pupils as to what they considered to be evidence; the teacher would use skills of assessment to ascertain whether or not her pupils fully understood these concepts. Most importantly, the energy and enthusiasm with which the teacher presented the task would be driven by her belief that this is an important activity for the pupils to do, and a distinction important for them to grasp. Teaching is not a matter of skill or competency alone. The kinds of deep understanding of several different knowledge bases, the processes of pedagogical reasoning, the skills of teaching and the beliefs of the teacher, comprise a sophisticated professional expertise. Of these components, the knowledge bases for teaching have been comparatively neglected, certainly recently in the UK, in contrast to the skills and competences needed for teaching.

The model of knowledge bases

When I first moved from teaching in a secondary school, to a primary school, I started by working as a supply teacher at the infant school which my own children attended, as do many women after having a family. On my first day teaching a Year 1 class, I found myself in the hall, doing PE on apparatus. I had observed the head teacher taking this lesson the week before, but nothing prepared me for the realities of taking such a lesson. Quite apart from the fuss which these five and six-year-olds had managed to generate over changing into PE clothes (as a new teacher I was fair game), I felt at a loss as to how to select and present activities in this subject and teaching context. I knew about warm-ups and got the children doing some, but the vague suggestions tossed at me by the head about working on balance, seemed hard to put into practice. I got through the lesson, but afterwards reflected on how the absence of subject knowledge about PE had led me to fumble my way through this lesson. I knew I could teach other subjects such as English fairly well, but I lacked the specialist professional knowledge to teach PE properly. Furthermore, I did not have the knowledge of how to set up class routines and expectations in a context so different to the one in which I usually worked.

What I was thinking about that day was in fact 'pedagogical content knowledge'. I did not meet the term for quite a while, until I read Shulman's 1985 presidential address to the American Educational Research Association (Shulman 1986a). His conceptualisation of it as an amalgam between content and pedagogy resonated with me immediately. I recalled that PE lesson and realised what I had been missing in terms of knowledge. Shulman (1986a; 1986b; 1987a) identified pedagogical content knowledge as being of special interest, because it is the blending of content and pedagogy into an understanding of how particular topics are transformed, organised, represented and adapted to the varying interests and abilities of learners. Pedagogical content knowledge is a powerful idea: it has been seized upon by a number of educationalists, who assimilated it, demonstrated its importance in teaching, reformulated it and criticised it. Shulman (1986a; 1986b; 1987a) suggested that there were seven categories of knowledge bases for teaching. These are listed in Figure 1.3.

Categories of knowledge bases

- content knowledge (subject matter knowledge)
- general pedagogical knowledge, with special reference to those broad principles and strategies of classroom management and organisation that appear to transcend the subject matter
- curriculum knowledge, with particular grasp of the materials and programmes that serve as 'tools of the trade' for teachers
- pedagogical content knowledge, that special amalgam of content and pedagogy that is uniquely the province of teachers, their own special form of professional understanding
- knowledge of learners and their characteristics
- knowledge of educational contexts, ranging from the workings of the group or classroom, the governance and financing of school districts, to the character of communities and cultures
- knowledge of educational ends, purposes and values and their philosophical and historical grounds

Figure 1.3 Categories of knowledge bases (Shulman 1986b)

Shulman identified pedagogical content knowledge as being of special interest, because it represents the blending of content and pedagogy into an understanding of how particular topics, problems or issues are organised, represented and adapted to the diverse interests and abilities of learners, and presented for instruction. The problem with this list, which appears in several publications, is that it is not clear how the knowledge bases interact, other than the brief sketch of ideas given above. In an article co-written with Wilson and Richert (Wilson *et al*. 1987), Shulman stated that:

> How these kinds of knowledge relate to one another remains a mystery to us . . . they are just boxes floating on a page. In our future work we intend to explicate the distinctions between different types and forms of knowledge, as well as the relationships between these entities.
>
> (Wilson *et al*. 1987, pp. 118–19)

The model of knowledge bases presented in this book goes further, in firstly trying to explicate with some clarity all of the knowledges bases for teaching, and secondly in offering an explanation of how these knowledge bases interact in the professional work of the teacher. This includes not just the 'active' phase of operating in the classroom, but the planning, evaluation and reflection phases as well.

A model of knowledge bases for teaching

Codes

- substantive subject knowledge SUB
- syntactic subject knowledge SYN
- beliefs about the subject BEL
- curriculum knowledge CUR
- general pedagogical knowledge GPK
- knowledge/models of teaching MOD
- knowledge of learners: cognitive L-COG
- knowledge of learners: empirical L-EMP
- knowledge of self SELF
- knowledge of educational contexts CON
- knowledge of educational ends ENDS
- pedagogical content knowledge PCK

Figure 1.4 Knowledge bases for teaching: the list

The model in this book, covering the knowledge bases listed in Figure 1.4, has been developed from a doctoral study (Turner-Bisset 1997) of postgraduate primary teachers learning to teach. It has further been developed through in-service courses, curriculum development, primary teacher education and through teaching in primary classrooms. A complete account of this more comprehensive model is given elsewhere (Turner-Bisset 1999a), but it needs to be described here as it forms the framework for this book.

Substantive knowledge, syntactic knowledge and beliefs about the subject

These are all aspects of content or subject knowledge. Schwab (1964; 1978) presented an analysis of academic disciplines in which he introduced the terms 'substantive structures' and 'syntactic structures'. *Substantive knowledge* within a discipline is the substance of the discipline: the facts and concepts of a subject. In addition, the substantive structures of a discipline are the frameworks used to organise these facts and concepts. Schwab described *syntactic knowledge* as the ways and means by which the propositional knowledge has been generated and established. It is the way in which new knowledge becomes accepted by a scholarly community, through various procedures of experimentation, and verification. It therefore involves more than procedural knowledge and routine enquiry. Syntactic knowledge means 'the scientific method' or in history it is the investigative and interpretative procedures of enquiry, or in literature the analytical tools of criticism.

Beliefs about the subject have been shown to be important by several researchers. Wilson and Wineburg (1988) described how four new teachers each with differences in their understanding of the nature of history used different approaches to teaching the same topic of the Great Depression. More recently Askew *et al.* (1997) have argued that the most effective teachers of numeracy had connectionist beliefs about the nature of mathematics, and Medwell *et al.* (1998) have found that teachers who placed a high value on the creation of meaning in literacy were the most effective. Beliefs about the subject would appear to be just as an important aspect of subject matter knowledge as substantive and syntactic knowledge, and influenced by one's understanding, or lack of understanding of these structures. Therefore they have been included in the model as a separate knowledge base.

Curriculum knowledge

This was described as the 'tools of the trade' by Shulman (1986b), meaning the materials and programmes of study available for each subject. Thus curriculum knowledge is knowledge of the curriculum in its widest sense, of the whole curriculum laid down for children, the programmes of study, and the kinds of curriculum materials used to teach each subject. These would include reading, literacy and maths schemes, teaching packs, topic books, visits to sites and museums: in short, all the materials and resources which might be used to teach aspects of the curriculum. Curriculum materials are not only what is available commercially or by government prescription: the concept is broader than this. Materials might be home-made, devised with a particular context or set of learners in mind, or to communicate an especially difficult concept. An important part of curriculum knowledge is the understanding that materials have flexible uses: sand might be employed in science, geography, art and in imaginative play which develops story composition.

General pedagogical knowledge

This is generic knowledge about teaching gained from practice. The sort of knowledge referred to here is knowledge of, for example, how to settle a class, how to attract and hold attention, and how to manage resources. Shulman (1986b) referred to 'broad principles and strategies of classroom management and organisation that appear to transcend subject matter'. Much of general pedagogical knowledge would appear to be procedural, and learnt from practice; yet it is also likely, given that it is grounded in practice, that general pedagogical knowledge is constructed from innumerable 'cases' of teaching, and has a substantive base.

Knowledge/models of teaching

This can also be described as beliefs about teaching and learning. These are ideas about how children learn and of what teachers do in order that they learn. Some of the substantial amount of research on teachers' thinking and beliefs (e.g. Calderhead and Robson 1991; Zeichner *et al.* 1987; Leinhardt 1988) indicated that knowledge about teaching from their own experiences of school shapes the student teacher's ideas and understanding of what teaching is, and hence their own developing practice. Common perceptions from one's own experience of schools are that teaching is telling and showing; learning is memorising (Calderhead and Robson 1991). Such views of the processes of education have an impact on what teachers do and how they do it. In the absence of clearly delineated models and understandings of teaching and learning, beginning teachers tend to fall back on what they know.

Knowledge of learners

This is more complex than Shulman's original category would suggest. It consists of different elements: *empirical knowledge of learners* and *cognitive knowledge of learners*. Empirical or social knowledge of learners is: knowledge of what children of a particular age range are like; their social nature; how they behave in classrooms and school; their interests and preoccupations; how contextual factors such as non-routine events or adverse weather can have an effect on their work and behaviour; and the nature of the child–teacher relationship.

Cognitive knowledge of learners consists of two elements. First there is the knowledge of theories of child development which informs practice. The second element is context-bound to a particular group of learners: the kind of knowledge which grows from regular contact with these learners, of what they know, of what they can do, and of what they are likely to be able to understand. From this kind of knowledge come the skills and processes of adaptation of activities and representations to the needs of particular learners; in other words of differentiation for difffering abilities.

Knowledge of self

Shulman did not include *knowledge of self* in his original list of categories of the knowledge base for teaching, but there is a range of evidence suggesting that it is an important knowledge base for teaching. Elbaz (1983) included knowledge of self in her five categories of teacher knowledge, and Lampert's (1981; 1984) category of personal knowledge combined knowledge of self with knowledge of children. Kagan reviewed a large number of learning-to-teach studies and identified the central role played by a novice's self-image, 'Indeed without a strong image of self as teacher, a novice may be doomed to flounder' (Kagan 1992, p. 147).

This sense of self as teacher combines the personal with the professional. Teaching in general and primary teaching in particular has always made huge demands upon the self. Nias (1989) argued for the centrality for primary teachers of the importance that they attach to sense of personal identity. The job has always called for enormous investments of time, energy and aspects of one's personality. The self is a crucial element in the way teachers themselves understand the nature of the job (Nias 1989). Knowledge of self is an important requisite for reflection at the higher levels (McIntyre 1992). It has some effect on teachers' ability to deliberate on their own practice. Teaching is a profession in which the self is a crucial element, which demands a heavy investment of the self and in which the self in evaluation and reflection plays an important part. Therefore knowledge of self is an important knowledge base and should be added to the categories of knowledge for teaching.

Knowledge of educational contexts

This is in the broadest sense knowledge of all settings where learning takes place: of schools, classrooms, nursery settings, universities and colleges, and the broader educational context of the community and society (Shulman 1986b). Contexts can very enormously: from the relatively privileged schools in a middle-class area, or with selective intakes, to the schools in inner city or rural deprived areas. Reception or nursery classes, and Year 6 classes can be very different contexts, yet they are both within the primary age-range. Teaching contexts have a significant impact on teaching performance, and there are a range of contextual factors which affect teachers' development and classroom performance. These include: the socio-economic level of the catchment area; the type and size of school; the class size; the amount and quality of support teachers and other colleagues give to each other; the feedback teachers receive on their performance; the quality of relationships in the school; and the expectations and attitudes of the head teacher.

Knowledge of educational ends, purposes and values

Teaching is a purposeful activity: teachers have short-term goals for a lesson or series of lessons; and the jury is still out over the long-term purposes of education. Some would argue that it is a purely utilitarian endeavour, aiming to produce efficient workers who will serve the needs of society well. Some see it as being of intrinsic worth in itself (e.g. Peters 1965). For some the moral dimension, or purpose, is of the greatest importance, in that education should produce morally upright and responsible citizens. Sockett (1987) claimed that the essential feature of teaching is moral. There is a socio-moral quality to teaching, but it is only one of many essential features. For many teachers working at the chalkface, the day-to-day business of teaching is so all-consuming, that they may have little time to consider the long-term aims of education. They may have aims, but these might not be explicitly expressed or discussed. However, in truly expert teachers educational ends should be explicit in their thinking and planning.

The amalgam of knowledge bases

In the model presented here the concept borrows an idea from set theory to describe what is happening when different kinds of teaching knowledge are combined in various combinations. The central idea is of an overarching knowledge base comprising all of the knowledge bases described above. They are represented as sets in this model, which can intersect, in the way the content knowledge and pedagogical knowledge do, or content knowledge and curriculum knowledge. These are forms of pedagogical content knowledge, but the most complete form is an example of teaching, in the broadest sense of the word, in which all of the knowledge bases are present in the amalgam. Thus the pedagogical content knowledge of the expert teacher is the set that comprises all of the other sets of knowledge bases (see Figure 1.5).

In beginning teachers it has been shown (Turner-Bisset 1997) that only some of the knowledge bases are combined: for example a teacher may have good subject knowledge in maths, but undeveloped empirical and cognitive knowledge of learners, and only the beginnings of general pedagogical content knowledge. In addition, her models of teaching and learning may be of telling the children maths

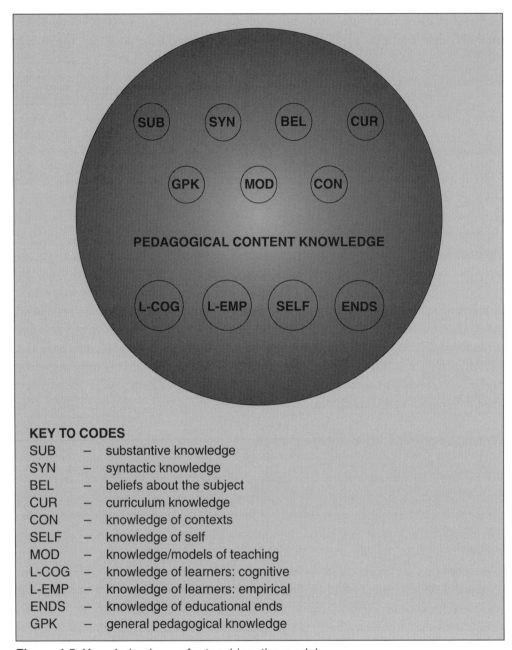

KEY TO CODES

SUB	–	substantive knowledge
SYN	–	syntactic knowledge
BEL	–	beliefs about the subject
CUR	–	curriculum knowledge
CON	–	knowledge of contexts
SELF	–	knowledge of self
MOD	–	knowledge/models of teaching
L-COG	–	knowledge of learners: cognitive
L-EMP	–	knowledge of learners: empirical
ENDS	–	knowledge of educational ends
GPK	–	general pedagogical knowledge

Figure 1.5 Knowledge bases for teaching: the model

procedures. Therefore she has few strategies on which to draw to teach maths; she does not know how to engage and motivate the children. Her understandings of investigation and proof may seem very distant from the basic maths she is teaching the children, and she does not seem able to use her subject knowledge. Another example is of a teacher with inadequate subject knowledge in art, but good knowledge of learners, both empirical and cognitive, and a broad range of teaching strategies based on good general pedagogical knowledge. His methods of art teaching might ignore his wealth of knowledge of learners and of pedagogy, by being based on his beliefs that art is about all the class making identical dinosaurs, or drawing pictures of Greek triremes to go in their topic books. These notions might be based on what is understood by 'good practice' in art in the context in which he works; he may have no other images of teaching art to inform him. Without an understanding of the processes of art, or its syntactical knowledge, he is likely to have the children doing busy work rather than real art.

Thus it is argued that all of these knowledge bases are essential for the most expert teaching, which demonstrates pedagogical content knowledge in its most comprehensive form. It is further argued, in the course of this book, that all of the paradigms suggested by Squires (1999) are present in this model, some more obviously than others. For example, the teaching as craft is clearly represented in general pedagogical knowledge; and teaching as reflective practice is represented in knowledge of self and in knowledge of educational ends. The case studies of teaching in this book, will demonstrate aspects of the knowledge bases for teaching, and their importance in the processes of teaching. They will be discussed mainly in the order in which they appear in this chapter, but some knowledge bases have been grouped together for coherence.

Summary

This chapter has discussed a number of paradigms of teaching and examined notions of effective or excellent teaching from early research in the 1960s to the present day. It has given an account of the kinds of knowledge considered necessary for teaching from medieval times to the present day. It offers a new paradigm of teaching as a knowledge-based profession, and gives an outline of the conception of knowledge which underpins it. It briefly sketched the knowledge bases for teaching, and more importantly a model of how these knowledge bases interact and intermesh in the processes of teaching. This book sets out to present a theory and a model of how the knowledge bases for teaching interact, through case studies of examples of beginning and experienced teachers.

CHAPTER 2

Subject knowledge: substantive and syntactic knowledge and beliefs about subject knowledge

Introduction

It is axiomatic that teachers need subject knowledge for teaching. Of course: how else could they be teachers? However subject knowledge means different things to different people, and it is important to determine exactly what is meant by subject knowledge. The White Paper *Teaching Quality* (DES 1983) can be seen as the key document initiating concern over the importance of teachers' subject knowledge. The Council for the Accreditation of Teacher Education (CATE) was set up in 1984, as ordered in the government Circular 3/84 (DES 1984) and reconstituted in 1989 (Circular 24/89, DES 1989b); in their criteria there was a more elaborated emphasis on subject study. The underlying assumption in these criteria was that a student's mastery of a subject and its application promotes effective teaching, and high-quality learning. The importance of subject knowledge in the eyes of government officials was further strengthened by publications such as Lawlor's (1990) pamphlet, issued by the Centre for Policy Studies, a right-wing think tank. In this document, she pointed out that: 'It was with the object of placing the mastery of the subject at the heart of the teacher's training, as the first prerequisite for good teaching' that the recent proposals to reform teacher training were introduced. For Lawlor, subject mastery was all-important. But for all her emphasis on subject study, nowhere in the pamphlet is there any indication of what is meant by subject knowledge, or subject mastery. The terms 'deep knowledge of the subject' and 'mastery of the subject' are not explored.

These terms continued to be taken for granted throughout the reforms of the 1990s, including Circular 9/92 (DfE 1992) which greatly enhanced the role of schools in the preparation for teachers, and Circular 14/93 (DfE 1993a). Following in the wake of debates about primary education, initiated by the discussion paper of Alexander *et al.* (1992), and continued in reports by OFSTED (1993a; 1993b) and the NCC (1993), Circular 14/93 laid down strict new criteria which all training courses must meet, focusing on the subject knowledge and teaching skills new teachers must have to be effective in the classrooom. It also set out in its proposals for reform a continuing need for study in higher education institutions of the subject knowledge necessary for sound teaching of the primary curriculum, and courses preparing teachers to work as subject specialists at Key Stage 2. At the same time, publication of findings from the Leverhulme Primary Project (Wragg *et al.* 1989; Bennett *et al.* 1992; Bennett and Carre 1993) drew attention to deficiencies in subject knowledge among students and teachers. The establishment of the Teacher Training Agency (TTA), a government quango, which oversees all routes into teacher education, moved control over the content of teacher training courses into the hands of government.

The TTA introduced the first ever national curriculum for initial teacher training, now published as Circular 4/98 (DfEE 1998a). This detailed document lists standards for the award of qualified teacher status (QTS). Section A, Knowledge and Understanding, includes knowledge of the National Curriculum. For English, maths and science, knowledge and understanding are defined in terms of the National Curriculum subject content. For specialist subjects, beginning teachers must have a secure knowledge of the subject to at least A Level standard; for other non-core subjects, they must have secure knowledge to a standard equivalent to at least Level 7 of the pupils' National Curriculum. Thus subject knowledge for primary teachers is defined by the TTA in terms of what pupils must learn, and in terms of A Level. It would appear that for the TTA, this is what mastery in a subject would seem to be. For various reasons, some to do with curriculum design, and some to do with knowledge and control (Young 1971; 1998), this seems a narrow conception of subject knowledge and of subject mastery. The curriculum is only ever selections from a culture, and selections from subjects: what is selected to be in the curriculum may depend as much on the beliefs and values of politicians at the time, as on content, processes and skills determined by experts in the field who comprise subject working groups. A good example of this is given in Phillips (1998) in his account of the development of the 1991 History National Curriculum. A Levels have been the subject of enormous debate in recent times (see e.g. Young 1998). There are two fundamental problems with A Level as an assumed standard for primary teaching. Firstly, despite the introduction of modular A Levels, much of the content and skills is determined by what is examinable in end of course exams. Secondly, it is quite possible to study a subject to A Level, and even degree level, without ever gaining a understanding of the essential structures of the discipline. The next section in this chapter deals with those essential structures, and it is argued that no notion of deep understanding of a subject, or of subject mastery, is complete, without understanding the structures of the disciplines.

The structures of the disciplines

Subject matter knowledge is sometimes characterised by critics of its importance and child-centred educationists as comprising only piles of 'inert facts'. However this is a narrow conception of subject knowledge, perhaps influenced by Dickens' (1854) satirical treatment of formal learning in *Hard Times* and perhaps by the very means by which subjects are taught, particularly in the secondary curriculum, for examination purposes. However most people would agree that the knowledge which individuals acquire over time does not exist in memory as many collections of disconnected facts. Humans have had to invent ways of organising knowledge, and ways of talking about its connectedness, or the ways in which ideas and facts, experiences and processes are grouped together. Ryle (1949) distinguished between propositional knowledge and procedural knowledge: two fundamental forms of knowledge. Propostional knowledge is the substance or content of the discipline: its facts and concepts, which are put together in propositions, for example heat is a form of energy; William of Normandy invaded Britain in 1066. Procedural knowledge comprises ways of proceding within the discipline: in other words, skills and processes. These are the skills of measuring within disciplines which use quantitative data, observational skills which are common to many disciplines, and intellectual skills which are such as the interpretation of evidence in history, or fair test design in science, handling a number of variables.

Substantive and syntactic knowledge

However, there is more to knowledge than this. We do not just have a bundle of disconnected facts and concepts in our minds within a subject. Schwab (1964; 1978) made the same useful distinction between propositional and procedural knowledge, but further defined propositional knowledge in terms of the structures of the disciplines. He used the terms 'substantive structures' and 'syntactic structures'. Substantive knowledge is the substance of the discipline, the facts and concepts of a subject. In addition there are the substantive structures, the way that facts and concepts are organised into frameworks, which are then used to guide enquiry. For example:

> In physics, concepts of atom, electron, subatomic particles are understood in terms of an organising framework called the Kinetic Theory. The model is an imaginative idea which we assign to unobservable atoms and molecules to explain how the world 'out there' behaves. The classificatory systems of chemistry and biology are other organising frameworks which help explain what may appear superficially as a profusion of disparate bits of information.
>
> (Carre 1995, p. 44)

Substantive knowledge

The organising frameworks are useful and powerful ideas. They shape conceptualisation and reasoning; they guide enquiry in the sense that they can influence the kind of data or evidence collected, and the observations made. In science they provide ways of thinking about the universe and what is in it, on which a whole-world view may be based. There tends to be one dominant framework or paradigm operating at a time in science. When new ideas appear, often generated by observations previously unmade, or new data which does not 'fit' into previously conceived frameworks, then they change existing paradigms and new ones are produced. The passage of acceptance of new ideas is not always smooth; sometimes, as the following examples show, publication of new ideas can cause an uproar, and the effects of the new ideas resonate in other disciplines, for example in art, literature, poetry, philosophy and theology.

Until the sixteenth century the accepted model of the universe was that of Ptolemy, in which the sun and the planets revolved around the earth. This was the dominant paradigm, and complex adjustments were added to Ptolemy's system to make it fit astronomical observations. Copernicus put forward the hypothesis that the earth moved and went round the sun, but most people did not take this seriously until the invention of the telescope. Galileo constructed the first powerful telescope, and his remarkable observations shattered old beliefs: the mountains and craters of the moon showed that the celestial bodies were not perfect spheres; that the moon was illuminated by solar light reflected from the sun; and that there were four new 'planets' moving around Jupiter. This new information from direct observation 'hath overthrown all former astronomy and next all astrology' (Galileo 1610 in Carey 1995, p. 14). He was welcomed as a celebrity at first, but became less guarded about Copernican ideas, until he was brought to trial before the Inquisition, found guilty, and sentenced to an indefinite term of imprisonment. Under threat of torture, he retracted his published ideas that the earth and planets moved around the sun.

Another example of the impact of observation on accepted ideas, was Newton's theory that white light was not pure, but a mixture of rays of different colours. This new idea met with strong opposition. A further example is Newton's law of gravitation, which remained the accepted theory of gravity until it was superseded by Einstein's General Theory of Relativity. In Newtonian physics, space and time were absolute; in Einstein's theory they became fluid: space–time continuum. When the news broke in 1919 of the testing of Einstein's theory, relativity theory became headline news across the world. It also caused shock-waves in literature and the visual arts, as well as in popular thought. It had some impact on the cubism movement in art: poems, both serious and comic, were written involving Einstein's ideas.

A final example of the change in the dominant paradigm in a branch of scientific study comes from craniology, a now rather discredited study, but part of the science and culture of the nineteenth century. The overarching structure of this study was based on the notion that the intelligence of human beings could be measured by the size of their brains and skull capacity: men having larger brains than women, it was argued, must be more intelligent. This notion was used to justify the position of women in society, as well as establishing that Africans, Asians and even southern Europeans were 'inferior' to Caucasian whites. This served as a justification for racism. However craniology was torn apart by its own internal contradictions: for example, how could they square the knowledge that whales and elephants had larger brains than human? Eventually when Alice Lee's study in 1901 (Steinem 1992), showed female medical students had larger skulls than some of the male authorities within the faculty, men had to choose between their own intelligence and accepted craniological theory. Her paper was so criticised by craniologists that as with many women academics of the day, her work had little impact until a male academic defended her. Craniology was based on false hypotheses of male and Caucasian superiority, and worked backward from these theories. Nowadays, craniology seems ridiculous, but it is important to understand that it was once a respectable branch of science (Steinem 1992). The processes of paradigm shift will be examined further in the discussion on syntactic knowledge. Before this, one final example from a different discipline is given to illustrate the changing paradigms within a field of study.

History as a discipline has been characterised by a number of paradigm shifts and competing paradigms. Medieval and early modern historians saw their function as the working-out of God's purposes in the world. The rationalist historians of the Enlightenment used a mode of historical explanation which rested on human forces, but they still saw their work as a kind of moral illustration (for example, Gibbon's 'Decline and Fall of the Roman Empire'). In the Romantic period, historians came to see the past as exciting because it was different, and also it provided an understanding of the institutions of state and society in the present. The lead in this shift in perspective was created by Leopold von Ranke (Evans 1997), whose contribution to historical scholarship was considerable. He helped to establish history as a separate discipline, independent from philosophy or literature. He saw that history's unique task was to establish essentially how it was in the past. He also stated that the past could not be judged by the standards of the present. Crucially, he introduced the importance of the use of primary sources to establish the facts of what happened in the past. History thus became established much as it is today, as an essentially scientific discipline, the difference between history and science being in the kinds of evidence on which facts and theories are based.

However, not all academic historians practised what they preached, i.e. the interpretation of primary sources on which to base narratives of the past, and the notion of a truly scientific history seemed shaky by the end of the nineteenth century. Another shift occurred with Trevelyan (1913) who stated that history was a mixture of the scientific (research), the imaginative or speculative (interpretation) and the literary (presentation). Since then there have been other shifts, some influenced by contemporary events such as the First World War, and the influence of new theories from science, such as Einstein's General Theory of Relativity. Historical objectivity was restored after the Second World War with the work of Elton (1969) and others. Popper (1961) also had some influence on ideas of historical objectivity. The development of the social sciences made some historians (e.g. Carr 1964; Stone 1981) push for closer links between history and the social sciences. Most recently postmodernism has had some impact on history, and debates continue as to whether it is possible to do history (Evans 1997).

Thus, within history as within science, there have been paradigm shifts as well as competing paradigms. The different disciplines which constitute all human knowledge have experienced shifts of precise content, of perspective and of structures, as for example in the sixteenth and seventeenth centuries when the distinction between philosophy and science became a separation thanks to the rise of experimental science. As well as separation, there can be union, as when branches of a discipline come together in new fields of study such as biophysics and biochemistry. In a sense we can 'slice up the subject matter pie of the universe as we so please', (Burns and Brauner 1962, p. 7) according to the structures we impose upon content. Knowledge is humanly and socially constructed. The processes of knowledge construction are the syntactic structures of disciplines, which will be discussed in the next section.

Syntactic knowledge
Syntactic structures are the procedures, the means and processes by which accepted 'truths' have become accepted. Schwab refers to three kinds of skills:

> First, and most commonly sought in a curriculum, are the skills by which one applies the truths learned from the discipline. Second, there are the skills of enquiry itself. In their primary use, these are the skills by which the master of a discipline contributes new knowledge to that discipline . . . Third, there are the skills of reading and interpretation by which one discovers the meaning of statements . . .

> (Schwab 1978, p. 236)

This sounds difficult, but is perhaps better expressed as the ways and means by which new knowledge becomes accepted by a scholarly community, through procedures of experimentation and verification. In science, this would mean the scientific method, including observing and inferring, reasoning, weighing evidence, predicting, asking questions and testing hypotheses. In history the syntactic structures include investigative and interpretative procedures of enquiry, and the use of argument. In literature, both the processes of writing and the tools of analytical enquiry are part of the syntactic structures, the nature of which are more complex than in history or science, because literature, like art and music is a productive rather than a pure discipline. It is important to understand as Schwab pointed out, that as well as procedures, there is 'the buried four-fifths of enquiry'. These are 'the manoeuvres which precede the collection of data and define what data are relevant' (Schwab 1978, p. 240). This part of enquiry is based on the substantive structures of a discipline and in this sense they can be said to guide enquiry. Understanding of syntactic structures is important for teaching, for if one attempts to teach science and history as a parade of facts and concepts then children will not come to understand the true nature of each subject.

Why should teachers know about the outcry which sometimes greets new scientific knowledge or new paradigms, as in the cases of Galileo, Einstein, and Lee, cited above? The end-products of scientific or historical enquiry, in the form of lectures and published papers, which may or may not be well-received, are part of the syntactic structures: the means by which new knowledge becomes accepted into the canons of 'truth' of each discipline. If teachers understand this, they understand the provisional nature of much human knowledge and the cultural embeddedness of knowledge. If teachers have some understanding of all of the syntactic structures of the disciplines they represent as subjects in the classroom, they will teach those subjects differently than if they treat all knowledge as accepted fact. Grossman *et al.* (1989) commented that:

> Novice teachers who lack knowledge of the syntactic structures of the subject matter fail to incorporate that aspect of the discipline in their curriculum . . . students need to know that mathematics is more than algorithms and that chemistry is more than the periodic table . . . A lack of syntactic knowledge may also seriously limit prospective teachers' abilities to learn new information in their fields.
>
> (Grossman *et al.* 1989, p. 30)

These conclusions were drawn from case studies of novice science teachers, who defined the nature of enquiry in very different ways, and social studies novices who perceived history variously as 'knowing the facts', or as involving very clear thinking about argument, logic, and evidence. It is clear that the novices' understanding of the nature of the subject, the substantive and syntactic structures of the subject, had an impact on their beliefs and the kinds of lessons they presented.

Beliefs about subject knowledge

Some of the research evidence on beliefs about subject matter has already been mentioned in Chapter 1: to this must be added more recent research. Both initial and in-service courses seek to challenge teachers' beliefs about subject knowledge, but there are problems. Teachers experience difficulties in adopting new practices without an appreciation of, and belief in, the underlying principles (Alexander 1992). Some teachers adopt the rhetoric of 'good' practice in a subject, for example mathematics, without changes to their actual practice (Desforges and Cockburn 1987; Eraut 1989). Brown *et al.* (1998) point out that beliefs about the nature of the subject have been explored in the literature (Ernest 1989; Lerman 1990; Thompson 1984; Carre 1993) but have not yet been shown to be as important as pedagogical beliefs. Cobb *et al.* (1988) argue that neither beliefs nor practice have primacy, but that 'beliefs and practice are dialectically related' (Cobb *et al.* 1988, p. 24). A similar view is held by Foss and Kleinsasser (1996). The main focus of research into beliefs about subject knowledge has been in English, maths and science; a certain amount has been done in history. The findings from this research are presented below to show some evidence for beliefs about subject knowledge being part of the subject knowledge base for teaching.

In science, there is a recognition that teachers' and students' understandings of the nature of the discipline are often inadequate (e.g. Carre 1993). They often define science as a process of exploration in which data are gathered to discover truths about the world. They tend to regard these truths as absolute, and 'out there' waiting to be discovered (Abell and Smith 1994). Without some notion that scientific knowledge is provisional and socially constructed, one cannot be said to be truly scientifically literate. In maths, the problem of a lack of understanding of the nature of mathematics, combined with a dislike and fear of maths, means that most prospective teachers enter teacher education with a view of maths as an unrelated set of facts, rules and skills, lacking any coherence or reason (Schuck 1997).

Recent research in the UK into effective teachers of numeracy, also points to the importance of beliefs about subject knowledge in effective teaching. In the numeracy project, it was found that what distinguished highly effective teachers from other teachers was a particular set of coherent beliefs and understandings which underpinned their teaching of numeracy (Askew *et al.* 1997). In the recent study of effective teachers of literacy in the UK, Medwell *et al.* (1998) reported that such teachers tended to place a high value on communication and composition in their views about the teaching of reading and writing: they believed that the creation of meaning in literacy was fundamental. In history, Wilson and Wineburg (1988) observed how new teachers' beliefs and understandings of history affected their planning and teaching. They concluded that for their teachers, knowledge of the subject was a much a product of their beliefs as it was an accumulation of facts and interpretation. Evans (1994) in his study of secondary school teachers found that teacher conceptions of history seemed to be profoundly related to teacher background, teacher belief and teacher knowledge. Newton and Newton (1998) from a study of students with science and history degrees intending to train as primary teachers, found that there were wide variations in their conceptions of history. They argued that knowing what counts in a subject is largely a process of enculturation. Turner-Bisset (1999b) found that it was possible to change intending teachers' beliefs and practice in teaching history through a carefully designed course.

It is important to understand at least some of this for teaching. What one believes a subject to be will inevitably shape one's teaching of it as shown in these two case studies. The first one presents a beginning teacher trying to teach poetry, without good subject knowledge, particularly of syntactic structures. The second presents the same teacher a year later, teaching science, his specialist subject, in contrast to the English lesson.

Case study 2: Tom: An engineer teaches poetry

Tom entered teacher education with a 2:1 honours degree in mechanical engineering, and A Levels in maths, further maths, chemistry and physics. His weekly work with children on a project, and running a swimming programme encouraged him to consider teaching seriously. It is clear from his educational background that his strengths lay in physical sciences and mathematics, rather than in the arts or language and literature. Nonetheless as a primary teacher, he found himself teaching across the curriculum in areas where he did not really have deep subject knowledge, particularly of syntactic structures of the discipline. The school context was not as favourable as it might have been for a student on his first placement. The teacher had had a student in this Year 5 class the previous term, and felt unable to 'let go' of the class, or give Tom a free rein. He also insisted that virtually everything Tom taught was linked to the class topic of Egypt, which proved a considerable constraint.

Tom's intentions for the lesson were to try to interest the children in writing poetry as an alternative to more conventional narrative. He thought that the children would learn that: language and pictorial description may be combined; language may be used in a more 'creative fashion' than the usual narrative or prose styles; and that poems do not have to rhyme. The task was to write shape poems on Egypt, developing previous work on caligrams. He had originally wanted the shape poems to be on any subject; the teacher wanted them linked to the current topic. The finished poems would go into the children's project books and the children 'would value them more'. He planned to take the whole class of 36 Year 5 children. There would be an initial class discussion, individual work and, if time, some sharing of work. Tom planned for differentiation only in that he thought that the high and low attainers would work at their own levels. The low attainers would need ideas given in an explicit and structured fashion to provide a foundation. Tom's plans looked as if he had at least some subject knowledge about language and poetry, but it was not clear how the task would be presented to the children, how the intended learning would result, or how he would organise this large group of children to help the low attainers.

Tom and the children had just returned from swimming, having walked back through a thunderstorm. They were all very wet. He had a heavy cold. He started the lesson by reminding them of previous work:

Tom: Remember what we did last week when we made up those words that I put up on the wall over here? We were thinking about words and what they meant, weren't we, and putting the words into the shape of the meaning, but today we are going to take that a little bit further, but this time we are going to concentrate on Egypt. So you're going to do this work and then you are going to stick it into your project books.

He then brainstormed the class for words to do with Egypt, which he wrote on the board. Most of the words were nouns such as pyramids, the Nile, camels, shadoof, sphinx. The only adjective was 'ancient'. He did not discuss with the children the kinds of words they had generated. Instead he moved straight on to giving them instructions:

Tom: So what I want to you to do is to choose a word that has a very strong link with Egypt, like 'mummy' and then write a little poem about it in your rough books. It doesn't have to rhyme; doesn't have to be very long, but once you've got your poem worked out in your rough books, then I am going to give you a piece of plain paper, and if you're writing about 'mummy', when you get your piece of plain paper, draw the mummy shape, and then you could write your poem inside the mummy in that shape, or you could write it round the outside.

He further suggested using a pyramid shape and illustrated a Nile shape on the board. The blackboard work was very badly presented and the children were totally confused about the 'shapes' they were supposed to fit with the words of their poem. There was much talk about 'Did it have to rhyme?' With little guidance and only six minutes into the lesson, the children began to write. Tom walked about giving encouragement and help, but did not appear enthusiastic. Noise levels rose. Children were shouting out and wandering over to speak to friends; he appeared not to notice. Queues formed. Children began to read their work to him:

Child: I am a mummy and I don't have a dummy and I sit in a box on the Nile.
Tom: Excellent! Good! Really good. You going to write any more to it? You gonna halt at that? So now you want to work out your shape, don't you?

He continued to look at work and suggest that the children put it on to plain paper:

Child: Practising messages, pitch black darkness all around, spiders crawling in the ground, Mummies and Daddies walking around.
Tom: Good. Right. You ready to put it on your sheet of paper now?

After 30 minutes, he told the children to pack away their things and indicated that they would return to the work. He then insisted on absolute quiet before they could leave for lunch. Not much work had been done; in fact no-one had completed a poem, and some had hardly put pen to paper.

When Tom came to evaluate the lesson, he thought that his intentions were fulfilled up to a point, and would be when the poems were finished. His strengths were that he had handed out paper well, avoiding the usual pupil attempts to do this riotously. Quite a lot of pupils had been interested and imaginations had been inspired. One boy had produced a particularly good piece of work. He would change the lesson, if he did it again, by improving his board work, perhaps using more brightly coloured chalks. He was not happy with the lesson, his presentation, or his inability to control noise levels or cope with their demands. He claimed he had assessed most of their work, but was really under pressure; so he had just glanced at some and given reassurance. He found that they got up to queue too much and were too demanding for him. He said he was not feeling too good at the time: he had health problems, the weather was poor and he found it hard to be enthusiastic. Despite this, he thought that most had worked up to their potential. He considered that they had learnt: that poems do not have to be long; and to use language more creatively (an ongoing process, part of a series of lessons). He did not think he had used specialist knowledge.

This lesson was observed by a researcher from the subject knowledge and teaching competence project. He thought that Tom's intentions had been poorly fulfilled. The children had learnt some specialist vocabulary about Egypt; some idea that poetry need not rhyme; and that it could be written in the shape of the word one was writing about. He thought that Tom had a good relationship with the children, but that his presentation was too brief and inadequate: there was no picture of a shape poem to give an idea of what was required. The blackboard work was appallingly bad and there was insufficient chalk. The children did not really know what to do. Tom had not controlled unacceptable noise. He had had only a very casual look at about half the class's work. The predicted difficulties with spelling had arisen. In addition the observer considered that the children had very little idea about getting to grips with appropriate language to express their poetical ideas about Egypt.

Tom's planning looked acceptable in some areas, but the actual presentation was so brief that there was no initial class discussion, only a brainstorming for words. Many children were not sure what to do: hence the excessive demands on his attention, leading to his inability to monitor the work effectively. There was certainly no discussion about using language in a more creative way. Tom's only response to the words suggested was praise. He did not realise that most of the words suggested were nouns or start to discuss words which might more effectively evoke an atmosphere. He had indicated in his planning that the low attainers would be given ideas in an explicit and structured fashion to provide a foundation for their own work. There is no evidence in the transcript or from the observer that he presented structured ideas at all. The children were simply told to get on with it. In his eager-to-praise response to the rhyming verses some of the children were producing, and his too-ready acceptance that the children were working up to their potential, there is evidence of a lack of syntactic knowledge about how poets work. The children certainly did get the message that a poem does not have to be very long, even if the message about poems not having to rhyme entirely escaped them. Most of Tom's evaluation was at a very basic level (see Case study 13, Chapter 7). He was certainly not happy with this lesson, but blamed much, including his poor presentation, on the weather and his ill-health. He recognised that the presentation and blackboard work had been very poor, but did not think beyond this to the fact that he had given the children no kind of example or representation of a shape poem. He did not connect this lack of representation to the large amounts of extra help many children were needing.

Case study 3: Tom: An engineer teaches science

Tom's planning for this lesson was very detailed. He listed several purposes: to introduce the class to a new aspect of transport (flight); to input ideas for the initiation of further practical investigative work; to get children thinking about air transport in general and parachutes in particular; and to satisfy the children's need to acquire and use various scientific and process skills, such as fair tests, keeping variables constant, and experimenting with dependent variables. He thought that the children would learn: the slowing effect of air resistance on moving objects; how something may be affected by a number of independent factors; that these independent variables are best tested separately; the concept of a fair test or reinforcement of that concept; and that *every* experiment contains inaccuracies in measurement (in this case, timing).

The plan of the task and presentation was very structured, listing the following activities in this order. He would give a demonstration of the effect of air resistance on a sheet and a crumpled ball of paper. He would talk about the slowing effect of air resistance on moving things. He would demonstrate the fall of a parachute, so that the children could observe what happened. He would repeat the demonstration, asking if it took the same time to fall. He would try the same thing again from different heights to illustrate the principle of a fair test. He would discuss what factors might affect how quickly a parachute falls to the ground (neglecting height). Finally he would explain that the children would investigate these, each group being given one factor, at a later time. All of these activities and discussion with the whole class constituted the presentation of the lesson. He had considered dealing with one group of four at a time, but this would have been inefficient in terms of his time. He also considered presenting the task on a worksheet, but this would have been very unsatisfactory for such a practical activity, and would have required much additional input from himself. He settled on the whole-class demonstration and discussion as being the most efficient and effective. He would cater for differing abilities in the demonstration and discussion by giving equal value to all ideas and suggestions, and by extending and 'opening' ideas. He thought that the later practical work was quite open-ended, but assistance from himself would probably be proportional to need. This practical work would be done in groups of four, while the rest of the class were engaged in other tasks. The children were quite used to working in this way.

He intended to assess them by talking with them individually and in their groups of four; by seeing what each child had written in her or his account of the investigation; and by hearing what the children had to say as a class in the plenary session at the end of the week. He had a comprehensive list of all the materials he would need. He foresaw practical problems, such as the cotton thread tearing through the corners of the parachutes, and problems in calculating area. He also thought that some children would have trouble dealing with the variables, and differentiating between dependent and independent variables.

The lesson started with Tom reminding the class that they were thinking about what it is that makes something stay up in the air while other things fall straight down through it. He asked what was the difference in the rate at which two bits of paper would fall, one scrunched up and one flat. He stood on the desk and asked the children to predict what would happen when he dropped them. Afterwards he asked them what they had noticed. The children were observant: one child said if he were to drop them again:

R: It depends how you hold the flat piece of paper because it could help like that.

The children were quiet and absorbed during the demonstration. When he asked why there was a difference, a girl offered the suggestion that it was something to do with the air stopping it. He reminded them humorously of previous work when people in Leonardo's Da Vinci's time were experimenting with parachutes and how dangerous it was with people jumping off buildings. He used this as a link to introducing the parachute he had previously prepared and asked the children to predict what would happen when he dropped it. The children were again observant:

J: When you held it the corners were quite close together, but when you let it go, it spread out because of the air pushing on it.

Tom: So you think the air pushed the corners out? Good. Well spotted.

He dropped the parachute again and asked if it took the same time. The children thought that it had done so; he asked them to estimate the time it took. When he dropped the parachute again with a child timing the fall, he challenged the children by suggesting he change the height: would it take the same length of time to fall?

Tom: What about from up here?

Child: It'll take longer because it's higher. That much higher.

Tom: Why do you want it to be there? Because it's fair?

Having introduced the notion of being fair, he was able to sum up:

Tom: So if I'm testing to see if it will take the same time, I have to drop it from the same height to make it fair: otherwise it's not a fair test.

He dropped the parachute several more times from the same height, to stress this point while the children timed the fall. After this he began to elicit ideas on what variables could affect the fall of the parachute. The children understood and helped him write a list of variables on the blackboard. During this, Tom challenged the children to explain exactly what they meant:

E: The size of the parachute and the size of the plane.

Tom: The size of the parachute, right. What do you mean by size? Do you mean how thick it is? How long is it? How wide is it? I've got wide and long. Can anyone give me another word that we might use for size? Jamie?

J: Diameter.

Tom: How about area? Have you heard that word before, last year? Right, so we've got area of the parachute: the size of it.

The children suggested height; the length and number of the strings; air turbulence or wind; the weight on the end of it; the material used to make it and the size of the person using it. Tom took all these suggestions seriously, restating them when it seemed necessary and acting in a chairman's role. When the children ran out of ideas, he mentioned *Dad's Army* to lead them into thinking about the shape of the parachute. He praised the children and explained that during the week each group would test one of the variables. At the end of the week in the Friday afternoon plenary session they would present their results, discuss what they had found out, and put all the test results together to see if they could come up with the ideal parachute. He asked each working group to decide which variable they wanted to test. The children had some element of choice as to which varible they chose to test. He wrote the group's names next to the relevant item on the board. He stressed again the points about fair testing, using vivid examples of parachutes made of tissue paper or cast iron, dropped from different heights, to emphasise not testing more than one variable at a time. He organised the groups of four to work at a range of tasks: in maths, the use of coordinates; in language, the history of flight (two groups); in geography, mapwork; in craft, designing and making a 3-D contour map with cardboard; and in science, investigating the fall of a parachute. This was the normal way of working for this class. Tom made use of peer tutoring, by groups who had already completed a task, to cut down on some of the explaining and reminding he might otherwise have to do.

He drew the attention of the small group to the design of the parachute: how at the corners he had put sellotape: that was so that the thread didn't just rip straight through. He also prevented this group from using too many variables and reminded them of the fair test. An unsolicited contribution from a child on using parachutes with boats led Tom to think aloud on saving the parachutes to use later in the term. Group work continued with him visiting groups in turn or when needed. Towards the end of the lesson he responded with caution to a child's request that the group test the parachutes from the balcony in the school. He pointed out that there might be a breeze, which would affect the fair test and challenged this group's thinking:

Tom: That could make a difference, couldn't it?
Child: Yes, but it's sheltered quite a bit. If we kept the weight and thought of that, and had the weight heavier when we were outside than in here . . .
Tom: But then you'd change the weight and that's another thing you're changing.
Child: But we'll keep the weight heavier, so that when the wind tries to go that way, it won't be able to.
Tom: Don't you think it would move a bit though? In the wind?
Child: Not really, sir, if you test with the right weight. If you can get the weight right, it would probably go right down.
Tom: What makes you think that?

The discussion continued with Tom listening to the children and taking their ideas seriously. He concluded by agreeing to do the testing with them from the balcony at a break or lunchtime.

In his evaluation Tom thought that his purposes had been fulfilled in that the children had learnt about the practical effect of air resistance. He had expected them to learn a great deal from this initial presentation. He thought that there had been no aspects of the work that they had misunderstood, and no misconceptions. He would not change the lesson, though he thought this presentation could have been a bit more polished. He considered that about half the class had made contributions and the fact that he had just wanted the children to observe closely and come up with their own theories meant that he had catered for differing abilities. He felt that strengths of the lesson were that the demonstration had appealed to their imaginations and that all the children would have the opportunity to do some practical investigation. He had been happy and confident with both the content of the lesson and with relationships: he commented that he had felt really happy to be up there talking to them. He was aware of individual children in the class: who was contributing and who wasn't; who was taking risks in contributing something; and who normally had a great deal to say. He felt he had used specialist knowledge of parachutes, air resistance, factors affecting the fall, fair tests and identifying the variables. His knowledge had given him confidence in talking about these things.

The observer thought that the purposes had been fulfilled well: the children had learnt that the resistance of air slows down movement, and that to investigate a problem in a scientific way, one has to understand fair testing. However, although everyone understood the inaccuracies involved in timing the parachutes, there were some who did not understand the idea of independent variables being tested one at a time. A start had been made on the concepts of dependent and independent variables.

He thought that Tom had assessed the children through many questions and genuine discussion. The presentation had been good and effective: it led to a discussion which formed the basis of the practical work. The children had been continuously involved and the materials had been appropriate, effective and motivating. All in all he felt that the excellent, animated, highly motivating presentation, and careful planning of resources, procedure and organisation, had led to a lively, productive atmosphere which stressed fun as part of learning. There was a pleasant relaxed atmosphere throughout, with a great deal of learning going on through continual involvement of children.

It is clear in this lesson that Tom was using his deep subject knowledge of science, in particular of syntactic structures, to inform his planning, presentation and task design. Through the simple demonstration of dropping a home-made parachute, he managed to get the children thinking about what might make something stay up in the air: this purpose was clear from his opening sentence. The children practised skills of close observation. He encouraged them to suggest variables to be tested singly. The lesson represented the syntactic structures of science fairly accurately. From the point of view of pedagogical content knowledge, Tom had moved from giving the children an open-ended task with no structure, as he did on his first teaching placement, to giving them a worksheet with the steps of the investigation outlined for them, to this much better stage of encouraging the children to select their own variable and test it. The lesson is remarkable for the length and quality of the children's contributions, in particular at the end where a group of boys were arguing for using the balcony. This lesson showed Tom's beliefs about science, especially his understanding of scientific enquiry.

Comment

There are clearly a number of reasons for the good quality of this science lesson in comparison to the weak poetry lesson. Some contextual factors must be taken into consideration. The fact that in the poetry lesson Tom was just setting out on the long task of learning to teach, whereas in the science lesson, he had been teaching for almost two years obviously had some influence. He was much happier about standing up and talking to children. In the first case study, he had a huge class of 36 children, and a teacher who did not really want to have a student. In the science lesson he was teaching his own class of 24 children. The class teacher did not really want to relinquish his hold over the children in the poetry lesson and wanted every piece of work to be linked to the topic of Egypt. In Tom's own class, no such constraints were operating: he was free to plan the work as he chose. Just before the poetry lesson, Tom had been swimming with the children, and had walked them back to their hut through a thunderstorm: they were all extremely wet. The science lesson took place in an large, airy, well-resourced internal classroom: the children were dry and comfortable. However, in additon to these factors subject knowledge also played a role in the success or otherwise of the two lessons. The weakness of Tom's subject knowledge in English, particularly of the role of grammar in writing poetry, the nature of poetry, and the syntactic processes of writing, combined with his poor pedagogical knowledge at this stage in his career, made for a very weak lesson. In contrast, his deep subject knowledge in science, and the attendant confidence such knowledge brought with it, made for a very good lesson.

These two case studies demonstrate the importance of subject knowledge, and in particular of substantive and syntactic knowledge. Two lessons have been presented here from the same teacher for the deliberate purpose of showing that teachers are not equally strong in subject knowledge across all subjects and aspects of the primary curriculum. This point has implications for what we might term expert teaching, and expert teachers, at primary level. This point will be addressed further in Chapter 10.

CHAPTER 3

Curriculum knowledge and knowledge of educational ends

Introduction

These two knowledge bases have been linked in this chapter because what is included in a curriculum needs to be linked to the aims and purposes of education. In some ways the primary curriculum has changed radically since the nineteenth century. However, as scholars such as Alexander (1984) have pointed out, the so-called freedom and flexibility of the post-Plowden era concealed a situation in which there were in reality two primary curricula, which he labelled Curriculum I and Curriculum II. Curriculum I is the high priority area of 'basic skills', defined as reading, writing, and mathematics; Curriculum II comprises the lower priority areas of creative and expressive arts, social and environmental studies, scientific understanding, moral and religious education and so on (Alexander 1984). This divide was in fact reinforced in the National Curriculum by distinguishing between core subjects and foundation subjects, although science entered the core at this time. It is further reinforced by the introduction of the high-priority literacy and numeracy hours (DfEE 1998b; 1999b), sharply defined in their relative frameworks, and made to feel compulsory even if there is some room for negotiation. It would seem then that primary education is about instruction in basic literacy and numeracy, much as elementary education was in the nineteenth century and early in the twentieth century: in fact, *plus ça change*. However, in aims and purposes of primary education and in versions of the primary curriculum, there have always been contradictions and confusions (Alexander 1984). These are related to tensions and misunderstandings: the tensions between the needs of society and the needs of individuals, between child-centred education and education in subjects; and misunderstandings about the nature of subject knowledge. This is not the place for an extended discussion on the primary curriculum, since we are concerned here with the curriculum knowledge of expert teachers. However, teachers need to be aware of the historical complexities and contradictions in the primary curriculum, and consider these in their reflections on teaching and in making professional judgements about what to teach and how to teach it.

Curriculum knowledge

The national curriculum for initial teacher training (ITT), and by implication for teachers, sets out the subject knowledge and curriculum knowledge required by teachers to meet the standards for qualified teacher status (QTS). They have to demonstrate that they:

(a) understand the purposes, scope, structure and balance of the National Curriculum Orders as a whole, and within them, the place and scope of the primary key stages, the primary core and foundation subjects and RE;
(b) are aware of the breadth of content covered by the pupils' National Curriculum across the primary core and foundation subjects and RE;
(c) understand how pupils' learning is affected by their physical, intellectual, emotional and social development;
(d) for each core and specialist subject covered in their training:
    i. have, where applicable, a detailed knowledge and understanding of the relevant National Curriculum programmes of study and level descriptions or end of key stage descriptions across the primary age-range;

                                        (DfEE 1998a, p. 10)

In addition, they are to have secure knowledge and understanding of the content of ICT within subject teaching; secure knowledge and understanding of the subject content in the ITT National Curricula for English, maths and science; knowledge equivalent to A Level for the Key Stage 1 and 2 content in any specialist subject; and in non-core, non-specialist subjects secure knowledge equivalent to Level 7 of the National Curriculum. These details have been given at length to show the pervasiveness of the National Curriculum in defining both subject knowledge and curriculum knowledge.

That it is important to have an understanding of the whole curriculum is not denied. Primary teachers have a unique role of being expected to teach all the subjects of the curriculum. It is important that they understand the nature of each subject, what it can contribute to a child's learning and development, and how the different subjects relate to each other. Otherwise there exists a situation in which Alexander's three related hypotheses about primary practice come into play:

1. What teachers do not adequately understand, they are unlikely to teach well.
2. What teachers do not value they are unlikely to teach well.
3. What teachers do not understand they are unlikely to value.

                                         (Alexander 1984, p. 73)

These can lead to a situation in which ignorance about subjects, lack of security in how to teach them, and low value attached to some subjects at the expense of others, are exacerbated and self-perpetuating. Knowledge of the whole curriculum, in terms of detailed understanding of the nature of each subject and its potential for children's learning and development is clearly essential. However, in this chapter, I am going to argue that the view of the DfEE is an impoverished one, a mere starting-point for consideration of the curriculum and related issues. In this chapter I propose a broader conception of curriculum knowledge which comprises several dimensions. These are: curriculum knowledge related to subject knowledge for teaching; knowledge of the curriculum as differentiated subjects and integrated subjects; and critical understanding of the curriculum.

Curriculum knowledge related to subject knowledge for teaching

This was characterised by Shulman (1986b) as 'the tools of the trade' for teaching – the syllabi: programmes of study; schemes of work, both those commercially available and those developed by schools and individual teachers; and the materials and resources. At its narrowest, this will simply mean knowledge of the National Curriculum in its current version, knowledge of, for example, the published frameworks for literacy and numeracy, and knowledge of the more common published schemes in each subject. It is perfectly possible for teachers to use these and nothing else. Indeed, where subject knowledge has been codified and set out in great detail in the core or high-priority areas of the curriculum, there has been a great reliance on these schemes.

   In core areas, the external pressures from society, reflected in previous and current concerns to 'drive up standards' in literacy and numeracy, have generated much research and curriculum development in areas such as maths, reading and writing. Deep investigation of areas of learning tend to make it more systematised. There is also the internal pressure from teachers who may be insecure in core curriculum areas, notably, maths and English. The problem with such commercial schemes as well as those produced by the government, is that teachers can come to rely on them. In the foundation subjects some teachers and schools can rely almost totally on the Qualification and Curriculum Authority (QCA) exemplar schemes of work, or on commercial schemes. The disadvantages of doing so are twofold. The first is that some of the content of such schemes is simply not very worthwhile or insufficiently challenging for children. Activities may be heavily based on reading and writing, without opportunities to operate within the syntactic structures of that subject. The second problem is that of of deskilling. Crawford (1996) carried out a study of commercially produced history schemes and came to the conclusion that they deskilled teachers in that they removed some of the thinking and professional decision-making. In order to appear as comprehensive as possible, such schemes promised subject knowledge, teaching ideas, assessment proformas, and photocopiable worksheets: in short a complete package designed to provide an instant 'solution' for that part of the curriculum. On closer examination, some of the activities proved to be fairly low-level and unlikely to assist children to achieve the required levels of attainment. Faced with planning for ten subjects, not all of which one is entirely secure in, to use DfEE-speak, it is an attractive solution to take an idea from the curriculum bank for the Tudors, or whatever topic is being taught, each week. What is missing in this kind of planning, is the deep comprehension of the subject matter, consideration of the particular learners' needs and attainments, and adaptation of subject knowledge for teaching these learners. There is often little planning for continuity or progression. Rather than work upon the material themselves, teachers can find themselves delivering a potted version of the subject based upon the interpretation of the scheme designer. Such materials employ a delivery model of the curriculum, in which the teacher presents what others have designed and planned. In this sense these schemes are deskilling. Nowhere is this more apparent than in the literacy and numeracy strategies, where even the timing, organisation and format of the lesson are pre-ordained.

Therefore, one needs to consider the National Curriculum Orders in each subject, the literacy and numeracy strategies and commercial schemes as mere starting-points. Curriculum knowledge can be infinitely richer than this. In the broadest sense, it can mean all those resources and teaching ideas which seem at first maybe to be unlikely. It is an understanding of what is possible to use in order to communicate knowledge, skills and understanding to children within a subject domain. It is closely linked to subject knowledge and an important knowledge base within pedagogical content knowledge, which is dealt with more fully in Chapter 8. For the moment, it is sufficient to say that the activities teachers plan and design for children, the resources and materials they use, and the visual aids are all ways of representing ideas and concepts to children; moreover, they are all ways of representing that subject discipline to children, who form an impression of what it means to do that subject from the kinds of tasks they are given to do in school. I have encountered many student-teachers and teachers for whom the realisation that history is an enquiry-based discipline is a revelation, for they were never made aware of the syntactic structures of history at school or university. They still arrive to train to be teachers with the idea that history is about learning dates and facts about dead kings and queens. For some children who experienced primary education during the 1970s, 1980s, and early 1990s, maths might mean ploughing through one workbook after another; in the late 1990s mental maths might feature more in their conception of maths. The curriculum as experienced by children is as much a function of the generic activities they are allocated as it is a matter of subject labels. Alexander (1995) suggested the notion of the curriculum as a series of generic activities, such as writing, using apparatus, reading, listening/looking, drawing/painting, collaboration, movement, talking to the teacher, construction and talking to the class. Children form their own impressions of what it means to do a subject, as illustrated in this extract from a practical lesson on maths.

Case study 4: Helen: The other sort of maths

Helen, a postgraduate student-teacher, was taking a lesson with a Year 4 class which involved three activities: language, history and maths. The class teacher was away ill, so she took the lesson herself with a supply teacher in support. However, although she fundamentally disagreed with this way of working, she had organised the class as the teacher did, with one group doing maths, one group language and the third group doing history. At the time of data collection, this multi-focus classroom organisation was commonplace; almost something of an orthodoxy in primary teaching. She had to conform to fit in with the expectations of the teacher and the school. Being a history specialist, she had devised her own activity linked to the class topic on transport. The children were to sort photographs of bicycles into date order, using reference books to help them, and devise a caption for each picture describing the changes made with each new model of bicycle. Thus, the curriculum resources she had collected were primary evidence, and the task of observing the photographs of bicycles in detail, looking at all the features, and sequencing them into date order was a genuine historical task. The children were enquiring into transport in the past by looking at primary evidence, interpreting it using their own knowledge and experience, as well as the secondary reference sources, and reaching their own conclusions. She had set up this task and the language task previously.

She then demonstrated the maths activity to the children. It was an investigation of shape: making hexagons and octogons out of folded paper. She wanted the children to have tactile, practical experience of producing 2-D shapes, and to learn that the more sides a shape has, the nearer it is to a circle. This lesson is described more fully in Bennett and Turner-Bisset (1993b). Although not a perfect lesson, the small groups of children with whom she was working did indeed realise that the more sides a shape had, the more like a circle it was. One boy commented that his shape looked like a 50-pence piece. One of the problems of this kind of curriculum organisation is that other groups' activities can sometimes look more attractive than one's own task, as the following transcript extract shows. One of the children in the language group asked the teacher what the maths group were doing:

Child: What are they doing, maths?
Helen: Yes, they're cutting out some shapes.
Child: Is it for maths?
Helen: Yes.
Child: So when I do maths, it's not maths like in doing maths?
Helen: Well, unfortunately this afternoon, you're going to be doing the other sort of maths.
Child: Oh!
Helen: But you can do this one perhaps tomorrow or the day after.
Child: Why are you doing this?
Helen: Because I'm being taped. The lady wanted to see me actually teaching some maths rather than just giving you work from books.

This is a fascinating piece of discourse. It shows that this eight-year-old child has a clear understanding of what it means to do maths normally in the classroom context: to work from books. It also shows his emerging understanding that doing maths might mean something else. There is maths, and there is the other sort of maths. Both teacher and child understood this. In her post-lesson interview, she was adamant that she would not organise her class in this way, but teach only one subject at a time to the whole class, even though the tasks might be differentiated for differing abilities. She was critical of herself in the fact that she had not been able to devote appropriate time and attention to each of the three subject groups. The extract does show however, that the curriculum activities can come to represent whole-subject areas, as well as ideas and concepts within a subject.

Tools of the trade

It has been stated that curriculum knowledge includes knowledge of the National Curriculum, literacy and numeracy strategies, published schemes of work and commercially available schemes and packs. What else might the 'tools of the trade' be in the broadest sense? Some examples are given below of curriculum knowledge in the broadest sense.

1. A Year 5 class teacher is planning to do some 3-D work with her class. She wants the children to learn more about line, colour and shape. An exhibition in the local gallery of Beryl Cook's paintings prompts her to buy some postcards and prints of these pictures. She also has an unwanted gift at home: a model of a very fat jolly lady reclining in a swimming costume boldly striped in orange and green. She takes in these items to use with the children. She wants them to develop observational skills so she types out short descriptions or accounts of how each picture came into being. The children work on an activity matching the pictures to the descriptions. The children present their findings to the class. She then uses the pictures and the model to initiate some creative work with clay in which the children make curvy figures.

2. A Year 4 teacher, working on a project on Tudors, finds some woodcut illustrations in a book on the Tudors, which she was thinking of throwing out because the text was too difficult for primary age children. The illustrations are copies of original Tudor pictures in black and white. She dismantles the book, and photocopies and enlarges the woodcuts to use as primary evidence of Tudor costume. This she uses alongside a pack of portraits from the National Portrait Gallery. The children are given a glossary of terms to do with Tudor dress to help them describe their pictures. They then produce a 'Who am I?' puzzle to go with each portrait and swap them in the class. The portraits and puzzles are used to make a display, designed and planned by the children themselves. Here the teacher is not only teaching historical skills and processes, but generic skills of observation and recording. Through putting the information they have gained into a different genre and medium, the children are working actively on the

evidence. In literacy she is extending their vocabulary and giving them experience of writing in a particular genre.

3. A Year 6 teacher is about to begin a topic on probability. He selects for his curriculum materials a clothes-line, pegs and some cards on which he writes words such as improbable, probable, likely, not very likely: in fact the full range of vocabulary related to probability. He also brings in a stale end of a loaf from home. He starts the lesson by opening a window and throwing out a handful of breadcrumbs. The class are intrigued. He asks them if they think it is probable or likely that some birds will come to take the breadcrumbs. The class are sure that this is very probable. They wait a little while and some starlings swoop down for the crumbs. He next asks how probable or likely it is that some elephants will arrive to eat the crumbs. The children laugh and assure him this is extemely unlikely, in fact, improbable! As the school is a few miles from the sea, he asks how probable it is that a seagull would take some of the crumbs. The children discuss this and say it is very probable. One boy points out that the starlings have had most of the crumbs already. The teacher throws out another handful and asks the question again. This time the starlings, three sparrows and two fat herring gulls swoop down for the bread. There is much laughter, and the boy says: 'Well, if you are going to throw bread out of the window all day . . . !' The teacher settles the class good-humouredly and sets up the clothes-line across the room. He asks them about each of the examples of probability they have seen and children volunteer to peg the appropriate card to the line for each one. He invites them to make up more examples for the cards in between the extremes of probable and improbable. Throughout the lesson the children are all having opportunities to use the language of probability and the clothes-line represents the gradations of probability. In this lesson, the clothes-line, pegs, cards, breadcrumbs and the birds themselves (albeit unwittingly) are all used as curriculum materials.

4. A teacher of a combined Year 1/Year 2 class is planning to teach about electricity and electrical circuits. She has the standard equipment of batteries, wires, clips, switches, paper-clips, bulbs, buzzers and small motors. She also has a moving toy, battery-powered, of a little clown which flips itself over. She show the children this to start with and asks for their ideas on what is making the toy move and how. As the children are so young, there is quite a range of ideas. They are all recorded on a sheet, for the class to refer back to at the end of the topic. She gets a child to open up the toy and reveal the battery. She further asks how this object can make things move. She demonstrates torches, one with light, and one with a light and buzzer, finishing off with her trusty AA torch, with a flashing red light for breakdown purposes at night. She asks the children for their ideas on how these work. They move from this into making a bulb light up and other circuit-making activities. At the end of the topic, which takes several

weeks, she shows the clown toy again and asks for their ideas on what makes it work. The children have much clearer ideas about electricity and electrical circuits.

5. A Year 5 teacher, wanting to teach concepts of urban and rural in a local study for geography and history, assembles some slides of cities, towns, suburbia, villages, rural landscapes and isolated houses. Most of the slides are taken from a coffee-table book on 'The Heritage of Britain' and some are from her holiday. She shows these slides asking the children whether they are cities, towns, or whatever. There is some discussion as to what makes a city, and the children state what each slide is. She then introduces them to the concepts of 'urban' and 'rural' showing these words with their Latin roots on the board. She asks them to classify the numbered slides again, into urban and rural. This is supported by aerial photos from the internet and maps of urban and rural areas. By now the children have the idea that it is the number and density of buildings which makes an area urban or rural. They compare two maps of the local area, one new and one old, and the children are able to say that the area used to be rural but has changed in the last century, becoming urban.

6. A teacher in a tiny rural school, has a mixed-age class of Reception, Year 1 and Year 2. She plans to do an integrated project on art, history and personal and social education. This rural area, located near gravel extraction pits and farmland, is very poor, and the children come from deprived backgrounds. There has been fighting in the playground recently, and she wants to involve them in making the playground a more pleasant place to be in. Her curriculum materials are: a set of laminated colour copies of Breughel's *Children Playing*, a Dutch picture from the sixteenth century; a set of magnifying glasses; art materials; Peter and Iona Opie's (1969) book on playground games and rhymes; a set of fivestones or jacks, some marbles and some skipping ropes. She starts by showing them the picture and asking them to work in pairs to make a list of all the games they can see. The children soon generate long lists, with the elder in each pair doing the scribing. They feed back their findings and the teacher asks them what games they play now: Are any of them the same as they were in the painting? Some indeed are still played and the class make up new lists of old and new games. The teacher wants to fix the ideas of the games more firmly in everyone's mind, so she asks them to stand at the front of the class and make a freeze-frame of the picture, standing in the pose of one of the children in the painting. They are given a few moments to choose their figure. The work then develops over several weeks: she demonstrates games such as jacks and asks children to demonstrate their versions of marbles and other games. They play street-games, such as What's the Time Mr Wolf?, the King of the Golden River, Ralevo, Grandmother's Footsteps, Hopscotch, Simple Simon, Gluepots, Red-letter Day and a variety of skipping games. In literacy, they work on letters of the

alphabet, writing instructions for games, and captions for their pictures of their favourite figure from the painting. In art, they attempt a crowd scene using simplified figures to show movement and activity and their beginnings of understanding about composition. In history, they re-enact old games, collect oral evidence from neighbours and relatives about the games they played when they were little and play all these games in the playground and at home. In PE they are developing gross motor skills such as coordination through the games; jacks provides a rich, incentive-laden activity for developing fine motor coordination, particularly of eye to hand. For personal and social education, the children are learning to cooperate with each other, the externally imposed rules of the games providing a framework to guide their behaviour in the different games. In addition, the games are a rich resource for the children to draw upon while in the playground, helping to reduce the popularity of kiss-chase which has caused many arguments and some bullying. Finally the class and teacher request some funds from the PTA to help realise the children's new designs for the playground, with designated areas. The children draw basic maps of the playground, showing where they would like the areas to be. In this case, the curriculum materials were as varied as the picture, the book, the play equipment, the games themselves, and the parents, and grandparents who supplied additional games.

One could continue with many more examples: the teacher who used a candle-powered boat to teach ideas about jet propulsion; the teacher who told the story of Boudicca up to the point of the Iceni deciding what to do about the Roman threat, and using drama and role-cards to set up an re-enactment of the tribe's full council meeting; the teacher who brought in her 'jazz-kit', comprising a variety of percussion instruments, to teach about vibration in sound and to use to accompany the historical dance music she played to the children; the teacher who told religious stories and used artefacts to teach central ideas about different religions; or the teacher who used a set of ten wooden skittles, and a wooden ball, brought at a car boot sale, to teach number bonds up to ten, through the children playing with these old toys. Anything can be utilised as curriculum materials: expert teachers use their deep subject knowledge and other knowledge bases to devise, adapt, select and create materials for teaching. The downside of this is that part of being a teacher can be the tendency to look on everything in life as a possible resource to use with the children, a predilection well known to teachers and their partners, in which it becomes almost impossible to 'switch off' from the job of teaching. This hazard of the job apart, it is one of the hallmarks of expert teachers to be creative and inventive in this way, in their quest for the best possible way of communicating and sharing their knowledge, skills and understanding with their children.

The curriculum: differentiated and integrated

In order for teachers to operate in this way across the primary curriculum, teachers need deep content knowledge in all the subjects of the curriculum. As well as knowledge of each individual subject, there is more. From their understanding of substantive and syntactic structures of each discipline, teachers need to be able to make connections between subjects, as in some of the examples given above. These are not merely the sometimes tenuous connections of thematic work (see for example, Turner-Bisset 2000a), but how the various skills, processes, concepts and attitudes from each subject relate to each other. In the examples above, the concepts 'urban' and 'rural' are used both in history and in geography. Skills of observation are involved in several of the lessons, as are design processes and processes of reasoning. Language and, to a lesser extent, maths play a part in the lessons too. Historically people have meant different things by the expression 'the integrated curriculum'. A curriculum can be merely non-differentiated: one in which subjects are subsumed under the heading of topic or thematic work without due regard for the essential nature of each discipline; while a genuinely integrated curriculum is one in which the differences, qualities and structures of each discipline have been differentiated (Pring 1976) and proper connections made. There is a difference. In addition to statutory requirements, including spiritual, moral, cultural, and social development, teachers also need to understand how provision for citizenship, environmental, health and personal and social education can fit into the existing curriculum; and coherent, sensible links made. This is rather a tall order, and has implications for the kind of people we would want to become teachers, which will be dealt with in Chapter 10.

Critical understanding of the curriculum

This third aspect of curriculum knowledge has been hinted at earlier in this chapter. Depending on when one experienced primary teaching, as a child or as a student or beginning teacher, one tends to have images or models of what the primary curriculum should be. In the 1950s, I experienced a rigorous curriculum which comprised maths, English and intelligence tests in preparation for the eleven-plus examination. The mornings were given over to this and copious religious instruction. In the afternoons, we had physical training, art and craft (sewing for girls and woodwork for boys), music, story and very rarely, some history or geography. Whatever one thinks of this curriculum, we did arrive at secondary school both numerate and literate, and with a thirst for the new subjects. During the early 1960s this type of quasi-elementary school curriculum continued, but later that decade, and in the 1970s and early 1980s, there was meant to be a Plowdenesque revolution: certainly rigid streaming was abandoned and mixed ability teaching became the norm. However, despite surface appearances of flexibility, what with multi-curriculum focus, the integrated day, group work, project work and topic work, the 'basics' part of the curriculum tended to be taught separately and granted a higher status in the curriculum (Alexander 1984). If one trained at this time, the individualisation of work, the multi-curriculum focus, and the emphasis on group instruction would have been perceived as the normal way of managing and teaching the curriculum.

The introduction of the National Curriculum in 1989, with ten foundation subjects, brought in for the first time the notion of 'a broad and balanced curriculum' for all primary age children (DES 1989a). However, maths and English were protected by being designated core subjects and thus effectively granted a higher status. Science was brought into the core, presumably to ensure the eventual production of future scientists and technicians. However, with each subject lobby arguing powerfully for its subject, the amount of content in the first version of the National Curriculum was impossibly large. The slimmed down version (DfE 1993b) improved matters somewhat, but the introduction of the National Literacy Strategy (DfEE 1998b) and the National Numeracy Strategy (DfEE 1999b) effectively gave English and maths a higher status than all of the other subjects, and split the curriculum into two again: the basics and the rest. To ease their intro- duction the statutory orders for the other foundation subjects were suspended (QCA 1998) and teachers were recommended to reduce, prioritise or combine the content of the other subjects. The new National Curriculum (DfEE 1999c) maintains the status of maths and English, but restores the statutory force of the orders in the other core and foundation subjects. The problem of curriculum overload is still with us (Turner-Bisset 2000a).

It is important that teachers have some kind of historical overview of the primary curriculum, some awareness of continuity and change over the years. It is not enough to take the curriculum as a given entity; instead teachers need to have an informed critical awareness and understanding of the forces which have shaped the primary curriculum in its current form. I would argue that this is an important aspect of curriculum knowledge for expert teachers: to have the knowledge which enables them to make informed judgements about what they might select from the curriculum to teach particular classes. Armed with a historical overview, teachers are aware of the central tensions in the primary curriculum between a broad and balanced curriculum and education in the basics of literacy and numeracy (and more recently ICT). They would know, for example of the cross-curricular themes from the first version of the National Curriculum; how they were intended to provide some education in the social subjects neglected by it; and how, if taken as a complete package, they could represent a whole alternative national curriculum. This kind of insight leads to the understanding, crucial in education, that the primary curriculum we have now is part of a historical tradition, and moreover, is only one of many possible curricula which we could be providing for primary children. There are many possible selections from a culture which may be deemed essential for primary children: much depends on the aims and purposes of education (which will be dealt with in the next section). Expert teachers are informed about the debates on curriculum issues: have read for example the National Advisory Committee on Creative and Cultural Education (NACCCE) report (DfEE 1999a), which stresses the importance of creative and cultural education, and the need to remove the distinction between core and foundation subjects. They are able to add their voices to the debate.

Two examples follow of expert teachers expressing their ideas about the curriculum, primary practice and their philosophy of primary teaching. The first is Katy, a final year BEd student who specialised in art, history and early years education during her four-year course. She received glowing reports from her four placements and a first-class honours degree. The interview is taken from a four-year study into the beliefs and practice of primary BEd students in teaching history. The second is David, the teacher whose lesson on the Romans is described in the Prologue (Case study 1). The interviews, part of a two-year study into the impact of 20-day courses in history subject knowledge, were recorded immediately following the course and two years later, subsequent to the lesson observation.

Case study 5: Katy (early years specialist): No gobbets

Katy had not been able to do any history teaching on her final practice, but in her final year interview she described the history teaching which she had done in a reception class during her third year practice. When asked what was good or bad about this teaching, she answered:

Katy: What was good was that all the children were involved. They all had a part to play in it and they all really enjoyed it. They loved the toys we brought in as well; they were enthusiastic on the subject, which was good. I think what was bad was maybe the time limitation on it. We couldn't really go forward. It was their obvious area of interest and they were very enthusiastic about it, yet we couldn't continue the work because we just didn't have the time.

Katy had talked earlier in the interview about the need for continuity and progression in planning and teaching history. For her it was an essential part of good practice. However, she clearly found this difficult, if not impossible to achieve with the kind of 'snapshot history' she was being forced to teach because of the limited amount of time available for subjects other than literacy and numeracy. This led her to question the role of, and the need for history in the early years curriculum, and the nature of the curriculum itself.

Katy: My main belief is, because I specialise in early years, I've found that particularly in reception there is so much more to do that history in becoming increasingly sidelined anyway. Also I think that you need to prioritise and I just think there's too much emphsis on literacy and numeracy, but I think that things like art, music and PE are really important for a young child. I think history is important too, but when you have got a limited time, you have got to find what's best really. I would probably take history to Year 1 and start with it there.

Interviewer: So what would be your rationale for say, PE, art and music rather than history?

Katy: I think there needs to be a balance between the more formal subjects and I think that PE is something that children need to do anyway. I think they need that physical activity, especially little children. You do PE and it does hype them up for the rest of the afternoon, but also they need to release that energy, and same with creative subjects like art and music. They are needed as balance. I think at the moment there are so many subjects being covered in the curriculum that it is very difficult to give them any worth. I think you should save it (history); so you can put more time into it. I felt that when I have been teaching history, it felt almost useless, because I was doing a quick snapshot. I feel I am not really helping the children in any way at all: I am not giving them enough time.

Interviewer: But you might be sparking up their interest?

Katy: Yes, but that's quite cruel, sparking up their interest in subjects that you're not going to follow up.

Katy here had strong views about the relative worth of giving children little gobbets of history, and the moral implications of doing so. This led her to question the role of history in the overcrowded early years curriculum. She made her own professional judgement not to teach it before Year 1 at the earliest. Her experience of children and learning contexts of this age-range together with her early years specialist training played an important role in her thinking, knowledge and judgement.

Case study 1 revisited: David: Creating a Roman galley

These extracts are taken from the interview that took place immediately following the end of the in-service course on history subject knowledge (Turner-Bisset and Nichol 1999). David was a geography specialist, who had attended the course because he knew so little about how to teach history. He was asked what he had learnt on the course:

David: If I could explain that when I started teaching history in the school, my style was such that I looked at the documents and thought you've got a thousand year breadth to teach in one term and all these different aspects to cover, and you think: well, I'll never do this. You become almost like pouring out information; you felt pressurised to get this information across in as quick a time as possible. So my method was, for the whole topic of Tudors and Stuarts, me putting up dates and talking about it and children listening and responding, but you know in your heart that they are not taking it in, and it's not working, but what choice have I got? You've got to get this covered. You go on the course and people actually know what they are talking about, saying: Well, you don't have to do that. It's the legal requirement but it's rubbish. They are not afraid to stand up and say that, and you think: Great, freedom to experiment! And my approaches to history have completely changed. It's also had a knock-on effect on other subjects as well; it's not just history.

Although his comments relate to history, there is a sense of emancipation as a teacher, and a restoration of his professional judgement, which had been eroded by the introduction of the content-heavy National Curriculum. The course empowered him through the new understanding of the subject, and the many ways to teach it, and reaffirmed him as a professional. He felt able to select what he thought was important for the children to learn, rather than trying to teach everything. He felt able to stand up, and say, like his course tutors (both academic historians with a wealth of classroom experience) that the legal requirements were rubbish. His knowledge of learners had informed him that under his old approach, the children were not actually learning anything, but he had felt powerless to do anything about it.

Comment

This sense of power as a professional is crucial for teachers, and is an essential part of being an expert teacher. The power is based upon the professional knowledge and understanding, in these two cases of subject and curriculum knowledge, knowledge of learners and general pedagogical knowledge. Both of these teachers held views on aspects of the curriculum which were informed by their professional knowledge and understanding. One may not necessarily agree with them: for example, I have argued elsewhere for the value of doing history with very young children (Turner-Bisset 2000b). Katy did not share my view, but what is important is that these teachers have views and can articulate them with an informed rationale. Katy felt that movement and creative activities were more important for young children, and she argued against giving them little gobbets of a subject. If teachers merely accept the curriculum as externally and legally imposed, without speaking up for the profession in which they work, and without adapting it according to their professional knowledge, they are disempowered, and reduced to 'deliverers', rather than professionals. Expert teachers' understanding of curriculum in the broadest sense must also be linked to their knowledge of educational ends.

Knowledge of educational ends

The curriculum is there for a purpose: it is meant to achieve educational ends. There are three kinds of educational ends. The first are the legal requirements, which are enshrined in government legislation. This is not the place to comment on these at length, but it is worth saying that the first version of the National Curriculum was remarkably brief and vague as to the aims and values of education. The new Curriculum 2000 (DfEE 1999c) is slightly better in this respect, but we are still in a position of having a curriculum imposed upon us whose aims and purposes have not been clearly thought through. The recent moratorium on change in the National Curriculum imposed post-Dearing provided a welcome breather in the climate of rapid change, but with the Dearing Report (DfE 1993b) and with the review of the curriculum for the year 2000, it has been assumed that the aims of education have already been decided. However, as will be illustrated in the following section, the different traditions of primary education make for a bundle of explicit and tacit aims which have not been fully examined: some of them reinforce each other and others compete. There is still a lack of consensus as to the purpose of primary education. The second set of aims are those of the school. Most schools have some sort of a mission statement which sets out what the school would like to achieve for its children in terms of different kinds of development. The third set of aims and values are those of teachers themselves. Given that teaching involves a heavy investment of the self, one's values, whether implicit or explicit, are going to play a part in one's teaching. To sum up, there are educational ends and values of society, of the school community, and of the teacher, which constitute an important knowledge base and interact with other knowledge bases in the amalgam of pedagogical content knowledge. Each of these will be discussed in term.

Educational ends of society

The curriculum is a means to an end in education. It exists to achieve particular goals and purposes. However, the matter is complex, for there are competing traditions and tensions as to the ends of education. Blyth (1965) suggested that there were three competing traditions in primary education. The old elementary school tradition, which is one of the foundations of today's primary education, was the education of the masses to meet the needs of society for an appropriately skilled workforce, one which was drilled in basic arithmetic, reading and writing, with a sizeable dose of religious instruction to bring them out of evil thoughts and behaviour. The elementary tradition also had the aim of keeping the working classes in their place in society: to educate them too much, particularly in human-ities and the arts, oracy and argument, would be to risk the social order, through producing articulate, thinking, well-rounded human beings. The preparatory school tradition aimed at preparing the future leaders of society via a curriculum which introduced children to the classical and academic cultural heritage, through study of subject disciplines. The developmental tradition argued for a curriculum which was structured around the physical, emotional and cognitive development of the child. This child-centred way of thinking about the purposes of education can be linked to the progressive tradition, in which the curriculum is built around the needs of the individual. Those who espouse progressive ways of thinking about education see childhood as a separate phase of life, not merely as a preparation for adulthood. The strongest element in this tradition is the vision of producing autonomous individuals, who have developed those aspects of themselves which they wish to develop, and who have the capacity to go on learning and developing as they wish.

To these traditions must be added others. Alexander (1995) further identifed three other traditions or ideologies in primary education. There is the behavioural or mechanistic tendency, which sees the purpose of education as producing easily measurable attainment or performance in children, usually narrowly defined as achievement in 'the basics' of the curriculum and present in both the 'Payment by Results' system of inspection of the nineteenth century, and its modern day equivalents of standard attainment tasks (SATs), league tables and OFSTED inspections. Related to the elementary tradition is the utilitarian tradition: education for the purpose of meeting the economic and technological needs of society, with a similar emphasis on education for labour needs. There is also the social reformist and egalitarian tradition (Alexander 1995) of the curriculum being to enable the child to both fulfil individual potential and contribute to the progress of society, in terms of a plural society, democracy and social justice. To these it is worth adding the political purposes of education and the curriculum designed to achieve these. This is not a tradition as such, but there is no denying that political purpose and ambition have a role to play in shaping the curriculum. Immediately following the election of 1997, we were left in no doubt that education was going to be high on the agenda of the Labour government. The declaration of goals in terms of achievement in literary and numeracy by the year 2002, the introduction of the National Literacy Strategy, and the National Numeracy Strategy, the temporary suspension of statutory orders in other foundation subjects, and the assessment procedures to measure achievement, have all had their impact on the curriculum as experienced by teachers and children.

Educational ends of schools

All primary schools will have some kind of statement of aims: some intention of what they hope to achieve with the young people entrusted to them. Most readers will be familiar with such statements. Sometimes, but not always, these will be translated explicitly into particular parts of the taught curriculum, for example: physical development to be achieved through a wide range of curricular and extra curricular sporting activities; or aesthetic development through arts and creative activities. Concerns about social and moral development will often be provided for through the hidden curriculum: what else is experienced in school apart from the taught curriculum. In addition to the explicitly-stated aims there are the cultural norms and expectations of a school. Every school has its own sub-culture; new members of the staff are expected to absorb the prevailing culture and usually to conform to it. Thus there might be particular ways of managing order, of promoting social and moral development, and even of teaching which are the sub-cultural norms. Embedded in these are expectations and aims for the children. This can be a benefical aspect of school life. One head of a middle school, in discussing the feeder first schools during the course of an inspection, remarked that children from one particular first school were easily identifiable. They had come from a school in which the ethos of caring for others was very strong; thus they tried to intervene in playground incidents and tried to promote harmony in the classroom. In addition, they had been encouraged to develop their own interests, and were more autonomous learners than some of their peers from neighbouring feeder schools. Thus each school has its own sub-culture and set of explicit and tacit educational ends for their children.

Educational ends of teachers

One does not go into teaching for the money. It is perceived as a job with intrinsic rather than extrinsic rewards: one goes into the job to help children learn, to improve their lives, and to have some impact upon society. It can be a job with enormous satisfaction and pleasure, attainable in aiding others to develop. However, material rewards are sparse, particularly at classroom teacher level in primary education. The management structure of primary schools is very 'flat' compared with that of secondary school, in which there is a tier of middle management comprising heads of department, and heads of year or house. Below head and deputy, there are posts of responsibility for curriculum areas, but the rewards are minute: one or two additional points on the scale, for sometimes considerable reponsibility such as maths or special educational needs coordinator. It is rare to be given additional points for excellent teaching. In addition there is a culture of altruism and humility which dates back to the elementary school tradition, in which school teachers, often recruited from the lower classes themselves, were to be kept in their place in society, and not encouraged to climb the social ladder.

In this culture, the desire to help others is prevalent and a worthy value held by many primary teachers. There are other values and ends, some of which may be concerned with society's needs, for example to produce self-motivated learners who will be able to hold down several jobs during their lifetime. Others may be concerned with the ends for a particular class or group of learners, such as tolerance of different races and genders; an understanding that violence and bullying are wrong; or using a wide range of registers in writing and speech, to give them entry to all levels of society. Whatever the individual teacher's educational ends are, she or he needs to have examined them, and to have made them explicit to themselves.

Conclusion

In Chapter 6 a case study (Case study 11) is presented of a final year BEd student, wrestling with the conflicting educational aims of politicians, society, the school and her own aims, beliefs and values. Although not yet a qualified teacher, she is aware of the conflicting educational aims and purposes of education, and she shows a sophisticated understanding of how to operate within the school sub-culture in order to promote her aims. In this sense, she is expert in this particular knowledge base: this kind of understanding will be immensely valuable in all the teaching jobs she undertakes.

I would argue, that expert teachers should have an awareness and understanding of all three sets of aims: not to leave them to politicians and the media, but to explore those understandings and be aware of how varying educational aims may impact upon their teaching. They should be aware of the historical basis of primary education, the traditions on which it is built, the tensions between these traditions, the aims of the sub-culture of the schools in which they work, and their own educational ends, which should be part of the process of reflection.

CHAPTER 4

Models of teaching and learning and general pedagogical knowledge

Expert teaching requires knowledge and understanding of a range of theories about learning and about teaching. Subscribing to one or two theories limits the options available to the teacher to connect learners and subject knowledge; having a broad range of theories extends possibilities and opens the mind to innovative ways of teaching. It is a common assumption that there is one theory of learning which is correct. However it is not the case that one theory is right and the others are all wrong. Likewise, there is no one correct way of teaching which is superior to all the others. Much depends upon the kind of learning involved. Presented in this chapter are: a sample of theories of learning; a sample of concepts of teaching; examples of both of these in practice; a discussion of the relationship between theories of learning and pedagogical strategies; and a theory of pedagogy as a teaching repertoire.

Theories of learning

We generally define learning as a process which brings about some sort of fairly permanent change of behaviour or way of thinking. Below are some examples of learning which are taken from experience as a parent and teacher: they are all multi-layered and can be considered in different ways. However one dominant kind of learning is meant to be represented in each example. It is worth reflecting on these examples of learning briefly, for they can inform our understanding of learning; they can and do inform the practice of expert teachers.

Examples of learning

1. Susie, an 18-month-old girl, on seeing a large outdoor paddling pool for the first time, notes the bright blue of the expanse of water, and attempts to walk

across it, but of course her feet sink into the water. She shrieks with astonishment (up until now all surfaces, whether black, brown, grey, fawn of green, have borne her weight and not made her wet). She spends some time in the pool, splashing about, coming out on to dry land and going back into the pool many times. She chuckles with glee. The next time she sees such a pool, she demands of her parents that they remove her sandals and she wades into the shallow water.

2. Emma, a three-year-old, visits the hairdresser for the first time with mother and older sister. She observes silently the procedures and actions of the hairdresser, and submits in her turn to the draping in a cape and sitting perfectly still while her hair is cut. Later that evening she astonishes her father by fetching a towel from the kitchen, draping it around his neck and proceeding to 'cut' his hair with imaginary scissors and comb. 'Keep still, Daddy!' she instructs him firmly. She then moves on to her mother and older sister and gives them the same treatment, each time whisking off the towel with a flourish and a shake.

3. Thomas, a four-year-old starting school, is enchanted by the classroom and the variety of things in it. When all the others are seated on the carpet, he is still in the home corner, talking on the telephone. The teacher fetches him and seats him on the carpet near her. This happens for several days, but each time she draws attention to the desired behaviour, and praises him for coming to sit on the carpet. She lets him take the register to the office, accompanied by a girl who knows the way. After a few days he is first on the carpet at her feet, cross-legged and arms folded, hoping to be rewarded in some way.

4. Matthew, a five-year-old, is seated at a table in the classroom doing jigsaw puzzles with a parent helper. One large puzzle with many pieces is of the four seasons and the boy struggles with it, unsure of where to start. The assistant suggests that he find all the pieces with the nest and birds on them, and all the names of the seasons. He does this, and she shows him how they form the top two corners of each section of the puzzle. He finds some more of the side pieces easily after that and soon they have the outline of the whole puzzle. There are fewer pieces left to sort through, and she suggests that he does winter first, with its distinctive snowy pieces. He does this, then tackles summer with its clear blue sky. All the while he chatters about the content of the puzzle, and she talks to him about the sequence of events with the birds in the top right-hand corner of each section. He places the last piece with great satisfaction. The next time he tries the puzzle, on his own, he searches deliberately for the bird and writing pieces, having learnt this strategy.

5. Harriet, a six year-old, receives the gift of a two-octave keyboard, tape of music and instruction manual for Christmas. She spends the first few days playing with the pre-recorded sounds and listening to the tape. Eventually she teaches

herself to play 'I'd like to teach the world to sing' from the manual on the black keys using the numerical fingering chart. At this stage she cannot read standard staff notation, but she is happy playing this tune and making up her own tunes. A few months later, her parents buy the spare school piano. Harriet sees it delivered, goes to examine and play with it, and runs to her mother shouting: 'Mum, this is just like my keyboard only it has a longer bit on each side!' Puzzled, her mother goes to see what the excitement is about. Harriet shows her the two octaves which match the ones on her keyboard and points to the other octaves on either side. She plays her party piece on the black notes in the centre of the piano. Her mother points out that most people play on the white keys first and suggests starting on a white key to see what happens. Harriet tries this, and with one or two wrong notes produces the same tune a semi-tone down. She also tries playing the same tune at different points on the piano, noticing how it sounds in each octave. A few months later, Harriet starts piano lessons. Her teacher is sensitive enough to listen and applaud the progress Harriet has made on her own, even writing down her 'compositions' or musical doodles in staff notation. Harriet begins to understand the relationship between the music she hears and plays and standard notation. In a couple of weeks she is reading music.

6. Rebecca, a seven-year-old, is out in the yard of the village hall trying to ride a bike without stabilisers. Her mother and a friend watch her. The mother is anxious: the child does not really want to do this, but all her friends have given up stabilisers. Time and again she sets the right-hand pedal to the high position to push off with and sets off, only to collapse sideways in a heap. Her legs are becoming bruised. Her mother is thinking she should give up, but her friend, who has given all three of her sons the opportunity to learn to ride a bike, tells her that it's going well. The child is learning to balance: she is learning through doing it, that if the bike leans one way, she must compensate with her weight to restore the balance and avoid falling over. She is also learning to think about this, respond, and pedal simultaneously, but not as yet to steer. From time to time, she almost manages a right and left push down on the pedals, before she falls off. Eventually she pedals, almost in balance for several yards, and jumps off, shouting with excitement.

7. A class of eight- and nine-year-olds are studying the Tudors. Their teacher sings to them one verse of 'Greensleeves' at the end of the school day. The words are on an overhead transparency, projected on to the classroom wall. They sing it through several times. The following week, some of the children come to the teacher and tell her they have learnt the verse by heart. They lead the singing, and over four weeks, the class learn the whole song in this way.

8. A group of children are playing a street game 'Cannon' in the playground. This is a variant of cricket combined with chase. A wicket is set up of clothes-pegs:

three uprights with one peg forming the cross piece, leaning against the playground wall. Members of one team take it in turns to aim at the wicket three times with a tennis ball. If they knock over the pegs, all members of the team chase the opposing team until one is caught: that person is then out. If they miss all three times or let the ball be caught on the rebound, the opposing team chase them until one member is caught. This continues until all members of the one team are caught. Whichever team wins has their innings. Rachel, a ten-year-old new to the school, watches and is eventually allowed to join in. She throws the ball underarm at first, but this rarely knocks down the pegs because there is not enough force. Furthermore it bounces so gently and high that the opposing team catch the ball regularly and she is 'out' almost immediately. She watches the best bowlers and realises they do it overarm. She tries this, but her efforts seem more puny than before. After watching some of the others bowl, and practising in her garden after school, she learns the arm movements and how to aim accurately with this method. Soon she is in demand for any of the teams which form on an *ad hoc* basis.

9. Small groups of seven- and eight-year-olds have been set the task of finding out how many different ways they can combine 20p, 10p, 5p, 2p, and 1p coins to make 50p. One child goes to the maths cupboard and returns with a pile of coins which the children handle and arrange into amounts of 50p. They are to record their work so each child writes down each method using addition signs. They all do it randomly at first. Another child, Tracy, suddenly throws down her pen and says: 'This is stupid!' She crosses out her work, and gets a fresh sheet of paper, muttering to herself: 'What did we do when we were in Miss Bird's class? You know, with the 20p?' Her friend, Joanna, hears her and says: 'We made a chart!' Tracy draws a chart with a column for each kind of coin and a tally system of each coin used. Each combination takes one line across the page and can be read at a glance. The others look at her system and copy her.

10. Toby is three-years-old when he starts this piece of learning and 11 when he finishes it. Aged three he watches his mother make mince pies at Christmas: she give him some pastry, a rolling pin and a variety of shape-cutters to make pastry shapes. He watches and enjoys making his own shapes to bake in the oven; this activity happens each year until he is five. His mother asks him to count the lids and put them on for her. He takes over this stage in the process, and learns from watching and trying, how to moisten the rim of each base to seal the pies. When eight he progessed to placing the bases in the greased bun tin, putting in the mincemeat and finishing the rest of the process, including brushing the lids with beaten egg. Around this time he learns on other occasions from watching and copying, how to break an egg successfully into a basin and beat it. He also learns how to make dough, first weighing and

measuring quantities of ingredients from the recipe for his mother; later getting his hands in the mixture and feeling what pastry dough should feel like when it is ready. Gradually, by the time he is ten he can do most of the different parts of the job. At Christmas when he is 11 he asks his mother: 'Mum, can I make the mince pies this year?' She agrees readily. He does the whole task, with her just watching and offering gentle reminders about using the timer to ensure he does not burn them.

Relating the examples to the theories of learning
In these examples of learning, some of which occur with teaching, and some without, can be traced elements of a number of learning theories. The first example could be explained by schema theory, which originated in the Genevan School, with Piaget and his colleagues. The essential notion here is that thought processes depend upon our ability to create mental representations of objects and people. The experience of these, and the way in which they relate to each other, is stored as schema: internal representations which can be quite complex patterns. They involve recognition, understanding, action and sometimes emotional reactions. Adaptation is the process by which schemas are changed. It has two aspects: assimilation and accommodation. When a person has a new experience, some sort of image or internal representation is made of it. But to become part of a schema, the additional process of accommodation is needed; it is not merely a matter of adding new knowledge. The new ideas, images, knowledge or experience need to be worked on in some way so that the schema is adjusted. This process is accommodation, and the process by which this happens is called equilibration. A child, this case Susie, may have an established schema for surfaces on which one walks: a stable notion that all such surfaces will bear one's weight and be solid. This is an example of equilibrium. A specific pattern of action is associated with it, in this case, walking on it. However, our environments are complex. For the 18-month-old, walking 'on' the water was an inadequate response to that part of the environment. This led to a state on uncertainty or disequilibrium. The novel element of the water destabilised her existing pattern of understanding, or schema. This state of disequilibrium may be accompanied by emotion, in this case shrieks of astonishment and chuckles of glee. Sometimes less pleasurable emotions are present, such as fear, anger or of not being able to cope.

There are various ways of coping with this cognitive and emotional conflict, or dissonance. One can ignore new information or experience which does not accord with our existing schema, as happens when people choose to hold on to beliefs which do not match the evidence in front of them. One can live with the conflict or disequilibrium, which can be rather uncomfortable. Alternatively, people can restructure their schemas to accommodate new information, ideas or experience. This restructuring is the process of accommodation, and it is important to understand that the learner has to take an active part in this. In the example of the girl in the paddling pool, she went into and out of the water many times, actively restructuring her schema. That it was restructured is shown by her actions the next time she saw a paddling pool. Thus, in schema theory, learning consists of restructuring or revising the schema in the light of new ideas, information or experience. Learning does not take place if the effort to restructure is not made. In this theory of learning, it is of crucial importance for teachers to find out what learners' existing schema are, and to present material and experiences which challenge them.

The second example, of the pretend haircut, is an example of learning through observation and play. Children have experiences of all kinds: they relive and rehearse those experiences as a way of making sense of them. Many a mother has observed her young children playing 'schools' during the school holidays. The children arrange furniture to represent a classroom, take on roles of pupil and teacher, and act out school activities. It is a salutary thought that much of what they act out are school routines, such as registers, dinner money, lining up, and going to have pages of sums marked. One needs to comprehend they they are making sense of the routines and the rituals of school. They are developing concepts of teacher and pupil, understanding what it means to function in a classroom context, and understanding of their role as pupils. In the same way, the three-year-old was developing a concept of a hairdresser and what a hairdresser did, through reliving the experience in the role of the hairdresser. The fact that the play involved motor activity is significant. Concept development occurs through physical and kinaesthetic activity as much as through language and pictorial means of communication.

Stones (1992) presented a useful analysis of learning. He distinguished between four types of learning: rote learning, concept learning, psychomotor learning and problem-solving. Each of these is associated with a particular kind of teaching. Rote learning is essentially memorising, learning to produce a response to a stimulus, such as giving the letter sound and name when presented with a letter of the alphabet, giving an instant response to seven times eight, or the French word for 'holidays'. It can be learning without understanding, and has received much criticism for this in the past, as images of children seated in rows chanting tables became an anathema to the teaching profession for some years. However, it has its uses, particularly in areas of the curriculum such as languages, where one is required to learn vocabulary. Memorisation of multiplication tables is better than working out the answer through say, repeated addition, in situations where multiplication is a means to an end, rather than the end itself. Rote learning is associated with teaching as telling, and learning as the simple recall of factual information. The example of children learning the song 'Greensleeves' is a kind of rote learning. The oral tradition of learning songs and stories is as old as humankind and as powerful as ever. It is no secret to advertisers that music in the form of jingles aids learning: the repetition of advertising jingles is employed to the full to lodge advertising claims in our consciousness.

Concept learning is a major part of what teachers are concerned with, and it is an integral part of all curriculum subjects. Concepts can be simple, such as 'dog', 'woman', 'hairdresser' or 'shell'. They can also be very complex: such as 'monarchy', 'melody', 'photosynthesis', or 'urban'. All of these concepts appear in the primary curriculum and it is important to understand that concepts should be actively taught; that learning them is not a matter of rote learning; and that teaching as telling is inappropriate for this kind of learning. The notion of experiental learning comes to mind as an obvious strategy, but as Stones (1992) points out, all learning is experiential. Sometimes intended concept learning can become rote learning. Children can learn to read and say the words, without forming appropriate mental representations. They have experience, as it were, of empty words, which are without meaning. Teaching children that Henry VIII's actions resulted in the dissolution of the monasteries, is of little use, unless the accompanying teaching activities ensure that the children understand what is meant by 'dissolution' in this context. It goes without saying that they would also need to understand the concept of 'monastery'.

The teaching of psychomotor skills is another category of learning which cuts across several curriculum areas, including physical education, dance, art, design technology, music and handwriting. The example of the girl learning to bowl overarm in the playground/street game is an example of such learning. This is a particularly rich example of learning, not least because of the kind of learning involved and the fact that it occurred without formal teaching. On the face of it she was learning a physical skill, but it was also psychomotor, as such skills generally are. Some aspects of it were motor, concerned with physical activity, and some were psychological; in other words, they involved the learning of a concept. The concept in question was the overarm throw or bowling. The girl had to learn to recognise the difference between overarm and underarm, which she did through observation and physical activity in the form of trying for herself. Next she observed those who seemed to have most success in knocking down the 'wicket'. In the absence of someone to teach her, she learnt through observation at school and practice at home, but it was essential that she first had a concept of the kind of throw she was trying to do.

Learning to ride a bike is another rich example of this kind of learning. It seems at first glance to be entirely physical, concerned with motor skills. It is something which children often learn to do for themselves, sometimes without any adult intervention or assistance. However, there is some conceptual learning involved: as well as the physical skill of pedalling, there is the skill of balancing itself, learning to shift weight almost inperceptibly and frequently to maintain the bike in an almost upright position. The child needs a concept of balancing which can be acquired through this physical activity, or it may have been acquired through cooking activities at home, or through weighing activities at school. Parents or peers calling out: 'You need to keep your balance!' will be offering little useful feedback if the child in question does not fully understand 'balance'. The obvious way to teach physical skills tends to be of 'show and tell'; however the element of concept learning within them can be overlooked. Conversely, an attempt to teach a particular concept may not meet with success because the child lacks a necessary motor skill. A further example is that of a sophisticated psychomotor skill such as phrasing in the playing of music. Motor skills are involved in the physical activity of singing or playing an instrument, but to phrase well, requires understanding of the concept of phrasing, and mental representations of how good phrasing might sound.

Stones (1992) final category of learning is problem-solving, which he regarded as one of the most important kinds of learning. It is fundamentally a variety of concept learning, but tends to mean the learning of complex concepts with less information than is normally available. It may involve the application of previous learning, of concepts, skills and strategies, or processes of elimination in finding a fault or a possible answer. It may simply be finding the best way to go about a task. The problem can be relatively simple, such as the jigsaw puzzle example given above, or the maths problem; or it can be much more complex, as in the simulation of the process to establish the best site for a pedestrian crossing, or whether or not a new out-of-town supermarket should be built and where. In the case of the jigsaw puzzle, Matthew was given strategies for doing such a puzzle, which he replicated when trying to do it unassisted. In the case of the maths problem, it was Tracy, a resourceful girl who devised her own strategy, with the help of Joanna. Between them they recalled encountering a similar sort of problem and applied their knowledge of charts and tallies to this new situation. Problem-solving such as this is seen as the end point in teaching, when the teacher withdraws support or instruction, and leaves the children to solve problems unassisted. However, it is important in problem-solving that children are given strategies with which to work on problems. Success is important, and it is a powerful motivator.

Motivation as a part of learning appears in several of the examples and is a crucially important aspect of learning. Rebecca, the girl learning to ride the bike, and Rachel, trying to learn how to bowl overarm, both had the powerful motivating factor of wanting to be like, and fit in with, their peers. Early psychological work on learning focused principally on motivation as a means of altering behaviour. The work of this group of pyschologists investigated the external, observable behaviour which was measurable in a rigorously scientific way. They hoped to discover general laws which would eventually lead to a scientific theory of learning. This approach to learning derived from a notion called the association of ideas. This was conditioning the mind to respond to external stimuli, in that the stimulus became associated with the reward from responding. From early experiments done with animals, the behaviourists developed the theory that the fundamental process of learning was the elimination or establishment of stimulus–response bonds. An important point about this theory was that the best way to ensure learning is not to give a reward or reinforcement each time the animal responds: it is the intermittent schedule of rewards which is most successful (Skinner 1938; Wood 1988; Brown 1995).

Skinner's work on behaviourist principles influenced the technology of programmed learning (Leith 1964). In this model of learning, complex behaviour is broken down into a series of small steps. Each time the learner masters a step, she or he is rewarded and moves on to the next step. The theory lay behind the 'drill-and-practice' computer software, which, it was once confidently predicted, would eliminate the human teacher altogether. That this has not happened serves to show the complexity of human learning and some of the inadequacies of behaviourist theory. Nonetheless, some vestige of this theory is found in the classroom as behaviour modification. Children are rewarded by ticks, house points, praise from the teacher or smily faces as a way of modifying their behaviour. Sometimes the teacher might give a special task or responsibility to a child as a reward for changing his or her behaviour, as in the example of Thomas starting school. This is particularly useful in settling new children into the routines and expectations of the primary classroom. It is used frequently also with children who have emotional and behavioural difficulties.

Bruner (1970) developed a theory of how humans develop mental representations of the real world. He stated that there were three forms of mental representation: enactive, iconic and symbolic representation. Enactive represen-tation is a way of understanding the world by acting out ideas and experiences. Iconic representation is understanding the world by pictorial means: pictures, drawings, diagrams, maps and plans. Symbolic representation is understanding the world through symbol systems, such as language, both spoken and written, mathe-matical symbols and musical notation. These can be extremely powerful in communicating meaning, but have to be mastered. The enactive form usually comes first, thus Emma above acted out her experience of the hairdressers as a way of understanding, and building a mental representation of what it means to go to the hairdressers. On another occasion, she watched the Olympic Games on television, and spent the next few days jumping off furniture. Her mother admonished her and suggested she did her jumping outside in the garden. This spoken language was an symbolic representation. At four she drew people doing high jumps: an iconic representation. Later still she was able to write the word 'jumping'; this was another symbolic representation. Bruner stressed that although enactive representation comes first in young children, then iconic and symbolic representation, as older learners and adults, we move between the three modes of mental representation. All three are important in learning.

The notion of these three modes of representation is useful in understanding another theory of learning: Norman's theory of complex learning (Norman 1978). The importance of this theory is that it attempts to explain how children learn large bodies of complex material over long periods of time. Norman's view can be compared with schema theory in that he thought that all learning is organised into schemes and new learning interacts with existing knowledge. Meaningful learning happens when new material in integrated with relevant schemes. The processes involved in the acquisition and organisation of new knowledge are accretion, restructuring and tuning. Accretion is the acquisition of new knowledge: facts, examples, concepts, skills and processes. Restructuring is the re-organising of existing knowledge. The learner gains new insights or sees new patterns of meaning. The third process is tuning: one in which skills or the uses of new knowledge become automatic. No one of these processes is superior to the others: they are simply different stages in the process of learning. They can be seen in the example of Rachel learning to bowl overarm. First there is accretion in the acquisition of new knowledge in seeing a game she has never experienced before. Then comes the process of restructuring in re-organising her knowledge of throwing balls and changing muscle movements to learn the new method: more accretion. Finally there is tuning in the practice to perfect her throw. The learning here happens through enactive representation of what the new way of throwing looks and feels like. Rachel's learning can also be understood in terms of schema theory. She assimilates new information about throwing. There follows a period of disequilibrium as she strives to learn the new skill. Her active attempts to throw the ball in this new way at first meet with failure. She persists, because her motivation is powerful: she is very keen to be allowed to join in the popular game and be accepted by her peers. The final stage is tuning, in which she perfects her throw. All are necessary stages in learning.

Another psychologist, Vygotsky, shared with Piaget the notion that children have to be active and constructive in developing their understanding of the world (Wood 1988). He argued that children who are unable to carry out tasks, solve problems or recall experiences, can often do these things with the help of an adult. Piaget took a negative view of the success children had with adult help, arguing that they were merely learning procedures, rather than understanding. In contrast, Vygotsky argued that the ability to learn through instruction was a fundamental feature of human intelligence (Wood 1988). Vygotsky's view, which placed teaching and instruction at the heart of development, revealed the importance of a child's potential for learning. This potential is often realised in interactions with others. This is one of Vygotsky's main contributions to educational theory: the concept of the 'zone of proximal development'. The term refers to the gap between what a child can do unaided and what he or she can do with the help of an adult, or one more knowledgeable or skilled than him or herself. This leads to a different conception of readiness to learn than that of Piaget, and a different conception of the role of instruction. Teaching then becomes assisted performance (Tharp and Gallimore 1988) as teachers or other adults guide children through their zone of proximal development in a particular area of knowledge, skill, or learning. Individual children may be at the same level of unassisted performance, but have different zones of proximal development; that is, different potential for learning in that area.

This is illustrated by the example of Harriet, who showed that she had a large zone of proximal development when it came to learning music. She was able to learn a great deal unaided, through observing, listening and experimentation. Through the timely intervention of adults at appropriate moments, she was able to move through the zone of proximal devlopment in learning music. Harriet's early stages of learning to play the piano and to read music are complex episodes of learning. Playing an instrument is a psychomotor variety of learning. She had to learn the concept of octave, through looking at the manual and the keyboard itself, to recognise the repeated pattern of notes which comprises an octave. This was a powerful iconic and enactive representation of the concept of octave; reinforced by the symbolic representations on the tape in the form of sounds and in the manual in the fingering system marked on a chart of the keyboard. She learnt the tunes by singing along with the tape. Practice enabled her to master the muscular movements and coordination required to play a single-note melody with one hand. The arrival of the piano made her restructure her schema about keyboards, for here were seven octaves, not two. This was accompanied by some emotions of excitement and pleasure. In other respects it was just like her keyboard, for she could play the same tune on it. Learning that she could play the same tune on the white keys altered her ideas about what she could do with this one tune. When she started lessons, her teacher took the trouble to discover her existing knowledge about music, and to value it by praising her and notating her compositions. Gradually through repeated experience of staff notation, Harriet learned to connect the sounds with the notes on the stave. This complex learning happened over a period of months, involving accretion, restructuring and tuning. She worked actively on her knowledge of music to accommodate the new knowledge into her schema.

Toby's learning to make mince pies is a classic example of assisted performance. He started at an early age by playing with the materials and copying the actions of his mother. He gradually learnt all the stages of the process, until he was able to do a number of them independently. This took some time, as Christmas comes but once a year. The learning involved psychomotor skills, such as rolling out pastry, eye-to-hand coordinaton in the fine motor skills involved, language and simple maths. Finally, after some years. Toby signalled his readiness to make mince pies unaided. The progression was one of demonstration by his more knowledgable adult, joint activity, supported activity and independent activity. This is learning as assisted performance.

This is not meant to be a treatise on children's learning, but some knowledge and understanding of all these theories is essential for the expert teacher. It is on our conceptions of learning that we base our pedagogical strategies. A simple model of adding knowledge to empty vessels leads to strategies such as teaching as telling. However, if we understand learning in terms of schema theory, or in terms of Norman's model, then the kinds of learning experiences we present for our pupils are very different. If we further bear in mind Bruner's ideas of enactive, iconic and symbolic representation, this adds another dimension to devising strategies and teaching approaches which ensure pupils will fully comprehend the new material and re-organise their schemas. The example which follows illustrates this point. Two teachers, faced with teaching about the structure of Egyptian society as part of the primary history curriculum to a Year 4 class, tackle it in very different ways.

Two examples of teaching 'hierarchy'

Jane finds a page in one of the topic books on Egypt which describes the hierarchical society. She photocopies it and prepares some questions on the passage of writing. The teaching approach is one of comprehension. She asks four of the most fluent readers to read a section of the page. She asks questions of the class, focusing on who was at the 'top' and 'bottom' in Egyptian society. Some of the children answer the questions; not all are involved. She goes through the answers and writes the heading and date on the board. The children get out plain paper and line guides. They copy down heading and date, and write the answers to the questions. She sits with the table of least able writers and prompts them with their answers. Children come to her frequently for spellings. Those who finish first can draw the picture of the Pharoah which accompanied the passage from the book. Children work diligently, complying with the teacher's rules for comprehension and putting borders around their work. Two monitors come round with glue sticks and topic books: early finishers glue their work into the topic books.

Jackie ponders for a while on the concept of hierarchy, and as in Stones (1992) notion of sub-concepts within psychopedagogical analysis, decides that the children will not understand the notion of hierarchy without understanding the sub-concept of authority. She realises that they may already have some notion of this, which may not be articulated as it is an implicit part of their everyday lives. She devises the following teaching approaches and variety of representations, enactive, iconic and symbolic, to enable all the learners in her class to have access to this difficult concept. The lesson starts with her suddenly shouting at the classroom assistant as if she were a naughty pupil (this has been pre-arranged). The children are astonished, and then laugh as they see the humour in the situation. When they have settled, she asks them: 'What gave me the authority to do that?' The children reply that she is the teacher and in charge. She asks who is in charge of them at home. They reply: 'Mum' and 'Dad', or 'my older bother', or 'my nan'. She then asks if they are ever left in charge of anyone. Some children might be left in charge of younger siblings briefly while a parent cooks a meal or pops to a neighbour's house. She moves on to who has charge of the country. Their suggestions of queen and prime minister are recorded on the board at the top of the ladder. She continues to elicit ideas on who is at the bottom of the ladder, and who is at various rungs. Many children contribute, including the less able in reading and writing. She writes the words 'ladder' and 'hierarchy' on the board and explains that a hierarchy is like a ladder, with people at different points or rungs in society and with authority over others. She gives out a sheet with eight different groups from Ancient Egyptian society on it, from Pharoah and high priests down to slaves. The task is to cut up the sheet, matching the words to the pictures, and then arrange them in a ladder of society or hierarchy. When most of the children have completed their sorting, she asks pupils to share their ordering or ranking of people. There is some disagreement. She chooses pupils to stand at different points in a line down the side of the classroom, each with a sign to show what group they represent. The children make suggestions as to who should stand where and justify their choices. Finally, she sets a writing task: an explanation of the hierarchy in Ancient Egypt. The intended audience for this piece of writing are tourists and this piece is to be an entry in the class sightseers' guide. The most able write their own passages; she sits and works with the least able, for whom she has provided a writing frame (Lewis and Wray 1995; Wray and Lewis 1997) as a means of structuring their ideas.

Jane's model of teaching is based upon a model of learning as simple addition to existing knowledge. The knowledge of learning which informs it is impoverished and thin. She has not understood that 'hierarchy' is not merely a word on a page; neither has she analysed the concept to realise that the children need to understand the sub-concept of authority, before being introduced to the idea of hierarchy. Likewise, her knowledge of models of teaching is threadbare in relation to what is being taught. Leaving aside the problems of lack of syntactic knowledge of history, and her only partial understanding of history as a discipline, she does not seem to have the pedagogical repertoire on which to draw to teach about Egyptian society in a way which tranfers her understanding of it to the children. The model of teaching she employs is that of an English comprehension lesson. This might be based on her own experience of learning history, or on what she saw class teachers doing when she was on teaching placement; it may simply be the norm for that school, and totally influenced by context and a desire to fit in with the rest of the staff. Cynics here might add that she could be worn out from teaching literacy and numeracy hours in the morning, and looking for a quiet life in the afternoons. A further possibility might be that the history lesson is seen as a way of practising for SATs (Turner-Bisset 2000c). It is important to trace such influences for they can add to our understanding of why people teach as they do. However, in Jane's case, the lack of a pedagogical repertoire and of knowledge of children's learning, make for a situation in which the completion of the work becomes the end goal, rather than the development of children's understanding. This is an example of the 'production line' kind of classroom, which appears at first sight to be an exceptionally busy and productive environment (Desforges and Cockburn 1987; Cockburn 1995). The aim seems to be to get completed written work to go in the children's topic books.

There is a great deal of rich knowledge for teaching in Jackie's approach. As well as models of learning and teaching, her decisions are informed by other knowledge bases, including subject knowledge in history and English, knowledge of learners, of contexts, of educational ends, and pedagogical content knowledge. The reader might like to trace these in Jackie's example. However, in this chapter, it is the knowledge of models of learning and of teaching which are being considered. A key point in the teacher's understanding is that 'hierarchy' is a concept: the children will either need to add to their store of concepts or change their conceptual understanding, depending upon their previous knowledge of this term, if any. Therefore, teaching as telling is simply an inadequate approach. The children will need to work on the concept, to make it part of their schema. The activities in the lesson, being a mixture of enactive representation (the role-play at the beginning, and the pupils representing different groups standing in a line at the side of the classroom), iconic representation (the pictures of different groups in Eygptian society) and symbolic representation (spoken language, reading the words, matching words to pictures), are all designed to help children assimilate this new concept and ultimately accommodate it into their schema. For some children in the class, the learning will occur in this lesson. For others, it will need to be revisited over a period of time. The writing task is intended to enrich the learning embedded in the physical and sorting activities. Subject knowledge in English also informs Jackie's task design here, in that the activity of writing for an intended audience, both encourages the children to communicate their understanding of Eygptian society and is an appropriate representation of what real writers do (e.g. copy writers for tourist guides or web-pages giving tourist information). The analogy of the ladder to explain hierarchy is of key importance in linking existing knowledge to new knowledge. The importance of analogy in teaching will be explored in Chapter 8.

The pedagogical repertoire

In recent times there has been much debate about the most effective ways of teaching. Some of this debate has focused on the relative merits of whole-class, group or individualised instruction. In a sense this focus is misplaced, for what needs to be addressed is the appropriateness of the teaching strategy, in addition to any consideration of the organisational strategies. Whole-class, group, pair or individual approaches are not teaching strategies: they are merely organisational ones, and it is important to make this distinction clear. Whatever form or organisation is chosen, the guiding criterion needs to be fitness of purpose for the kind of learning intended to happen. Any notion of teaching approaches being only organisational ones, is an impoverished understanding of pedagogy. This kind of understanding is often present in beginning teachers. When one asks them what kind of teaching approach they used in a particular lesson, they will often reply: whole-group or group work. If one pursues the question further, beginning teachers are often at a loss to explain their teaching approach in terms of generic methods. Instead, they will describe what they did, without analysing it or classifying it. In contrast, expert teachers use a repertoire of strategies, selecting the most appropriate for use in a particular context and adapting it if necessary for a particular group of learners.

Some of these strategies might strike beginning teachers as unnecessary. For example, the use of a drama or role-play activity to teach a concept, whether of trade or of food-chains, may appear to be both extreme and demanding. There is the further consideration of order: can discipline be maintained throughout activities which involve children leaving their seats and moving around? These concerns should not affect experienced teachers however. Expert teachers present a wide range of learning activities in their classrooms, based on their rich understanding of learning and on their pedagogical repertoires. A pedagogical repertoire consists of two aspects (see Figure 4.1): approaches, activities, examples, analogies and illustrations for representing facts, skills, concepts, beliefs and attitudes to others; and the skills and strategies used as an integral part of these approaches. To make this distinction clearer, examples of the approaches are: storytelling, Socratic dialogue, drama, role-play, simulation, demonstration, modelling, problem-solving, singing, playing games, and transformation of knowledge into other forms, as well as the more obvious question-and-answer, instructing, explaining and giving feedback on children's oral contributions and written work. The other kinds of strategies or skills might be termed 'acting skills' as indeed some scholars have described them. Tauber and Mester (1995) likened teaching to acting, seeing a considerable parallel between the two professions, in that both are performance arts, and in both, the performer has to hold the attention of the audience and convey conviction in what they are doing. They suggested that teachers had a 'toolbox' comprising top tray tools of voice or vocal animation, body language or physical animation, and effective use of classroom space. The bottom tray tools are humour, role-playing, use of props and the elements of surprise and suspense. To these one might add observing and listening to children and generally responding to the audience's responses. Thus a teacher might employ the approach of storytelling, in order to teach ideas about taxation, and information about a particular period in history, but use humour and suspense as part of the strategies for holding

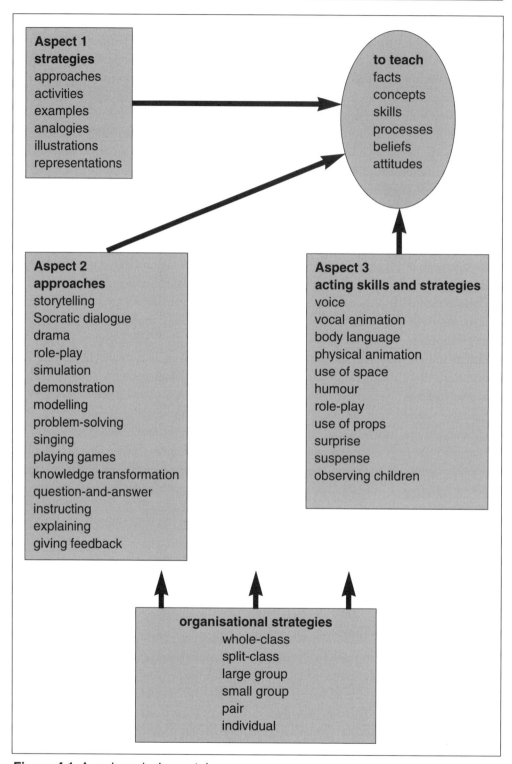

Figure 4.1 A pedagogical repertoire

his or her listeners' attention. Tauber and Mester identified enthusiasm as the key element in effective teaching, for it is fundamental to effective communication:

> Teacher enthusiasm plays a central role in holding students' attention, generating students' interest, and developing students' positive attitudes toward learning. Highly enthusiastic teachers are highly expressive in vocal delivery, gestures, body movement, and overall energy level. All of these are crucial ingredients that, in turn, contribute to greater student achievement.
>
> (Tauber and Mester 1995, p. 11)

Teacher enthusiasm is an item on many a list of aspects of effective teaching, but what is important here is that the 'tools' listed by Tauber and Mester demystify an obvious, but hard to define quality. Some idea is given of how to convey it. What is clear is that teachers' engagement with the material to be taught, their deep understanding of it, and passion for the subject, are important for the communication of genuine enthusiasm. Equally important are the use of voice, body language, physical space, non-verbal channels of communication, and the rest of the 'bottom tray tools' listed by Tauber and Mester (1995): humour, role-play, use of props and elements of surprise and suspense. All of these can be seen in operation in the lesson presented in the Prologue (Case study 1).

Case study 1 revisited: David: Creating a Roman galley

During this lesson, David used a variety of teaching approaches. An analysis of the teacher discourse shows that he used language for all of the following:

- restating classroom routines
- introducing the activity
- acting as storyteller
- directing the role-play
- taking part in the role-play
- giving information
- asking questions about previous work
- asking questions about the size of the ship on the OHP
- demonstrating drumming, whipping and rowing
- working out the size and shape of the ship
- introducing the written task
- giving examples of headlines.

In fact as teacher he took on a number of roles, including manager of order, questioner, playleader, storyteller, actor, and commentator. He was clear about this in the post-lesson interview:

David:　. . . my role was a multi-various one. One to be a guide and to ask the right questions to get them thinking about what it would be like at the time of the battle; what the boat was like; what it would have been used for; to keep order (chuckles); just really to inspire them as well; . . . to be a guide and steer the whole thing together and keep it on course; and to provide the resources; have some idea of where the lesson would go; but really to get them thinking, and enthusing, and wanting to do it; . . . story telling is very important. So running through the whole lesson there was a story about the invasion.'

David employed a range of approaches from his teaching repertoire, as well as a number of roles, and moved seamlessly from one role to the next. He started with a dialogue about the purpose and size of the ship. He moved into storytelling about the Roman invasion. He acted out the role of the drummer and of the man whipping the slaves. He was a guide for the children in their thinking: it is interesting that he used the metaphor of steering the class like a ship, and keeping them on course. He was a playleader briefly in the classroom, leading the children in the shout for help. He took this role again in the playground in the creation of the ship, the allocation of roles to children, and conducting the role-play itself. He also managed the children and instructed them in the writing task which was to consolidate their new knowledge. It is significant too that he talked of enthusing the children, making them eager to do the task he had planned. His teaching approaches reflected some of the theories of learning discussed earlier in the chapter. The children were active participants in the learning: they had the opportunity through the presentation of new ideas to build a mental representation of what a Roman galley was like and how it was used. All three of Bruner's (1970) forms of representation were used to teach the concepts of galley, invasion, the propulsion of the ship and so forth. Their active engagement with the ideas in the lesson is shown by their enthusiastic participation in the drawing out of the ship and in the role-play. Their imaginations were fired. In terms of assisting performance, he guided them through this experience and role-play as a more knowledgeable adult. Afterwards they would be able to use the chalk outline to repeat the play again and again, on their own, which some of them did.

David occupied physical space by standing at the OHP and using a pen to point to things on the screen. He moved around the room gesturing, using the metre rule; at one point, going to get the drum out of the cupboard. He used other gestures, such as the drumming and the whipping action, which generated some humour and some amusement. He laughed at the funny moments. He looked as if he was enjoying himself and having fun. His voice held a sense of urgency, when he was questioning the children about the ship, as if he was burning to know what the children thought. It also meant that the lesson moved at a brisk pace. He used simple props such as the drum to create atmosphere, suspense and tension, which was then released. Role-play was both a teaching approach and a 'bottom tray' strategy. He also used surprise in just putting the picture on the OHP and starting the lesson from there. As observer, I wondered what would happen next. This is not to argue that there is anything wrong in putting up a list of objectives at the beginning of each lesson; only that it is important to vary one's strategies and teaching approaches, so that the element of surprise can be employed from time to time. Above all, his strategies generated interest, motivation and enthusiasm. His organisational strategy was whole-class teaching, which was fitting for the purpose and tasks of a story and role-play in which all could participate.

Conclusion

This chapter has presented a selection of theories of learning, and a concept of the pedagogical repertoire. I have argued for the value of knowledge of a whole range of theories and models of learning, to inform one's planning and teaching. Understanding of learning is crucial to good teaching. This obviously is a cliche, but in the current focus on competences and skills, somehow the importance of this knowledge base can be submerged. The knowledge of learning underpins the knowledge of models of teaching, and gives rise to the employment of a wide range of teaching approaches and strategies. This is presented in this chapter as the pedagogical repertoire. It is as important to pedagogy as all the other knowledge and skills of managing the different age-ranges of classes within the primary phase (one uses very different approaches for managing order with five-year-olds than one does with ten-year-olds), and managing the learning context. This is not to deny the importance of knowledge and skills in classroom management. However, it is possible to learn to manage classrooms without ever properly learning to teach: 'By concentrating on the interactive side of classroom teaching, however, student teachers may learn to manage pupils and classrooms without learning to teach' (Feiman-Nemser and Buchmann 1989, p. 367).

Using such a pedagogical repertoire as presented here, in conjunction with knowledge of models of learning, and with the other knowledge bases in this book, one can ensure a focus on teaching and learning, rather than on classroom management.

CHAPTER 5

Knowledge of learners: empirical and cognitive

Empirical knowledge of learners

All knowledge is not equal in value or worth. Different kinds of knowledge have a different status in society. Thus the 'hard' quantitiative data of national tests, regardless of how flawed they might be, is preferred by some to 'soft' qualitative data, or using formative assessment to find out a great deal about what children know, can do and understand. Likewise, for the likes of Lawlor (1990) and the right-wing think tanks of the early 1990s, subject matter was seen as being of prime importance for teaching, and other sources of knowledge for teaching, such as knowledge about culture and society, about children and about pedagogy, were seen as being of little importance. To regard one knowledge base as being of greater importance than all the others is to misunderstand professional knowledge for teaching: each part of the amalgam of pedagogical content knowledge is as important as the others. This point is significant when one comes to examine the kind of knowledge I have labelled as empirical or social knowledge of learners. This is knowledge of what children of different ages are like; what interests or preoccupies them; their social nature; and how contextual factors can affect their behaviour and learning. It is this part of teachers' knowledge which is most likely to be characterised as common sense, and dismissed as a potentially important knowledge base because the knowledge seems so obvious (to some) to acquire, so trivial, and so straightforward. It is sometimes characterised as intuitive because it is based on close observation, and indeed teachers may not be able to articulate this knowledge or reasoning which led them to teach in a particular way.

Empirical knowledge of learners tends also, in primary teaching, to be particularly the province of women, perhaps because embedded within it is some element of caring for one's pupils as people. This is not to say that male teachers do not care, only that society as a whole still regards child-rearing and child-care as women's work. The deep, detailed knowledge which those in regular daily contact with children have, of their interests and preocupations, their moods and dispositions at different times of the day, the TV programmes they watch and the music they like, and their families and siblings, is important for the design and timing of tasks and the conscious, deliberate selection of representations and language in classroom discourse, which is one of the hallmarks of expert teachers. Presented below are a number of examples of empirical knowledge of learners: it needs to be understood that as this is part of pedagogical content knowledge, there are other knowledge bases informing teaching decisions.

Teachers talk to children informally about their interests and pastimes, their holidays, if they have them, their pets, younger or older siblings, how they spend their weekends and what has happened in their lives. In addition, they closely observe children, both in the classroom and around the school, and build up knowledge of their behaviour, their moods, their states of activity or lethargy, their social interactions and their play. They see how wind can make children hyperactive and jittery; how indoor play made necessary by rainy weather can have a similar effect. They are aware of incidents in the playground, and know when to split up children who may have fought at playtime. Children may also need to be seated apart because they may egg each other on to show off, or even bully others. Teachers are aware of home circumstances, for example, there may be children in the class who have not had breakfast because there is no food at home. If home circumstances are truly appalling, they may need teaching tactics which are designed to develop their self-confidence and self-esteem. At the opposite end of the social and economic spectrum, children in another school might be so loved and pampered that their massive self-confidence might come across as irritating or threatening. Such children may need a great deal of 'squashing' verbally if order is to be maintained.

At first glance it would seem that such knowledge is peripheral to the business of teaching, to do with the management of order, or with caring, and with the whole rather feminine world of primary teaching. However empirical knowledge of learners informs our teaching decisions and impacts on our relationships with children. Both of these are crucially important for successful lessons. For those who do not have a well-developed empirical knowledge of learners, its lack can mean unsuccessful lessons. Case study 12 in Chapter 7, shows how the lack of empirical knowledge of learners can impact on the lesson, as well as the lack of knowledge of self.

Examples of empirical knowledge of learners

A teacher of a mixed Year 2/3 class in a small village school, has read a report in the educational press of the latest research into the relationship between inactive children and obesity and heart disease in adult life. She talks to her children in news time one morning about what physical activity they do, and finds there is much more TV watching and computer gaming going on than active play. Talking to a parent one day after school in the playground about the party she is running for her child that day, they discuss what sort of music and groups that children like. They laugh together when the parent says jokingly: 'All seven-year-old girls like Michael Jackson!' Dated or not, the teacher digs out her videos of Michael Jackson; she also watches the latest all-boy and all-girl manufactured pop groups and works out a couple of simple routines. Then she tells the children that every morning for ten minutes, they are going to have 'Healthy hearts'. She puts on a tape and demonstrates the routines. Because the exercise appeals to their own interests, they all join in. Dancing to loud music makes it enjoyable.

There are several interlocking knowledge bases present in this brief example. This teacher is informed about the broader educational contexts in which she works, in this case, that of society as a whole. She reads evidence which suggests that the lack of exercise among children and young people is laying up a store of future health problems. Her educational ends for these children are both short- and long-term ones, of providing, amongst other things, opportunities for physical and mental development. She knows a variety of curriculum materials for PE and dance, but the chance conversation with a parent started her thinking about which materials she might use, or what might be adapted as curriculum materials. She does not consider this activity to be only about healthy hearts, but also about sequencing a number of movements in time to music, using memory and physical coordination. Thus she is employing her subject knowledge of dance, and the skills and processes which this subject can contribute to a curriculum. The role that empirical knowledge of learners played in this example is threefold: first, she has some general theoretical knowledge of learners gained from her reading; second she has the detailed knowledge of this group of learners gained from discussing exercise and play activities with them; and third, she has the knowledge of popular music and culture which enables her to design activities which have a built-in appeal to children.

Another teacher, with a strong personal interest in interior decoration, is looking for ways to enrich and restructure her Year 6 children's understanding of basic mathematical operations, but in a way which will attract their interest and motivate them to work hard. She decides that some task or series of tasks with an end product would achieve this end. A TV programme called *Changing Rooms* sets her thinking about the possibilities. At the same time, a friend in the throes of househunting alerts her to the fact that whole interiors of houses may now be viewed in estate agents' details on the internet. Knowing that her children like computers, she devises a task for them which involves art, design technology, ICT and maths. As well as designing a new interior for a room they find on the internet, the children have to plan out the materials and quantities for the dimensions of the rooms, and cost them, using either online DIY catalogues or the ones she has brought in from the local stores. The cost has to be within a particular budget. This task is set as a problem-solving or restructuring task once other work is completed. The children are motivated to get on to this novel, absorbing task.

Again, as with the first example, there are other knowledge bases underpinning this teaching example. There is the subject knowledge of the disciplines involved. There is the sophisticated understanding of what might be employed from the 'real world' as curriculum materials. In the short term her educational ends are to prepare the children for the language and presentation of maths problems in national tests, by getting them to work on real-life problems. Long term she is preparing the children for the opportunities and responsibilities of adult life. They may be faced with the very real problems of home-making on a limited budget in their adult lives. The teacher also employs knowledge of learning in the task design. She is choosing to use a problem-solving approach, as a way of getting them to apply, or restructure their existing knowledge of maths operations. Furthermore, she is intending that they work actively on existing knowledge in these subjects to assist the process of accommodation, and to ensure that real learning takes place. Her pedagogical approach uses the elements of surprise and challenge: she shows the children a number of slides of interiors: not the normal start to a maths lesson. The children are intrigued and engaged. Her empirical knowledge of learners is shown in her selection of curriculum materials: she knows that some of her pupils watch this programme and discuss the sometimes bizarre taste shown on it. The element of internet searching, while being a rather low-level usage of ICT, nonetheless holds appeal for many in her class. They like finding information on the internet.

Case study 6: Melanie: Composing a class poem

One of the lessons which will be revisited in this book is Melanie's poetry lesson. Although this was a lesson given by a beginning teacher, while on her second teaching practice as part of the Post-Graduate Certificate in Education, it is extraordinary in demonstrating many examples of knowledge bases in action. The class teacher was away ill, and she took a class of 33 Year 3 and Year 4 children for a poetry lesson. The activity planned was to write a class poem collectively, in order to model the process of writing poetry. The children would be able to see the process of drafting and redrafting literally in front of their eyes. This would give them some skills and experience on which to draw in attempting to write their own poetry. She would also be modelling for them that the choice of words was important: that this is one of the crucial aspects of writing poetry.

She seated herself on a table by the blackboard, and gathered the children about her in a semicircle: on the floor, chairs and on tables. She first of all read a couple of poems, for enjoyment and for examples of the vivid use of language. The first, about two giants was funny and employed rhyme in a spectacular array of words for fighting. She reminded the children of earlier work: a game with a cat in a hexagon, and the children had to put a describing word in each adjoining hexagon. She asked the class to give examples of describing words they had used in this game. The second, was concerned with feelings about a playground being closed to children. She discussed how the poem made them feel, and reminded them of another game called 'Preferences', in which they had lined up in two lines: one for love and one for hate. Some of them had said 'I love . . .' and some had said 'I hate . . .'. She reminded them about how they had talked about poetry being about what they felt.

She stated that she was going to introduce them to something called revising. When she realised that the children did not understand this, she explained that they were going to write a class poem and she was going to show that when people write poetry they need to swap things around sometimes. 'We need to change things and look at it more carefully to make it effective.' She steered the class towards the topic of homelessness: the children had been much interested in items in the news about people living in cardboard boxes, in cities such as London. She offered the example of a character from a soap opera which was immensely popular with children at the time (it still is!) who had run away and lived for a while in a cardboard box. This generated more words. Melanie either accepted words if she felt they were suitable or gently challenged the children's ideas if they were not.

She asked for their ideas on putting these words into a poem, concentrating first on how the poem should start. She accepted phrases from the children, who were quick to proffer ideas and added line after line until the difficulty arose of getting the image of 'slums' into the poem. In the exchange which followed, in which the children were invited to share their ideas on equal terms with the teacher, children and teacher wrestled with the problem of where to place words and phrases in the poem. During this process, the writing on the board became very untidy, with words crossed out and arrows inserted to show where words had been moved. One child suggested rubbing it all out and starting again. Melanie replied with a challenge to this idea:

> Melanie: No, this is what you've got to do. This is your rough work. This is what you've got to do when you're writing poetry. You've got to think where the different lines go to make sense. You've got to balance it up.

The lesson continued with Melanie eliciting contributions from the children and responding to them. She read the whole poem, but the last line was weak. She asked for ideas, and although some children suggested words to do with dying and drugs, which is not really what she wanted, as the poem was about homelessness, the discussion stimulated Carly to suggest 'dying of distress' as a final line. Melanie gave a warm positive reponses to this and praised her. She asked Ruth to read the whole poem aloud and praised the class. Her timing was not perfect, for they finished the poetry-writing activity with ten minutes to go. She used the time to tell them about word-processing this poem, the class poetry book she was planning and sharing poems. Two girls volunteered to say a short poem they had learnt by heart. She used the last few minutes for silent reading.

This is not a 'perfect lesson' but it is remarkable for many points of interest. It will be revisited and analysed in depth in Chapter 8. For the moment, it is worth commenting on the children's engagement and interest in this activity, which lasted about 45 minutes. There are many different knowledge bases in this teaching performance.

Melanie demonstrated substantive knowledge of English in the various activities she used to elicit and extend the children's vocabulary. Her syntactic knowledge of English is shown in her clear understanding of the processes of writing poetry. Her curriculum knowledge is particularly rich: in her selection of materials for the lesson, she shows good knowledge of poems which are likely to appeal to this age-range. The games with language and with feelings done in previous lessons are part of a rich repertoire of teaching strategies. In terms of general pedagogical knowledge, she understands that children will not understand a term such as revising or redrafting, without having some kind of demonstration or experience of it. The model of teaching and learning employed is that of assisted perfomance: alone and unaided, these children could probably not all produce a poem such as the class one, but with the aid of the teacher and peers, many children contribute towards a joint product. Her short-term aims were for them to enjoy hearing some poetry and to experience the drafting process. Long term, she wanted them to have an enjoyment of poetry which would continue into their adult lives, providing a source of pleasure and enjoyment for them. In addition, she wanted them to be able to write poetry, to be able to evaluate their own writing and redraft in response to their own judgements of their writing, again an important skill for adult life.

Her empirical knowledge of learners is shown in two aspects of the lesson. First, she selected a topic for the poems which was part of popular culture of the moment. At that time, there was news footage of 'cardboard city' in London, showing homeless people living in boxes and on the streets. This was something in which the children were interested, and about which they were concerned. She also knew that virtually all the children watched the particular TV programme from which came the episodes with the 16-year-old girl running away. As a means of engaging and holding the children's interest, she used the topic for the writing, and used the runaway girl as a representation of somebody homeless to whom they could all relate. Second, her empirical knowledge of these learners meant that she valued the children's ideas and contributions, and made them feel that their ideas were useful and important. Although she was the only person in the class writing, they were all engaged in the aspect of writing known as composing. Melanie responded to each child valuing all contributions. She acted as guide and leader, reminding the class of their focus. The classroom discourse generated in this lesson is remarkable for the length and frequency of the children's contributions, particularly in the drafting activity. Her relationship with the children was both relaxed and firm: the children felt able to offer ideas and make comments freely. This comfortable relationship at least partly stems from her empirical knowledge of them as learners, and how they were likely to respond to this kind of lesson.

Cognitive knowledge of learners

This consists of two elements: the generic knowledge of child development, which informs practice; and the specific knowledge of a particular group of learners, which grows from regular contact with and assessment of these learners. Both of these aspects are problematical for different reasons. Generic knowledge of child development is linked to knowledge of models of learning. Specific cognitive knowledge of a group of learners can be acquired through both formal and informal assessment, as well as what Alexander (1984) has termed 'grapevine information'. However, assessment is far from being an exact science, and it is possible to underestimate or overestimate learners' ability and attainment, with serious and far-reaching results. Nonetheless, this is an important knowledge base for teaching, fraught though it is with problems.

Knowledge of child development

Eraut (1994) gives a useful distinction between public and private theory: 'public theory' is publicaly available in books, libraries, institutions and the media; and 'private theory' are ideas in people's minds which they use to interpret or explain their experience. One of the difficulties of teaching theories of any kind is that there is a tendency among some people to treat theories as absolute knowledge, and not recognise their provisional nature. A theory about how children learn, or about child development, can become hardened into belief after several years of classroom practice. Beliefs can be very hard to shake. The other major problem is that theories can undergo a kind of sea change in the minds of those learning them, partly as a function of incomplete comprehension, and partly as a function of inaccurate language being used to remember or explain theories.

One of the most pervasive theories of child development, which permeated primary ideology in the 1970s and 1980s is Piaget's idea that there are natural stages of development through which children pass. The stages were thought of as kind of natural 'blueprint' for teaching and teachers attempted to fit their teaching to this blueprint (Fox 1995). The idea of readiness to learn is often associated with notions of sequential developmentalism (King 1978). Various kinds of learning, such as reading or mathematics are considered to be too difficult until a certain stage of readiness has been reached. The disadvantage of this theory, when it is adopted too slavishly, is that teachers can greatly underestimate what children can achieve, particularly in the areas of logical reasoning and abstract thought. Nowadays, stage development theory is less pervasive. Donaldson's seminal work on 'decentring' demonstrated that if the research procedures and language of the researchers were changed then very young children could give evidence of deductive reasoning abilities. She argued that to assert that children had limited capacity for reasoning and abstract thought was both inaccurate and damaging (Donaldson 1978).

More recently, other theorists are likely to be invoked by primary teachers. Vygotsky shares with Piaget an emphasis on activity as the basis for learning and for the development of thinking (Wood 1988). However, he placed far greater emphasis on the role of communication, social interaction and instruction in determining the path of development. His main contributions to educational theory: the zone of proximal development and the importance of cooperatively achieved success might be said to be part of primary ideology. Instruction whether formal or informal, in a variety of social contexts, given by more knowledgeable others, is the the vehicle for the cultural tranmission of knowledge (Wood 1988). The more knowledgeable others might be parents, peers, siblings, relatives, friends, youth leaders and teachers.

> Knowledge is embodied in the actions, work, play, technology, literature, art, and talk of members of a society. Only through interaction with the living representatives of culture, what Bruner terms the 'vicars of culture', can a child come to acquire, embody and further develop that knowledge. Children's development thus reflects their cultural experiences and their opportunities for access to the more mature who already practise specific areas of knowledge.
>
> (Wood 1988, p. 25)

Another theorist with whose ideas teachers are likely to be aware of is Bruner. He explored the nature of creative thinking and originality, not only in acquiring information, but also in 'going beyond the information given' by inventing codes and rules. For Bruner, learning involves the search for pattern, regularity and predictability (Wood 1988). The fundamental difference between Bruner's theories and those of Piaget is that Bruner (1970) rejects the view that symbolic thinking is constrained by stages of development. For example, Piagetian theory suggests that children will only be able to perform tasks using abstract ideas of algebraic notation when they reach the stage of formal operations. Bruner (1970) argues that much younger children can, if they are given appropriate instruction, learn how to understand and perform these intellectual activities. Hence in Bruner's theories there is a much greater emphasis on the role of instruction.

The crucial point here is that expert teachers are aware of a range of theories, understand that they are only theories rather than hard facts, and use them as threads of thinking in the planning for teaching and reflecting on practice. They also need to be aware that aspects of theories conflict. For expert teachers, the ideas of Bruner and Vygotsky are potentially the most important and exciting. They have crucial implications for the role of the teacher and indeed make teachers' possible contribution to learning much greater. In addition, the understanding of the role of culture and of language in child development can enhance the quality both of curriculum provision and of classroom discourse. However, while an absolutist interpretation of stage theory might lead to serious underestimation of what children might be able to achieve, some notions of typical levels of progress in specific subjects or complex skills such as reading, can be useful to teachers as long as they are not thought of as prescriptive. Two examples of these are Sulzby's (1988) model of levels of reading development; and Feldman's (1980) pattern of development in young children drawing maps. These models show a slow process of developing skill and knowledge, which results from repeated engagement with the activity over a period of years. Each study shows the gradual nature of developing competence over a period of years, with periods of consolidation, elaboration and innovation (Fox 1995). The interesting point about these studies is that understanding of development in a particular skill or area of knowledge arises from close observation in that subject: and is subject-specific. What may be of more use to teachers is subject-specific knowledge of child development, closely linked to subject knowledge. It should be imbued with the understanding that sets of levels are like common pathways, and that individuals may diverge slightly from the most usual route. This kind of knowledge can powerfully inform teaching approaches and strategies, and may be more valuable than a kind of global theory of child development.

Cognitive knowledge of particular learners

This is the kind of knowledge of learners gained from assessment. Most readers of this book will be familiar with forms and methods of assessment; it is not the intention to explain these here. Instead, there will be a focus on its problematical nature, and how expert teachers use such knowledge to inform their teaching. Assessment is not an exact science, and furthermore, one's assessment of a child's attainment or abilities may be subject to what Alexander called 'filtration' and 'signal interference' (Alexander 1984, p. 38). This is the viewing of a child through a particular set of lenses created by the teacher's beliefs about teaching, children and subject knowledge, their knowledge of self, the schools' and classroom context, and their enculturation. Such knowledge of children is neither absolute nor objective: bound up as it is with all these elements and the teacher's relationship with the child, it is most likely to be subjective.

There are three types of information on which teachers may draw for their knowledge of particular groups of learners. These are: pupil records, or baseline assessment, which are handed on to each new teacher; information from commercially available tests such as NFER (National Foundation for Educational Research) or Richmond tests, or national testing; and information gathered from informal assessment in the day-to-day work of the teacher. Pupil records can be subject to the same processes of filtration as any other form of assessment, although they can give a useful starting-point. Formal testing can only deal with specific and limited areas of the curriculum, usually certain aspects of maths and English. Informal assessment can yield a much greater amount of information, but it is affected by the same processes of filtration. Perceptions of behaviour and qualities such as the ability to pay attention, concentrate and persist with tasks can have an impact on judgements of attainment and ability. In addition, one's subject knowledge, or lack of it, can affect informal assessment and the thinking which informs decision-making about the next tasks or series of learning activities.

What distinguishes the expert teacher from others in using cognitive knowledge of learners? There are several points. Firstly, the expert teacher, while skilled in all the methods of assessment: administering tests; scoring tests; interpreting results; close observation of children; questioning to ascertain understanding; talking to children about their work; and assessing written work and spoken activities, treats all information gathered from these methods as both provisional and problematical. It is provisional in that children do develop and move on so it is constantly having to be revised in the light of new information. It is problematical in that expert teachers have self-awareness of their own role in assessment processes: they are aware that it is imperfect, subjective knowledge, filtered through the lenses of their other knowledge and beliefs.

Secondly, such knowledge is not always easy to acquire. Cognitive knowledge of learners can be difficult to gather in the busy, complex world of the classroom. As one experienced teacher pointed out in his evaluation of a course on assessment: 'The mystery is not how to do it, but when to fit it in!' He was referring to the kind of informal, formative and diagnostic assessment, which gave him detailed knowledge of a few individuals in his class. The course released him to work with these children for five days a year in one subject area: he pointed out the difficulty of doing this for all of the children without this kind of release from teaching. Of course teachers assess while teaching, and teach while assessing as part of the normal flow of classroom life, for example, in the kind of conversation in which a teacher assesses and gives feedback to a child, while offering new strategies for an activity or problem. However, classrooms are such busy places, that it is not always possible to give children the kind of extended attention which would lead to better assessment information. The tendency remarked on by Bennett *et al.* (1984) for teachers to be constantly available for even the most trivial of requests and spellings can absorb time which would be more valuably used in assessment.

The final point which distinguishes expert teachers is the speed and appropriateness of their response to newly acquired cognitive knowledge of learners. The following brief example of teaching illustrates the point.

Case study 7: Rosie: 'Oh, but they'll never do that!'

Rosie, a curriculum developer, intending to teach the Tudors to a Year 4 class, wanted them to make a concept web of background knowledge of the Tudor period. She had access to the children's reading records which showed that 17 children out of a class of 28 had reading ages below their chronological ages, including 5 children with specific language difficulties at stages three to five of the Special Educational Needs Code of Practice. The class teacher looked at the plan and made it clear that she thought it was too ambitious for these children. Rosie decided that in terms of learning history and organising information, the children could gain much from the activity, and went ahead despite the anticipated problems with literacy. The lesson started with her asking the children what they knew about the Tudors: next to nothing. She set them the task of writing down three interesting facts about the Tudors from the topic books provided. The class shared the new information, and then sorted it under topic headings such as Town Life, Crime and Punishment, and Henry VIII placed at different sites in the classroom. The children physically sorted their facts under the right headings. She modelled for them the process of making a concept web on the board, using the headings and facts. The children revisited each heading, literally, to record a fact from that heading. The final stage was for each child to make a concept web, using the collected facts. The class teacher sat throughout the introduction to the lesson with a sceptical air, clearly disbelieving that her class could do this.

This was the first lesson with an unknown group of learners. For Rosie, empirical and cognitive knowledge about these children was almost non-existent. She modelled the process of browsing through a book, finding an interesting topic, and reading aloud facts she might like to record. She used her empirical knowledge of children in general in selecting crime and punishment, for she knew that children of this age enjoy the 'gory bits'. She checked for understanding: the five SEN children wanted further explanation. Seeing some of the other children looking lost, she went round and asked if they would like to return to the carpet to work with her. Four more children joined the little group of five on the carpet. Realising that most of these children would find difficulty in both finding and recording their facts, she simplified the task by asking for only one fact each. She suggested that she find the facts and they could put their hands up if they wanted that particular fact. She read aloud bits of information and the children thrust their hands in the air with enthusiasm. She wrote down each one and handed it to a child. Soon all nine children were clutching a card and asking her to read it to them again. While this was happening, she observed the other children; seeing they had finished, she recalled them to the carpet to share their facts. Because of her rapid adaptive strategy with the children who found the literacy aspects of the task too demanding, all of the class were able to participate in the information-sharing. She ensured that all of these nine children were able to participate in this sharing, by asking them to read their facts first. It also enabled them to join in the fact-sorting under the various headings, with the help of herself and the class teacher, who had by this time abandoned her scepticism. The class went on to watch the process of making a concept web and to try it for themselves.

There is much to comment on in this brief example. Other knowledge bases are, as ever involved, not least knowledge of models of learning and teaching. In the finding, scribing, sharing, organisation and recording of the information, the children were enabled to work actively with the new information. They revisited the information several times, and the plenary showed that they had assimilated, at least temporarily, the new knowledge about the Tudors. It was also a collaborative activity in that children pooled the facts they had found out, both verbally and physically in the organisation of information. Possibly this activity was ambitious and aimed at the most able children; however, Rosie found ways for all the children to participate and gain something from the lesson. The expertise came in the teacher's ability to rapidly assimilate new empirical and cognitive knowledge about the children, within the classroom context.

Processes of classroom interaction are complex. Lortie (1975) pointed out that teachers do not establish separate relationships with each child in the class, but that the relationship with individual children is mediated though the public encounters with the whole class. The other point is that teachers are bombarded with a mass of information daily in the classroom. It is very easy to notice only those children who demand attention in some way, or to make hasty judgements based on inaccurate information. The skill lies in being able to pay attention to what is important or significant, and responding rapidly with appropriate managerial or teaching strategies. An analogy can be drawn here with research on information processing, and on chess players. Novice chess players and Grand Masters were asked to look for a few moments at a chessboard with the pieces arranged in a 'state of play'. The Grand Masters were able to recall the position of all the pieces even when most of them were in play; the novices were only able to remember a handful of pieces (Van De Groot 1965). This was not simply a feat of memory. It appeared that the novice players tended to recall isolated chessmen, while expert chess players were able to 'chunk' the information, to see the pieces as configurations or patterns. They encoded the meaningful configurations in their memory. Thus they did not only have good strategies for playing chess; they had also developed an organised memory, which enabled them to assimilate much more of what they saw (Wood 1988). This applies to other activities, such as reading. The expert reader perceives and processes larger chunks of text than the beginning reader. Expert teachers are able to read and process the complex mass of information which any classroom provides, much more rapidly and meaningfully. It is this which lies beneath qualities attibuted to expert or effective teachers such as 'withitness' (Kounin 1970).

To return to the example of teaching given above, Rosie observed some of the children looking around the classroom, apparently not settling to the task of finding out three facts. This could have been attributed to naughtiness, or disinclination to settle down to work, but she read it as needing help, recognising the reason why children might not immediately engage with a task. The swift response, to add them to the group requiring much additional help demonstrated that she was assimilating knowledge of these learners rapidly, and adapting her teaching strategies to differentiate the task for them almost instantaneously. This might be termed 'reflection in action' or 'knowing in action'. The expert teacher is able to adapt in the very act of teaching to the unexpected, unanticipated needs, and to employ a suitable teaching strategy instantaneously. Of course there will be occasions when the need arises for further reflection on such teaching problems and the more gradual devising of strategies over a longer period of time, but it is these knowledge bases of learners, both empirical and cognitive, which underpin part of the teaching and reflection processes. They are important, though problematic, knowledge bases in the amalgam of pedagogical content knowledge. In the case study presented next, a teacher is seen using her empirical and cognitive knowledge of learners, in conjunction with other knowledge bases, teaching the concept of ratio in a maths lesson.

Case study 8: Kirsty: Enjoyment of maths

Kirsty was one of the teachers identified by the local education authority as an expert teacher of maths. She visited other schools to give in-service training, and gave demonstration lessons in her own school. At the time of the research she had been teaching for about seven years. Originally music was her specialist subject, but she had become enthused by the numeracy strategy, and had developed her maths teaching. The context was a multicultural school in a north London suburb. In this school they placed the children into sets for maths; Kirsty taught a Year 5 upper set for maths. The lesson was planned within the numeracy strategy framework, with a mental/oral session, a main activity and a plenary. The aims for the mental maths part of the lesson were for the children to be able to recognise the links between decimals, fractions and percentages. For the main activity, she wanted them to be able to solve simple problems involving ratio.

When Kirsty said: 'Right, children. Eyes this way!' there was an instant response. They had just sat through an hour-long assembly, and she praised them for settling so quickly after this. The objectives for the lesson were written on the whiteboard. She explained them, and introduced 'Syd's Game', reminded them of the rules, and the strategy of holding up the cards if someone did not know an answer. She warned that this time she was using the timer, to try to complete it in five minutes. The game started: all children were totally involved. The game works like a game of 'Dynamic Dominoes', one answer leading to the next. All went well until they got to 75, where there was a hiatus. Kirsty asked three children to explain how they got to 75: one had used 5 times 12 and added 15; another had multiplied 25 by 3; and a third child had used time knowledge. Kirsty praised all these methods, careful to comment on the strategy of partitioning for the first child, long multiplication in his head for the second child, and the time knowledge for the third child. She confirmed all the strategies and emphasised that there was no 'right' one: they were all ways to work out answers. The game ended after almost seven minutes.

She told them to move to the carpet area where she went through some percentage problems written on a small portable whiteboard. The children were to wriggle their eyebrows if they got the answers. Later she used the gesture of thumbs up in a similar way. The children explained their answers using fractions, percentages and decimals. She checked understanding of 0.05 and 0.5. A child explained it would change one-twentieth to a half. Kirsty then introduced the main activity on ratio, using the problem of a mother seal eating two fish to every one which her baby seal ate. She swivelled the whiteboard: strips were stuck to it with the key vocabulary and a definition of ratio as 'numbers comparing the size of two or more quantities'. She worked through the seal example, writing on the whiteboard, showing how if she multiplied the mother's two fish by five, she had to do the same to the baby's fish. A child pointed out that there was an inverse relationship. Another child added that you could have a function machine to express this relationship. Kirsty praised and confirmed these ideas, writing them on the board. She checked understanding, before moving on:

Kirsty:	What if the baby seal ate 15 fish? How many fish did the mother seal eat?
Children:	30.
Kirsty:	If I wasn't sure of the answer, how would you convince me?
Child:	I doubled it.
Kirsty:	Do you need to use double? This is a multiplying question: you need to use multiply.
Kirsty:	We've got some of your favourite stuff up there (points to a balance with stars and squares stuck to the main whiteboard).
Children*:	Algebra!

(* only some of the children)

Kirsty introduced a trading game to demonstrate some of the group activities which would follow. She had strips of card with quantities of sweets typed on them. One Mars Bar was equivalent to 5 Milky Ways, which was equivalent to 2 gobstoppers: these in turn equalled 10 cola bottles. Selected children stood at the front holding up these strips. She went through an example on the board, showing that if she had 4 Mars Bars, she would be able to trade them for 8 gobstoppers. She flagged up that this was important by asking the children to watch carefully as this was a strategy they might like to use: multiplication. The final example she worked through was of 25 Milky Ways being equal to 10 gobstoppers. She collected the strips and introduced the tasks. Two groups had a market bartering worksheet, using the same ratios. The purple group had a different sheet with other ratios. When they understood how the ratios worked she sent them to their tables and settled them. She then worked with the yellow group of most able children on the balance activity. Using squares and stars as algebraic symbols she went through the operations they were using, which were multipying and dividing, to get each answer. She checked that they all understood the concept of inverse operation. Once this was done, they went to their tables to work on this algebraic worksheet using the same symbols.

As the groups worked, she stopped children wandering about, kept them on task and worked with individuals, getting them to explain answers. Eventually she stopped them, asking for pens down, eyes this way and listening, and warned them of a plenary in four minutes' time. All were to pick their favourite problem to explain to the class. Kirsty moved to another part of the room and stopped the class. She asked them to clear away and return to the carpet. A group of girls were all sitting together and one boy commented out loud to the class:

James: Look, it's the row of girls! It's the mothers' meeting!
Kirsty: James, this is the time when we listen and show respect.

Kirsty shook her head and grimaced to show her disapproval of this comment. There were rather more boys in the set than girls and the girls were somewhat subdued in this context. Kirsty chose a girl to explain her problem first, asking her to teach the class. The girl explained it but did not use the whiteboard. Kirsty scribed for the child and added more explanation. She showed the class a black and white metre rule, which she called a counting stick. She suggested that above it were multiples of three and below multiples of two and asked them to count through the two tables. She asked them how would they know if they had got it right at the end. For homework, they had to go home and teach this idea to their parents: also choose their favourite table to say on Wednesday. This test would be timed for each child: the aim was to do it in the shortest time. She then dismissed the set, class by class.

This lesson was remarkable for its evidence of knowledge of learners, both empirical and cognitive. Much of this emerged in the post-lesson interview, and is bound up with knowledge of contexts, and of educational ends. She had known this year group for two years, and had taught all the children at some point. There were far more boys than girls in the year group and set. The girls were somewhat subdued in this context, and tended to stay together on the carpet. Kirsty commented on the huge social and relationship problems within the year group, and how her colleague and herself had grouped and regrouped the children several times in order to solve problems and create better relationships.

In this lesson she had concentrated on teaching a new concept, that of ratio:

Kirsty: It was a concept of ratio today, but it was using number facts as well. They are just using so many skills now; they have built them up. I've had

> these children for two years now. It's great to see them bringing it all together and applying them in different contexts. So it's a variety of all those things really.

The progress they have made over the two years is clear from this. Although she was teaching a new concept, she was encouraging the children to apply existing knowledge to problems involving this new concept. Thus the learning was incremental, conceptual, had elements of practice; yet the children were engaging in problem-solving in selecting strategies, skills and operations to use in manipulating number. In addition to this Kirsty was deliberately teaching positive attitudes towards maths, towards learning, and towards each other:

Kirsty: I think in every lesson, I try to get the children to develop a positive attitude towards maths, and value maths, and value each other's contributions towards the maths lesson as well. I also try to let them know that it's OK to take risks, and have a go; to really encourage this risk-taking, because that is how they are going to make steps forward really. So I am really hot on that, and I jump on children that snigger or laugh. I hate that in lessons because it stops other children contributing. In fact having that ethos is very important to me.

The last point was illustrated by the incident when James sneered at the girls in the group. She made it absolutely clear that this behaviour was not to be tolerated:

Kirsty: I listen to them, and I show them respect, and I expect them to show me respect, and I expect them to show each other respect. I often say to them to show respect, like to James. He is a bright child, but has behavioural problems; he is stage one for behaviour. I sit him at the front and I have to touch him just to get his attention. He's one of the children that I target. I have two that I target each lesson and I have to do that or they will stop working.

Here she was using her empirical knowledge of this learner in devising strategies to contain him and motivate him. At the same time she made it clear that he had a role to play, as all the children did in maintaining the positive class ethos. Kirsty's comments about teaching attitudes and values in maths are very interesting because of the blend of knowledge bases which underpin them. Both in the short term and long term she wanted these children to succeed at maths, to like it and enjoy it. This was important for their immediate needs, for the following year to do well in the SATs, for their own self-confidence at being good at one of the core subjects, and for their future lives both at work and at play. Thus she was thinking long term of the educational ends of the children, the school and society. She had positive attitudes about maths herself and wanted to transfer these to the children. At the same time, the ethos of respecting each other and valuing each other's contributions had two purposes. The children would continue this in other lessons and subjects on the primary curriculum. It also increased their potential for learning. In Kirsty's knowledge bases of models of learning, it was through taking risks and 'having a go' that they would push forward their learning. Her cognitive knowledge of these learners was shown by her remark about them applying existing knowledge and skills learned over the past two years to deal with the new concept.

In fact her knowledge of these learners was so detailed, that she differentiated both in the main activity of the ratio work and in the mental activity of 'Syd's Game', where Kirsty selected the card for each child, and tried to smooth difficulties by two strategies: that of having the number on the back of the card to be referred to, and for the child to hold up if stuck; and by having the routine that children holding up a card could be helped by their peers. A striking and important part of her classroom organisation and ethos was that she talked of using the children as a resource.

Kirsty had assessed the children informally in the lesson and knew which ones were still uncertain. She intended to look at the work, give feedback, and 'fine tune' her teaching next time on the basis of those assessments, perhaps 'pulling' the least able back to the carpet for lots of oral and practical work to ensure they understood the concept before sending them to their places. She was explicit in several different ways about how her knowledge of these children, in particular her cognitive knowledge, both informed and drove her teaching. She talked of this in conjunction with the variety of pedagogical strategies she used:

> Kirsty: Last year, they were asking me if they could sit at the tables more than being on the carpet, and I was explaining to them why I like them around me. It hit me why I liked them on the carpet around me. It's because of their eyes. I can often see if they understand through their eyes, and I know if I need to give them more input. If there's one child looking at me like this (puzzled facial expression); then I know there's other children in the room like that too, and I need to rephrase it or repeat it in a different way. So that's going on all the time. I think it's a lot more intimate as well.

As well as immediate non-verbal feedback from the children, she employed a range of organisational strategies and approaches based on previous assessments:

> Kirsty: I used whole-class teaching, group work, individual work and paired discussion. I use quite a lot of that to get the vocabulary and the discussion going. I set up carpet pairs at the beginning of the year. They are ability-linked: they are with a partner of similar ability. They know if their partner is away, to sit with their hand up and another person with a partner away will join them. Sometimes I choose random partners. It depends on the activity; but there's value and benefit in that as well. I try to get as many involved as possible, because it's constant question, question, question. I use the thumbs up/thumbs down to get them all in. I do wriggling of eyebrows sometimes because it takes the pressure off children who maybe need a little bit more time to think, and if they see other children with their hands up, they think: 'Oh, well, what's the point? I'm not going to get asked.' So the eyebrows sometimes takes pressure off the children. I have children coming up and being the teacher. They love that. I say: 'Go on! Teach me!'

Here Kirsty was moving from organisational strategies to pedagogical ones, but she demonstrated a good understanding of how to get every child involved and motivated. There is an emphasis on language and discussion in this class, with the children doing much of the explaining, for example, of their various methods of working out a problem. The tactic of putting the child in role as teacher has echoes of the Socratic method, whereby the learner is encouraged to explain his or her understanding to the teacher who is a collaborator in learning. Through discussion and the critical testing of ideas, the learner comes to understand ideas better.

Kirsty also talked of the importance of making maths relevant to their lives, and in doing this revealed some knowledge of self and of her own attitude to maths. She spoke of the reasons she had chosen the market trading game:

Kirsty: I chose that context because it immediately sprang to my mind, and I thought that if I made that link, it would be easier for children to make that link. It's ease of access for the children, and it's relevant to them in their lives. I always try to make the lessons relevant to them. I used to get quite incensed at school that I was taught things that I did not know that I would be applying in my own life. So I try to say to them: 'Have you achieved it yet? How will this be of use to you? How will you apply this knowledge?' So they can apply it in their own lives and it has a meaning to them.

She had clear views about children's learning in maths and how to move them on in their learning:

Kirsty: The value of discussion and sharing work should not be underestimated. This is how children learn and develop confidence in their own thoughts and ideas – and that's where the confidence comes with children. I think the biggest block on children's mathematical ability in most cases is confidence in having a go. It is a real barrier.

This influenced her underpinning philosophy of teaching:

Kirsty: It's really giving them an achievable, accessible goal, but setting high expectations, and trying to push them to their limits at all times. Sometimes you do it, sometimes you don't, but that's the real skill of teaching: getting it spot on! And improving the number of times where you get it where they're just on the cusp of where they're just starting to push forward, at the top of their limit of understanding, and go a bit further.

The most obvious knowledge base in this statement is knowledge of learners. To know that children are just on the cusp of pushing forward their understanding or skill requires detailed cognitive and empirical knowledge of learners. Both are necessary, for it is knowledge of those such as James who would easily destroy the carefully constructed ethos essential to this kind of learning, and of those quiter less confident children who would not be able to 'have a go' if conditions were not conducive to it; if the whole classroom context did not function on a basis of mutual respect. Other knowledge bases are clearly present as well, such as knowledge of self, of context, of educational ends, of models of learning, of general pedagogical knowledge and subject knowledge. However it is striking how much of this teacher's discourse post-lesson focused on how her knowledge of these children informed and 'drove' her teaching and herself to do better:

Kirsty: One big influence on me was the numeracy strategy. Another was having students. One student I had in kept talking about DRIPs (DRies up If not Practised) and having a DRIP-DRIP. I was fascinated and started it, and the response from the children was huge. Just by changing my lesson at the beginning with a DRIP: they loved it. And that led to introducing more games and fun activities, quick activities. That gets the children's attention. And I think if you start, and you do something like that, even if it's a one-off, you get a response back, and that's what spurs me on and drives me and drives me. That's what feeds me to go out and put more effort into my work to make it much more fun for the children: it's the children ultimately.

The term 'DRIP' may need some explanation. At the university from which these students came, long before the numeracy strategy was conceived, tutors on the maths course encouraged students to use short, quick activities, oral and mental, to practise mental arithmetic: hence the name 'DRies up If not Practised (DRIP)'. The children were an important reference group for Kirsty. In seeing how they responded to this variety and approach in her maths lesson she was encouraged to develop the approaches even further. Thus by the time the numeracy strategy arrived, she was already teaching in some of the ways suggested. The children were a powerful reference group and had an impact on herself as teacher, on her pedgogical repertoire, and on her understanding of how children learn. The enjoyment which the children gained from the new approaches also contributed towards their developing positive attitudes towards maths. It was a pleasant and enjoyable experience for the teacher too, and spurred her on.

Conclusion

The three case studies presented in this chaper show the importance of these two knowledge bases. In particular they show the contribution which they can make to expert teaching through understanding children and their development, assessment of the attainment and potential, using that information to operate as Kirsty expressed it 'on the cusp of the where they are starting to push forward'. The skills of creating high expectations, positive attitudes towards subjects, positive attitudes towards learning, and a classroom ethos where respect is universal and mutual, where confidence, speaking out and risk-taking are the norm, are all underpinned by these knowledge bases.

CHAPTER 6

Knowledge of educational contexts

Introduction

The educational context with which teachers are most immediately concerned is that of the classroom. The major part of this chapter will deal with the classroom context, but the wider contexts of school, community and society will also be considered. Knowledge of contexts is vital for expert teaching, but as with other knowledge for teaching, it is linked to other knowledge bases, in particular, knowledge of self. How one functions within a classroom and school context is inevitably bound up with one's self-image as a teacher. At the same time, the prevailing orthodoxy of how a school or local authority organises classrooms can promote tensions between personal and public beliefs about how learning should be managed. Varieties of classroom context are also connected to methods of classroom organisation and management: the layout of furniture and work areas can have an impact on the kinds of teaching and learning which go on in classrooms. The following discussion presents issues and dilemmas of classroom contexts and organisation of which expert teachers need to be aware, in order to make informed judgements about the creation and management of contexts which promote learning. Classrooms are complex environments and expert teachers are able to 'read' them with an informed understanding of the forces which have shaped them, as well as the awareness or 'withitness' described by Kounin (1970).

Classroom contexts

Transport a visitor to any primary classroom in the country, and she or he would probably see some of the same things, whether the room is in a modern open-plan school, a Victorian triple-decker, a small village school or that most celebrated misnomer, a temporary classroom or hut. There will be a square or rectangular room, with one area carpeted. The walls and sometimes the ceiling and windows will be covered in displays of children's work. The tables will almost certainly be arranged in groups. There may be a teacher's desk, either in use as a centre of activities, or pushed against the wall as a repository of work and resources. There will be units with trays for storage, either for materials, or marked with the children's names. There may be a reading corner, or classroom library. There should be a large sink for the cleaning of art and science materials, but in the huts, frequently there is no sink. In infant classrooms there will be a home corner, sometimes arranged as a shop, café or castle for imaginative play. In some rooms, there may be work bays, designated for particular areas of the curriculum, such as maths, art, language and science corners. Depending on the age of the building, there may be a blackboard, a whiteboard or flipchart for the teacher to write on.

These are the outward trappings of the primary classroom context. In that so much is common, it might seem that there is not much for the teacher to know about or be aware of. However, these outward trappings represent a bundle of tensions and contradictions about teaching and learning, the curriculum, play, and classroom management. Furthermore, they are the consequence of historical changes in primary education. Finally, although they are the externals of the classroom context, they can have considerable impact on the kinds of activities and on learning. It is important that expert teachers have a broad historical knowledge and understanding of classroom contexts: this both helps them to set the apparatus of primary education into context, to understand the possible effects of context on learning, and to have the confidence and ability to vary contexts to promote the best possible learning.

Classroom contexts communicate and are informed by images and models of teaching and learning. In the nineteenth century, mass elementary education was education on the cheap. It was also an education in religious instruction and the basics, for the civilising effect of religion on the children of the poor, and sufficient grasp of reading, writing and number to equip them the kinds of work generated by the industrial revolution. Oracy did not feature in this canon of requirements, for the working classes were not required to think, reason, or be articulate: such an education might be dangerous in giving them ideas above their station in life. Schooling was to be done cheaply: to this end there were class teachers often with huge classes of 50 or 60 children. The class teachers were supported by pupil monitors. Much of the work was rote learning and practice of basic skills. Thus the teacher would speak from a dais to children sitting in rows, sometimes in raised banks. Thus education as imparting knowledge to the masses was translated into the physical context of platform and rows. The modern classroom communicates a different prevailing orthodoxy: the primacy of groups. This is not to say there was no group teaching in elementary schools; it was done by pupil monitors. However groups as both an organisational device and a setting for learning are very much part of current primary ideology. Hence the current ubiquitous form of classroom organisation of children sitting in table groups.

However, there is a fundamental paradox in this form of organisation. Children sit in groups, particularly in junior classrooms, but the work is individualised (Galton *et al.* 1980). The rhetoric is that children will cooperate in groups and help each other with their learning; ideas which were inculcated by the Plowden Report (CACE 1967) as a response to the difficulties thrown up by the individualisation of children's work. The idea was that children at roughly the same stage would sit together, assist their peers, inspire each other and engage in the 'cut and thrust' of conversation focused on the learning in hand. These groups were not to be firmly fixed. They were envisaged as being totally flexible, their composition changing according to subject area and progress made by the children. However, in practice, groups tend to be much more fixed than originally envisaged. In addition, they are useful neither for the completion of individual work nor for cooperation. There is evidence from studies such as ORACLE (Galton *et al.* 1980; Galton and Simon 1980; Galton 1987) and PRINDEP (Primary Needs Independent Evaluation Project) (Alexander 1992) to indicate that children working individually in groups rather than as groups means poor involvement in tasks, low-level interaction and lack of cooperative activity. Children are arranged so that they make eye-contact with ease; in humans this leads naturally to conversation. Yet they are discouraged from off-task talk even though their physical arrangement promotes it. When adults want to carry out some reading or writing task which requires sustained concentration, we tend to isolate ourselves from social contact and distraction. Children are expected to work in conditions which actively encourage distraction. A further problem is the nature of tasks set, which are largely individual. Genuinely cooperative tasks need to be set (Bennett 1995), which acknowledge the social nature of much of children's learning, and which encourage talk and collaborative activities. Other than that, by reflecting on the nature of classroom learning, we might devise more radical solutions to the problems of managing and promoting learning in classroom contexts. The following two case studies present, firstly, an analysis of the difficulties in teaching and learning in overly-complex classroom environments and, secondly, an example of teaching which suggests an alternative mode of classroom organisation. The first case study, is from Melanie, a newly qualified teacher in her first job, encountered previously as a student-teacher in Chapter 5. The second is from Rosie, the history curriculum expert, some of whose work is also described in Chapter 5.

Case study 9: Melanie: Science in a complex context

Melanie had been appointed through the county pool system to a permanent post in a large middle school to teach 9–10-year-olds. The whole year group of three classes was to move into new open-plan accommodation at the start of the year. The three teachers including Melanie worked collaboratively on planning but the organisation was very complex: children moved between areas in the year base according to what lesson they were having. She found this very challenging and in a telephone interview in the first week of term explained:

Melanie: A hectic beginning . . . difficult to get used to the system. The children seem to be going here, there and everywhere. I felt a bit panicky at first.

In the autumn term, Melanie was recorded teaching a science lesson planned by the whole team. She did not have good subject knowledge in science, and neither did she feel confident about it. The purposes were to introduce the topic of density and to have an investigative group activity. The task was for the children to see how different liquids (syrup, cooking oil and water) form different layers when put into the same jar, and how they mix together when shaken but separate back into the different layers afterwards. She thought that the children would learn that liquids have different densities and that this affects the floating and sinking of objects explaining why some objects float and others sink. However, she did think that the chidlren would have difficulty understanding the concept of density.

Although Melanie was working with her group of 12 children, she was responsible for the rest of her class who were doing art and humanities. Throughout the lesson they called on her for assistance. The area in which the 12 were working was screened off from the rest of the year base by a curtain, but their noise and movement was distracting. She started the lesson before the rest of the year base were properly settled. The 12 children stood around Melanie at the sink, where she showed them the three liquids, asked them to feel and taste them, and estimate which was the heaviest. The children moved into threes to carry out the investigation, but much of Melanie's talk in this part of the lesson was concerned with organising the children to look at the worksheets and carry out the instructions. She moved around the groups, monitoring their understanding of the task and what they saw:

Melanie: Listen. The oil goes above the water, even though we put the oil in before the water. Now why do you think that is? Why do you think then oil goes above the water?
Child: Because the water is heavier than the oil.
Melanie: Right.

Although the child's answer seems reasonable, the language in which it was expressed might not be that useful for concepts of density which Melanie later brought into the lesson. The next part of the task was to predict where each of three objects, a cork, a grape and a piece of candle, would float in the three layers of liquid. One child immediately predicted that they would float above the syrup, They tried it:

Melanie: Why do you think the grape floated?
Child: It floated on top of the syrup?
Melanie: So the grape went quite low compared to the candle and the cork, didn't it?

In this exchange, she is rushing the children to a conclusion, before giving them enough time to observe in detail. During this time she was dealing with queries from the arts and humanities groups. After almost half an hour she called the 12 children together to review what they had found so far. She summed up for them what they had done, but although she involved the children to some extent, she tended to answer her own questions. She continued to question her group amid interruptions from other groups, as to why objects floated at different levels:

Melanie: Did they all float in the same place? Why not? Why is thegrape down at the syrup, and the candle and cork at the top? Why? Think about the floating and sinking we did last term.

Child: I know. It sinks . . . it . . . mmmm, up the top.

Melanie: Yes, Natalie. Some things are heavier. The cork, Richard, is very, very light, isn't it? So it can float on top of the cooking oil. Even though the cooking oil is light, the cork can float up there because it is very light. The grape . . . a grape is not as light as a cork, is it? So that will sink below the cooking oil, and it actually sank below the water, didn't it?

She monitored for recall of a word she had used in the previous half-term:

Melanie: Do you remember the word I said when we were doing floating and sinking? Do you remember what density means? No? It basically means heaviness. Right, so which has the most density – cooking oil, water or syrup?

Children: Syrup.

Melanie: Which has the least density?

Children: Cooking oil.

Melanie: Cooking oil. Right, so although you've been doing about heaviness of liquids, and the way liquid layers are formed, what we call it is: density. Right, when you're writing up, write 'Liquid Layers' as your title. OK. I want an explanation of all the different things you've done today, please. All those three things. Right, the same order as usual. Same full workout sheet.

The children returned to their tables to write up their findings according to a fixed format.

In reflecting on the lesson afterwards, Melanie commented on the noise levels at the beginning of the lesson, but as this was part of the team teaching situation, she could do little about it. She should have waited until everyone in the year group was settled. She thought of changing the task if she did it again: demonstrating the pouring of the liquids into the jar, as some of them had shaken their jars too soon. She felt that one purpose of the lesson had been achieved though: that of the children doing group work. She considered that the children had learnt about the heaviness of different liquids, building on earlier work on floating and sinking. She thought that the concept of density was quite difficult and she had only introduced it at the end, tending to use the word 'heaviness' to make it easier. She mentioned that one very able child's description of the activity was confused. The strength had been the group work: the weaknesses were her not giving enough explanation, or letting them follow up their interests in the first part of the activity. She had not felt able to pursue the children's ideas and questions, such as what would happen if they put in washing-up liquid first, because that would have meant everyone being at different stages and she was worried about getting them back together again.

On the face of it, this was a well-managed lesson in which the children did manage to begin to explore the properties of different liquids, and cooperate in small groups.

However, there are serious weaknesses, some to do with lack of subject knowledge, and some to do with the context. The lack of subject knowledge requires some brief consideration, before moving on to the contextual problems. There is evidence that Melanie did not fully understand the concept of density. She stated that it basically meant heaviness. A more accurate definition would be that it is mass in relation to volume. It would have been necessary to deal with the sub-concepts of mass and volume before introducing the new concept of density. In addition her representation of the concept was not ideal. It might have been better to use three objects of exactly the same volume. The main problem was that there were too many variables for the children to cope with. If she had concentrated on the three liquids, or floated the objects in one liquid, there would have been fewer variables. If she had chosen to do the first part only, the children would have had time to pursue their own questions, and even devise their own experiment, rather than the recipe science they were doing. This would have been a more accurate reflection of the discipline of science for they would have been writing up their own investigation.

This was a challenging context in which to carry out any practical work. There were the physical problems of the 90 or so children moving and making noise around the base, and there were the constraints placed on Melanie by the team planning. Throughout the lesson, Melanie was plagued by children coming to ask for help in arts and humanities. This is an oddity, for if the base was being managed by three teachers, could not the other two have taken responsibility for the other children? Alternatively, more of the 90 children could have done the science activity, but possibly they were constrained by lack of space near the sink. As it was, the other children were an added pressure, and Melanie was inclined to rush the children through the activity without giving them time to investigate. They had to follow steps on the worksheet: a kind of investigation by numbers, or recipe science. A major concern seemed to be to get the activity done and written up, regardless of the children's learning. The complex context and team planning may have contributed to this. One of the difficulties of working in this kind of organisation is record-keeping: keeping track of which children have done which activities. To keep children on task a worksheet explaining the steps of the investigation had been provided, and this in itself was a constraint. The children asked genuinely scientific questions such as 'What would happen if we put the syrup in last?' However, they were not able to pursue these because of the pressure from the context to 'get things done' regardless. Melanie, as a newly qualifed teacher, doubtless felt constrained to complete the experiment and have the work written up neatly in science books, partly as a function of the context, and partly to give the impression to her more experienced colleagues, that she was able to manage this sort of activity in the time available. Learning became very much a secondary consideration in this context.

This is somewhat of a paradox when one considers that the aim behind the three-teacher year base context was that the learning environment should be child-centred. In fact the context had presented Melanie with some problems when she first started her new job, for it had an impact on the way she taught, and it made her reflect upon her role as a teacher. She had always been confident in teaching the whole class on her teaching practices: now it was rare for her to work in this way. In the beginning she had felt 'redundant and like a supervisor'. She had felt guilty if she had not been teaching the whole class. It is significant that in this context, she felt less of a teacher, and more like a task manager. It calls into question the role of the teacher, and what a teacher should be doing. Thus, one's whole self-image as a teacher is affected by the contexts in which one works: it would take an exceptionally determined beginning teacher to maintain a different view of the teacher's role in such a context. It is true that in this supposedly 'child-centred' environment, the focus of attention was on the children, but the logistical difficulties thrown up by the complex organisation meant that more attention was given to organisation and completion of work than to children's learning. Melanie devoted much time in planning to thinking about groupings, which had to be mixed ability. More time could usefully have been devoted to thinking about how the children were going to begin to understand the concept of density, and whether or not the experiment was a good representation of the concept.

The pressure to get all of the children through the activity during say, the course of a week, was too great to allow for high-quality planning, which would allow children to do a genuine investigatory activity based on their own questions and hypotheses. In this context, the very aspects which were supposed to make for flexible child-centred learning: multi-curriculum focus, organisation of an entire year group together, flexible groupings, and children working through a schedule of tasks, actually made for a more rigid kind of organisation, and paradoxically fostered less learning, given that the teachers were so caught up in the complex organisation. This is not to say that in some hands, complex classroom contexts do not work (see, for example Case study 13 of Tom in Chapter 7). However, complex forms of organisation can add considerably to the demands on teachers, and reduce both planning and teaching time.

Another aspect of the context in which Melanie found herself working was the tendency towards production line working (Cockburn 1995) or the importance of 'getting done' by both children and teachers alike. There is an emphasis in classroom life on completion of work. Cockburn summarises classroom life in this way. Classrooms are busy industrious places. They are also crowded. There can be many delays and interruptions in the work programme. Teachers are outnumbered, and they tend to manage learning rather than focus their attention on learning. Children often complete their work in ways not intended by the teacher. Sometimes there is a great deal of routine practice work. Children try very hard to please their teachers to gain praise. Another facet of this is the 'completion of workbook' syndrome, whereby children talk about how many pages they have done today. In classrooms where all children are engaged on making dinosaurs for design technology, or identical Easter cards, the classroom may come to resemble a production line. Learning can become pushed aside in these environments, and both teachers and children have to learn to adjust to them. In the second case study, we see the learning and teaching approaches used *dictating* the form of classroom layout and organisation, which is perhaps as it should be.

Case study 10: Rosie: Drama and oracy – making the space

Rosie, the history curriculum expert, had been teaching a Year 5 class in history and literacy. The class had been working on the Romans in Britain, focusing on the invasion, everyday life, and the revolt of Boudicca. The ideas with which she wished to experiment were: using storytelling as a means of teaching much factual information about the revolt; using drama as a means for the children to understand the historical situation from the inside, as it were; and whole-group talk, in role as ancient Celts, to explore the central ideas and concepts of this part of the history of Britain. The children would need to understand: Roman, Celt, chariot, taxes, loans, queen, royal descent through the female line, temples, legions and battle formations. They would need to know the main characters in the story. Rosie was also influenced by the work of Rosen (1990), Fines and Nichol (1997) and Bage (1999) among others, in using storytelling as a major means of communicating ideas and understanding. Rosen, in particular, gets children to write the story in their own words. From the point of view of theories about teaching and learning, this would seem a powerful method of teaching, for the children take from the story what they understand, blending it with their own perspective on life, often lifting some detail of the story and making it more central, or finding from the words of the storyteller meaningful phrases which 'lift' their writing. Through the process of writing, they are working on the information in the story, and on the emotions which the story conjures up, as part of the process of assimilation and accommodation.

However, in order to do this lesson, the classroom had to be reorganised. The tables, arranged in groups, were far from ideal for storytelling, an activity in which you need all eyes to be on the storyteller. In order to see the teacher, children had to swivel in their chairs: the temptation to turn back inwards to the table group, fiddle with equipment, and talk to neighbours was too much. One possibility was to have had them on the carpet, but these were Year 5 children and physically quite large. What is suitable for infants may not be suitable for upper juniors. In teaching Year 5 and Year 6 classes, Rosie had often been hemmed in by a sea of arms and legs, unable to move about, as storytelling demands. Thus she organised the children to move all the tables to one side of the room, and bring their chairs to sit in a large circle.

Once the furniture was arranged and all the children seated, she began the storytelling, at first seated, later getting up and moving around, using gesture to empha-sise meaning. She paused in the telling at the point in the story, after the death of King Prasutagus, husband of Queen Boudicca of the Iceni, when the tribe must hold a full council meeting to decide what to do about the recall of the loan from Seneca. At this point, she told the class that they would act out the meeting. She had ready a number of role-cards, ranging from names of key people in the story, such as Boudicca, to characters merely named as council elders. There was scope for all the children to take part. She explained that she would be in role as the chief elder, who would start the meeting. The allocation of parts proved very interesting: many children asked for roles, including those with special educational needs. One boy, Aaron, who was identified by the class teacher as having particular difficulties with literacy, begged Rosie to be allowed to play Boudicca. Sophie, another child with difficulties, was given a major role. Boys and girls alike volunteered for male and female roles and these were allocated without reference to gender.

With the whole class still seated in the circle, Rosie gave the signal and began the drama. In role as chief elder, she gave a speech telling the tribe that they were there to decide what to do about the action of the Romans, and the threat to the tribe if they did not repay the loan. She did this as a chairperson, to get the drama underway. Aaron, as Boudicca, kept looking across for reassurance as he spoke, but he grew in confidence, and as Queen of the tribe, took over the role of leader and chair quite naturally. Many suggestions were offered, first from key people and elders; later all of the tribesmen were invited to speak. Rosie had not presented them with historical alternatives: thus their ideas were grounded in their limited experience. This could be a criticism of the lesson, but on the other hand, they were trying to make sense of the dilemma of the tribe according to their own knowledge. There were some ideas which linked directly into the historical information given. For example, they knew the tribe was rich in horses and minerals, so several children suggested selling these to raise money to pay off the loan. There was much emphasis on fund-raising, which the teacher later explained to Rosie was because many of them sat on the school council, where fund-raising was a perennial concern. (This in itself says something about the broader educational context.) The most impressive were the performances of Aaron and Sophie, especially Aaron. He listened intently to all the suggestions, challenged them if he thought they had weaknesses, argued his points, invited further ideas, dismissed silly contributions, of which there were few, and generally acted as a confident and knowledgeable chair-person. He was totally in role as Boudicca, contrasting sharply with his silliness the previous week. Sophie did not say a great deal, but her suggestions were sensible, related to the historical information they had heard in the story, and she challenged others once or twice. Rosie ended the drama when the children began repeating ideas. She gave them a couple of minutes to talk among themselves after a period of such intense concentration; then she told the rest of the story. The children rearranged the tables and chairs back into groups and began the writing task, of retelling their own version of the story. All of the children were immediately engaged in the writing, despite it being the end of a long wet day. Their stories showed a good understanding of the revolt and its causes.

This lesson is described in some detail for several reasons. It was clearly a lesson in which much learning took place. There is evidence that the children understood the story from the ideas and suggestions in the drama. All the children were able to take part, and virtually all of them offered contributions to the council meeting. Released from the pressure of writing, the children with special educational needs demonstrated their historical understanding impressively. Their regular class teacher was delighted. However, without moving the furniture, this lesson would have been very difficult to do well. The inward focus of the circle for both the storytelling and the drama was very important. Thus the physical re-organisation of the room and of the children within it shaped the activity and made it possible. In terms of social inclusion, this was also a good learning activity, for everyone was able to be involved, without pressure, to say as much or as little as they wanted to say, and to make a contribution. All could think themselves into the historical situation: what would they do if they were the Iceni? It was not necessary to set different activities for different table groups according to ability.

Working with this kind of classroom organisation and experiencing its success made Rosie reflect upon an article by John Fines (1994). Over a period of several years he worked with a class in a middle school teaching history through storytelling, drama, visits and numerous other approaches. The school was fortunate enough to be allocated some money for refurbishment of several of the classrooms. Given a free hand to produce the kind of classroom environment he wanted, he worked with the class teacher to produce an original design, which was duly executed. He reasoned that when the children were working on writing tasks, they needed peace and as much isolation as can be achieved in an often overcrowded classroom. Tables seating two were fixed against the wall all round the room, with dividers between each table. Above the table was a shelf for each child to store books and other equipment, doing away with the constant movement to collect books, pencils and other materials from the tray units. Each child was given her or his own place, which they looked after and kept tidy. Thus, while engaged on individual work, they faced the wall, or window, and were not in direct eye contact with other children. They all had stools on which they could swivel to face the teacher. The central area of the classroom was kept clear for drama, role-play and other activities. The carpeted area was adapted as a library and reading area. The children were taught as a whole class, using the kind of activities described in this case study. From time to time they would need to discuss things in pairs, or produce something in pairs, which would then be fed back to the whole class. The transition from whole-class to individual or pair work and back again was swift and efficient (Fines 1994).

The reader may well be wondering: What about managing group work in such a classroom? Given Fines' preference for 'working' the whole class as a unit, he did not use group organisation a great deal, but occasionally he asked pairs and threes to form fours and fives for a particular task. They used some spare tables which were stacked against the wall for this purpose, with a couple of groups working in the library area. This example of a totally different form of classroom organisation, designed for the kind of teaching undertaken in the context, is given to show what might be possible. Just because primary classrooms have been organised in a particular way for some years, it does not mean that this is the only way of organising them. Of course, post eleven-plus, after the demise of rigid steaming in the primary school, the problem of teaching mixed ability classes made the use of groups a pragmatic solution. However, as noted, groups are often for organisational purposes only: the children in them are more often than not engaged on individual tasks and the group setting can prove a distraction. Moreover, for children to work collaboratively in groups requires two things: firstly, a training in collaboration and group work, including an awareness of roles and behaviours in the group (Bennett *et al.* 1991; Bennett and Dunne 1992); and secondly, the right kinds of tasks which lend themselves to collaborative work. Much of classroom work is not of this nature, and teachers need to understand the capital investment of time and preparation in order to make genuine group work happen.

Comment

The purpose of the case studies and this discussion is to show the relationship between classroom organisation, both physical and in terms of the children, teaching approaches, and models of teaching and learning. Contexts do matter in teaching, and they can have an impact on the kinds of teaching and learning which happen. Generally speaking, the wider experience teachers have of a range of different classroom contexts, the more knowledge they will have of the advantages and disadvantages of different forms of organisation. In Turner-Bisset's (1997) study of beginning teachers, it was apparent that the two student-teachers who made most rapid progress in learning to teach were those who had experience of a much broader range of educational contexts with primary age children. This was not of course the only factor in their relative success, but one of a set of contributory factors.

The situation in Melanie's first job (Case study 9), with the three classes in the open-plan year base, had proved almost too much for her initially. When interviewed at the end of the year, she stated that the team of teachers had in fact cut down on movement around the year base, and she was getting to teach her own class more as a class. The value of this experience for Melanie is in the material for reflection: the impact of classroom contexts on teaching and learning; the uses and misuses of group organisation; the relationship between self-as-teacher and context; the roles of significant others such as teachers in the same team, parent helpers and classroom assistants; and how these can affect one's teaching. For expert teachers, the foci of reflection should be the same. The value of experiencing a wide range of classroom contexts lies in the fact that one becomes aware of what is possible, in terms of creating and adapting contexts and creating the conditions for learning. One needs to be able to stand back from contexts, and not accept them as an immutable aspect of classroom life, but ask instead how a particular context might be adapted to promote a genuine learning environment, rather than one in which the ethos of pleasing the teacher and the work ethic of busyness actually detract from the quality of what happens in that room.

Other contexts: school

Teachers have to fit into school contexts much as they do with classroom contexts. One is not always so publically exposed in one's teaching as Melanie was in the three teacher base in her first year of teaching: nonetheless, one has to manage things, so that one appears at least to conform. Schools would appear to be essentially conservative places; certainly one of the major concerns which students and beginning teachers have is of fitting into the existing school context, and being accepted as a colleague. They are often acutely aware of how delicately this has to be managed. Nias (1989) in her study of primary teachers at work, has explored this area fully, and has identified 'impression management' as one of the coping strategies used by teachers whose models of teaching and learning, and teaching approaches do not concord with those of the school. Schools, no less than classrooms, are complex environments, and the same broad rule applies to both: that a wide range of experience of different schools, gives ample material for reflection about organisation, managing groups of children and teaching and learning. It also can enlighten one as to what is possible. This is not to say that one cannot be expert at teaching without knowledge of many different school contexts, only that it is an enriching aspect of this knowledge base.

The relationship betweeen knowledge of contexts and knowledge of self is worth exploring, for it can impact upon one's classroom practice and image of self as teacher. The problems of fitting in to classroom and school are obviously particularly acute for beginning teachers, but they can also have an effect on the performance of experienced teachers moving from one school to another. The case study of Sarah, a final year BEd student is presented below to illustrate some of these points.

Case study 11: Sarah: Impression management

Sarah was a science specialist who took history as a second specialist subject. The foundation course had changed her view of history and her understanding of it to realising it is an enquiry-based discipline. In addition, the specialist course, which revisited the nature of history and its substantive and syntactic structures, had deepened her understanding as she made clear in her final year interview:

> Sarah: It has really made me look at history, because although I had an understanding, it wasn't as deep as it is now. It was very useful to me because I had done historiography in my A Level as you know, but I never really understood what it was for, what the use of it was, and by looking at the assignments, made me think about it, especially the activity when we did the statement at the beginning, and it sunk in as to where those views, and why I am teaching, comes from, and that really helped me, because before it was something on a bit of paper that I had to do, and now I have a far better understanding of where it comes from and why people want to do it.

Here she was referring to an activity in which the students had analysed the quotations about history presented at the beginning of the Curriculum 2000 (DfEE 1999c). She had begun to see from which views of history these had come; more importantly, instead of seeing it as an official public document, to whose pronouncements she had to conform, she began to look at it critically, with an informed understanding.

She had always had strong views about teaching, and how to teach, but despite being an able student, had actually failed one teaching experience. I had been her supervisor on the first teaching practice, where I had observed two lessons of outstanding quality for a beginning teacher. She was placed in a complex environment, a combined classroom area accommodating a mixed Year 3/Year 4 class. There were about 60 children, two teachers, a classroom assistant, a specialist helper for a partially-sighted child, Sarah and a fellow student. Sarah taught two science lessons, working in a side room off the main classroom, in which she elicited ideas from a group of about 12 children about how they would test variables in growing seeds, got the children to plan their investigations, and carry out the practical work. The children were very engaged, and Sarah exuded confidence and enjoyment in what she was doing. A year later it was a different story. I heard she had failed her second year practice. I was stunned at the news, for I had considered her a very promising teacher. However, she went on to pass the repeat practice at another school; so it seemed to be a problem with not fitting into the new context. She continued with the course, but was quieter and more subdued. Perhaps these experiences had made her very wary when it came to the final long placement. At any rate, she was extremely careful to try to convey 'the right impression' to the staff, and made this her top priority. As she explains in her final year interview she had some difficulties with her teacher, who tended to plan things very much at the last minute:

> Sarah: . . . with time constraints I was finding teaching practice very difficult, particularly as I wasn't that far ahead planned, because my teacher was very last minute; so I found it hard to actually plan as well as I would have liked to have done. I was probably trying to tackle that problem more than my actual teaching.

Sarah had been placed in a Year 2 class, and the topic that year, was the Millennium. The school also taught literacy through its topics; thus much history work was done in literacy. This presented Sarah with some problems. For children so young, there is difficulty in understanding notions of 100 or 500 years, let alone 2,000 years. The other problem was that there was a tendency amongst teachers to devote something like half an hour to each period of history, giving for example the Anglo-Saxons just one lesson, in order to get through the mass of content which 2,000 years of history contains. Sarah did not feel that much of the time she taught history:

Sarah: The school actually had literacy and it was taught across the curriculum, and although I feel that you can teach history and literacy, I feel that it is quite a difficult task, and you have to be very focused on what you actually want them to do. I feel that the school is actually pushing the literacy objectives much more than the history ones; so I felt that I wasn't teaching history but literacy.

The two teachers planned the content and Sarah had to teach what they planned. Much was taught using 'big books' to convey historical stories, and information. Sarah had introduced them to the primary source of the Guy Fawkes letter, an anonymous letter warning of the Gunpowder Plot:

Sarah: We used the letter, but the focus was much more on literacy. It was much more about letter writing than it was about finding out the history of Guy Fawkes, which most of them knew the full story of anyway. I would have liked to use the letter more in a historical way, but I wasn't allowed to do that. I found it really difficult actually. I found it was really against what I believed in, about teaching and how I would like to teach.

Sarah was fully aware that teaching history through literacy was problematical, and that even with only one history objective and one literacy objective, the children could achieve both with some difficulty. She used the commercial resources and big books provided by the school, but when the teacher was not present in the room, she used other teaching activities:

Sarah: We did Christopher Columbus . . . I actually did a hot seat activity where I pretended to be one of the sailors, and they could ask what it was like. They really enjoyed that and then they went off and wrote about what it was like to be a sailor on the boat. They found that quite difficult, but they managed to get to grips with it. I gave them time to work in groups and they asked some really good questions; each group asked me different questions. They did some nice work for me. I think that contributed to the success of it, because if I had just given them questions to answer, I don't think that they would have got the feel for it. It was having someone there for them that was actually on the ship: I feel that really added to their work. It gave them a new dimension. The teacher wasn't there in the room, but she read the work that they did, and she was very impressed and pleased with it.

However, Sarah had not wanted to tell her teacher about the hot-seating activity and how this good work had been achieved:

Sarah: I didn't like to tell her, but she never asked and I kept it to myself.

Sarah was treading extremely carefully here, in her detemination to fit in with the teacher and the school. She talked of how the school context can have an impact on one's beliefs about teaching, and they can even change:

Sarah: I think, when you go into schools, you can sometimes lose what you believe. You get so wound up in everything you have got to achieve, and everything you have got to do. I think sometimes what you firmly believe in sometimes gets lost. I am hoping that when I am teaching my own class it will be much easier to do what I feel is appropriate.

In this final year interview Sarah spoke of the value of the course in reaffirming her beliefs about teaching, which has implications for experienced teachers as well as for beginners. It is easy for the context to be so overpowering, and the need to fit in to be so great, that without external in-service training, one can become immersed in the norms and orthodoxies of a school context, and find it difficult to step back from one's present reality. Sarah described the process of fitting in as a student, but the same might be true for a newly qualified teacher, or a teacher in a new school:

Sarah: They are a very tight knit group: they are very close and they believe the same things, and when I first entered the school I found it very difficult. I didn't feel that I was accepted. I didn't feel I could teach how I wanted to, and I found that extremely difficult. Then as I started teaching and doing things the way they expected them to be done, and with them vetting what they wanted to, I was accepted. Now I can go back and they are delightful; they are the nicest people in the world and I would work with them, but I had to do what they wanted me to do first, before I could go off and do my own teaching in the way that I would like to.

She showed acute awareness of the realities of fitting into a school, and how that could be achieved:

Sarah: I don't think you can walk straight into a very well-organised and well-structured school with staff that have been there a long time, and just say I am doing this, and this is the way I am doing it, because it will get their backs up completely, because they think: 'Hang on, this person is coming in with their new ideas, which is lovely, but they can't just come in and do what they like.' I feel I will probably drip my ideas in occasionally and gradually work them into the way I work in time; so they can become accepted.

The danger with this, as remarked earlier, is that over time, one can lose sight of what one believes, about teaching, children, subjects and classroom management. Sarah understood this as well as what was needed to be able to withstand the assault on one's own beliefs:

Sarah: I think, that definitely, to go against the grain you've got to be a really strong person. You've got to be really strong with your beliefs and a really strong person: you do.

This case study shows the problems in fitting into school contexts as a new teacher and the kind of impression management which can be necessary. Although about a beginning teacher, this can often be true of moving to another school. It illustrates how it is possible to lose what one believes in, in the mass of tasks and priorities which have to be tackled and the immediacy of that context. Teachers can also lose part of their 'teacher selves' in the effort of fitting in; it takes an exceptionally strong personality to withstand such erosion of beliefs. Alexander (e.g. 1984; 1995) has written extensively on the pervasiveness of primary ideologies, and this case can throw some light on how accepted practices in some schools can assume the status of absolute laws about what constitutes good practice. Expert teachers need to be aware of such problems, the processes of change within themselves, and how to have an influence on the school contexts and norms, without offending others. This can be achieved by stepping back, physically and figuratively, from the immediacy of the school context, and reflecting on it.

Other contexts: community and society

Schools are part of the broader community, both the immediate vicinity of the school and the catchment area, which these days even for primary schools can be relatively widespread. Such contexts can vary hugely, from the depths of inner city or rural deprivation to affluent suburbs. Sometimes the community genuinely exists: there are schools where the local postmistress goes into school once a week to teach Arabic dancing, a parent comes in to teach weaving or the local community association helps out on sports days, or holds money-raising events. Some schools are well-supported or sponsored by local businesses. In other places, the community as such exists in name only. I visited a school on the outskirts of a midland city, where the head teacher told me about the drug-running going on blatantly in the street outside the school, and the occasional battles which ensued. About a third of the houses on this estate were boarded up; nearby warehouses and factories, relics from the industrial revolution, stood empty and vandalised. These are extremes, and there is much in between, but an understanding of the local context of the school, and what kind of a community exists outside the school gates, is important for understanding children, parents, everyday lives and futures. One common factor in the wide range of community contexts is the need for fund-raising: all schools seem to need to do this to provide extras, and even basics for which the budget will not stretch. This shortage of money in primary education is historical: to an extent it is still education on the cheap for the masses, only these days, all kinds of consumers of education want much more for their money.

This is moving from the community context to the broader context of society, but all of these contexts are related. If in the broader context of society, primary education is underfunded compared with secondary education; then this impacts on all other contexts. Since the introduction of the National Curriculum, it has been acknowledged by all except the Government that the present funding arrangements, a historical legacy of primary needs being considered 'less' than those of secondary education, are inadequate for the new ten-subject curriculum. There does not seem to be much hope of a genuine review and assessment of the real costs of primary education currently. Hence the need for fund-raising at whatever level of society. It is important that teachers understand this aspect of society's context, for they need to set themselves and their work within that context. Teachers have always tried to do the best they possibly can with inadequate funding and resources, and frequently felt guilty if they did not achieve the goals they set for themselves. I would argue that guilt is one of the enemies of expert teaching. In a state of guilt one can lose the sense of professionalism which is essential for expert teaching. One must understand this aspect of the societal context, in order not to succumb to guilt.

There are other aspects of the societal context of which one must have knowledge and understanding: for example, the central tension in education between the needs of society and the needs of the individual. There is nothing natural about state schooling. It is a hot-housing of the raw material of future society in order to meet the predicted needs of that society. At the same time, the developmental and progressive traditions in primary education stress the needs and development of the individual child. At school context and classroom level, this may come down to an emphasis on the basics rather than on a broad and balanced curriculum. Such tensions sound irreconcilable, but need not be so. Much has already been written (e.g. Wragg 1997) on the need to produce flexible, adaptable people, who may have a portfolio of jobs rather than one job for life, for the uncertain future which lies ahead of us. It is in everyone's interests to promote the needs of the individual and those of society: in producing well-rounded flexible people with curiosity and enthusiasm for learning, society is benefitted as well as the individual. At the same time, the basics, probably better conceived of as maths and English rather than the narrower literacy and numeracy, are essential in empowering future citizens to function well in society. Expert teachers must be informed about such tensions and able to use this knowledge to devise their personal educational aims and curricular activities, without recourse to guilt. The value of knowledge of the broader contexts of education is a sense of perspective.

CHAPTER 7

Knowledge of self

The self is important in teaching. Teaching as a job involves a huge investment of the self: this is true in two senses. Firstly, teaching involves one's personality as a means of communication. Whatever kind of person one might be, is projected, even amplified in the business of teaching. Secondly, teaching has an impact on the self: the learning involved in learning to teach is affective as well as cognitive. Emotional engagement is necessary for teaching as much as intellectual engagement. Good or bad lessons generate feelings: in good lessons those of euphoria, excitement, relief, satisfaction, hope; in bad lessons, or those that do not 'go well', feelings of sadness, guilt, disappointment, even despair. Through the responses of children, one can learn about oneself. Thus teaching encompasses a two-way process as regards the self: one both invests one's self in the job, and learns about one's self through teaching.

The literature on teacher thinking and on reflection recognises the emotional impact of teaching, and the importance of the self in teaching. Early work on teacher thinking characterised teachers' knowledge as a reliance on intuition and impulse, implying that teaching is irrational (Jackson 1968). Perhaps it is more likely that because teaching is an intellectual as well as a practical activity, much of what appears to be intuitive and done on impulse, is actually the result of metacognition. Later research on teacher thinking focused on the propositional knowledge of teachers rather than on the processes. In some of this research (Elbaz 1983; Lampert 1981; 1984), there is the notion that teaching is also an affective activity, in that it engages the self and the emotions in ways which cannot be ignored. Elbaz included knowledge of self in her five categories of teacher knowledge, and Lampert had one category, personal knowledge, which combined knowledge of self with knowledge of children. Kagan (1992) in her review of learning-to-teach studies identified the central role played by a novice's image of self as teacher: 'Indeed without a strong image of self as teacher, a novice may be doomed to flounder' (p. 147).

There is also research in this country which underlines the importance of the self in teaching. Nias (1989) contends that one can best understand how primary teachers construe the notion of work and their developing relationship to it by grasping the importance that they attach to a sense of personal identity. Teachers exist as people before they become teachers and their work calls for a massive investment of their 'selves'. Nias points out that to be a teacher in the primary school system means working in a historically determined context which encourages individualism, isolationism, a belief in one's own autonomy and the investment of personal resources. Thus the self is a crucial element in the way teachers themselves construe the nature of the job. Teaching has a perceptual basis, in the same way that learning does. Teachers' perceptions of their role are modified by experience and activity. Since one's perceptions are different, each teacher 'sees' children and interprets children according to their own unique perceptual patterns. Because of the historical, financial, cultural and philosophical traditions of primary teaching, teachers usually expect to invest themselves heavily in the job.

To acquire self-knowledge, one must reflect on events and experience. The two contrasting case studies which are presented in this chapter illustrate the necessity for reflection upon the self, as well as on subject knowledge, purposes, learners, curriculum materials and the teaching performance itself. The case studies suggest a possible link between the ability to reflect on teaching performance, knowledge of self as teacher and development. There follows in the next section a brief critique of reflection. Its purpose is to set the scene for the importance of the notion of reflection in teaching. Two crucial questions for anyone concerned with expert teaching are: How does one become expert?; and, What are the factors involved in promoting development towards being firstly, a good teacher, and ultimately an expert teacher? For the purpose of these questions, the term 'teaching performance' comprises all activity related to teaching: the pre-active, interactive, and post-active phases of teaching. The word 'development' carries in it the notion of change, with the implication of change for the better. For teachers to change their classroom practice, or any aspect of it, there has to be a perception that current ways of teaching are not the best possible ones; in short, that there is a need for improvement. To arrive at this kind of perception, teachers need to engage in self-evaluation and reflection on their performance, knowledge and understanding of teaching-learning processes.

Reflection is a notion which has been widely and eagerly adopted by teacher educators both in the USA and in this country. Part of its appeal lies in its seemingly ready applicability to a range of professions and to teaching in particular. The conceptual confusion which surrounds reflection is expressed in the wide variety of terms used to describe teacher education courses based on notions of reflection, such as: 'reflective practice, inquiry-oriented teacher education, reflection-in-action, teacher as researcher, teacher as decision-maker, teacher as professional, teacher as problem-solver' (Calderhead 1989, p. 43). There are diverging views on what should be the most important content in reflection, ranging from technical considerations to moral and social emancipatory concerns; and on the very processes of reflection. Schon in his seminal works of 1983 and 1987, originated the debate.

Schon espoused a new theory of how professionals operate, delivering a powerful critique of the then dominant model of professional knowledge: the 'technical rationality' based on positivist epistemology. This was contrasted with a celebration of the artistry of professional practitioners whose work demonstrates instead professional creativity rather than technical rationality. In his examples, he focuses on the problematical elements of professional work, not the general unproblematical aspects. He describes two kinds of reflection: reflection-in-action and reflection-on-action.

Reflection-in-action, according to Schon, is the process in which professionals engage when involved in ill-defined incidents out of the normal routine, during which they draw upon their own practical experience in a highly intuitive manner. Reflection-in-action has three important features: it is conscious, in that we consider both the unexpected event and the knowing-in-action which preceded it, turning our thoughts back on the unusual event; it has a critical function, questioning the thinking which put us into this problematical situation; and, it provokes on-the-spot experiment, in which we try out new actions to improve the situation. 'What distinguishes reflection-in-action from other kinds of reflection is its immediate significance for action' (Schon 1987, pp. 28–9).

Reflection-on-action is a more straightforward term. It is the process of making sense of an action after it has occurred and possibly learning something from the experience. This notion would seem to have a ready applicability to teacher education programmes, especially if we are are concerned with the processes of change and development, yet there are criticisms.

The difference between the two kinds of reflection would seem to be one of time-scale: if one is reflecting-in-action, this is of necessity rapid, and intuitive; if reflecting-on-action, one is deliberating on past events with a view to modifying future actions in similar difficult situations. If this is the distinction, reflection-in-action is perhaps the application of knowledge or understanding in an apparently intuitive way. Munby and Russell (1989) have criticised Schon's work for the lack of elaboration of the psychological realities of reflection-in-action. Eraut (1994) has stated that the difficulty is exacerbated by Schon's inconsistencies in sustaining the differences between the two forms of reflection in the examples he cites.

One further criticism: can we extract attributes of reflective behaviour, such as reframing a problem in an architect's studio, engineering workshop or musician's master class, and apply the theory to teaching, which is perforce a very specialised context? A teacher may realise as she or he monitors a writing lesson that the children have not really understood the concept of audience, but she or he may be so caught up in the immediate demands of such a lesson (requests for spelling, difficulties with ideas for stories, off-task behaviour), that the problem is stored, to be deliberated upon and new representations devised in order to communicate the concept more effectively. In other words, teaching as an activity has its own peculiar problems; typically one is not thinking about one design problem in the quiet of a studio. A teacher is more likely to be juggling immediate demands in complex settings.

Yet theories of reflection can be useful. Schon's term 'reflection-in-action' is probably better replaced by 'knowing-in-action'. As to the nature of that knowing, Eraut (1994), argues that the term 'reflection' is unhelpful, and regards all of Schon's work on professional knowledge as a theory of metacognition. The deployment of knowledge-in-action is metacognition, which is itself developed through deliberation on action. The three attributes of this metacognition, that it is conscious, criticial and gives rise to immediate or later experiment, are essential for changes in one's practice to occur. In order to develop one has to be aware that one is thinking about a teaching or learning problem, critical of one's previous performance and intending to experiment with other ways of working.

To develop, teachers need to be able to reflect or deliberate on their performance, carrying out self-evaluation and evaluation of the children's performances. To exercise some kind of metacognition, they need to be thinking about their teaching in ways which are conscious, critical, and embody the intention to experiment with alternative ways of teaching. Knowledge of self is an important element in the process of reflection or metacognition; being consciously critical of one's performance implies that one can 'stand back' from one's performance and assess it without rationalisation. The latter is an early stage of reflection, in which beginning teachers try to explain classroom events or teaching decisions in terms of external factors over which they have no control; therefore they cannot be blamed for poor or unexpected outcomes. The highest stage or level of reflection is that in which teachers reconceptualise the curriculum, subject knowledge, knowledge of self, and models of teaching and learning, in the light of political, social and ethical considerations. To illustrate the levels of reflection and the importance of self-knowledge in learning to teach, two contrasting case studies are presented of student-teachers learning to teach in their postgraduate teacher education course and the first year of teaching.

Case study 12: Mark: A study in denial

Mark was a maths semi-specialist, aged 23 at the start of the course. He had a 2.1 degree in psychology and A Levels in maths, physics and English. His hobbies were musical and church-related activities. In terms of subject knowledge tests administered at the start of the course, he scored very highly: his subject knowledge was outstanding among his peers. Unfortunately he did not sit the music test, but he had Grade 8 violin, which suggests a a high level of musical experience and knowledge. He considered that his psychology degree gave him a good understanding of children. Mark sounded like an ideal candidate for teaching. In terms of Lawlor's (1990) notion that only good subject knowledge is required for teaching, he seemed an ideal person for the job, someone who might progress rapidly to a state of expertise.

Mark reacted to his curriculum courses with initial enthusaism, which quickly waned. While he appreciated the attempts to encourage the student-teachers to think through broader issues about teaching subject matter, he really wanted practical input, closely related to lesson planning and what to do in the classroom. Above all, he wanted practical ideas and activities which would work in the classroom. He was uncomfortable with discipline on his first teaching placement. One's attitudes towards discipline are bound up with the self and one's image of what sort of teacher one wants to be. Mark admired his teacher's seemingly effortless control, and tried to emulate it, only to discover that it was not so easy. Close structured observation might have enabled him to deconstruct how his teacher managed order. He wished to be like her, but did not know what lay beneath her control and relationship with the children. He resorted to shouting, but was clearly uncomfortable with this: it did not fit in with his image of the sort of teacher he would like to be, or with his perceptions of himself. His discomfort is related to the fact that he has no clear image of himself yet as teacher: his ideas of teaching were almost evangelical, of someone 'guiding others towards new truth', a notion that probably sits unhappily with the reality of badly behaved children.

This lesson shows Mark struggling with discipline with a whole class. He was placed for his first teaching practice in the same Year 4 class in which he had done his serial day's placement. He had been giving a series of music appreciation lessons and so far had played them pop and rock records. In this lesson he planned to play them classical music. His purposes were: to encourage imagination and reflection; to get the children to see music as meaningful; to get the children to express personal ideas and images; to break down musical barriers; and to encourage enjoyment and appreciation of a wide range of music. He also thought that they would learn some sense of the geographical, social and historical context of the music and the composer. The task was to listen and respond to 'Winter' from Vivaldi's *The Four Seasons*. He intended to ask them to close their eyes while listening, and give impressions and ideas. He would encourage response and avoid repetition of ideas. He intended to increasingly structure and direct their thoughts.

Unfortunately for Mark, the children were very excited, having just been involved with preparations for a special assembly with parents. He started the lesson by telling them that he had some more music for them and that they were to listen with their eyes closed. For the first eight minutes of the lesson while the music was playing, at least a quarter of the children were fidgeting, giggling and being disruptive. Mark tried to control them and when they had become a little more settled, he gave a mini-lecture on musical tastes, which did not engage their interests or improve their behaviour:

Mark: About your age a lot of children start to decide what kind of music they like and what sort of music they don't like. And an awful lot of people, Scott, an awful lot of people decide they like all this loud pop music, unlike this boring, classical violiny music. All right. I for one think that's very sad indeed, Stevie, because I think some of the most beautiful music, some of the most interesting music is in the classical music era. I feel it's very sad really. People just ignore it; so that's why I want to play some of that today. Come back here, Matthew!

Mark tried to elicit imaginative responses, but these were low-level: there were some responses about girls doing ballet or slow gymnastics, but most of the children found it difficult without any guidance. A little later he told the class that the composer did actually have something in mind when he wrote the music, but did not tell them what it was. The children continued to play him up with rude and disruptive behaviour. Mark did not carry out his threat to send Stevie out, and continued to ignore rudeness from the children. At this point he did try to give them some information about the composer and when he lived, but the children had little understanding of 300 years ago. He used no aids to help them understand and, in any case, they were not really listening or taking him seriously by this time. By the time he got to the third playing, he finally told them the title of the piece, thus giving them a clue as to what it might be about. The children made loud noises and giggled. Mark finally sent out one child. He played the music again, and elicited responses of 'water running through the forest', 'people playing violins', and 'ballroom dancing'. He still wanted ideas to do with winter:

Mark: Anything to do with winter though, Sam?
Sam: Old people inside, drinking tea and watching outside because it's snowing.
Mark: Right. What do you think? Did you hear the sort of pitter patter of the dum dum dum throughout the whole piece – there's a whole lot of violins very quietly plucking the strings rather than bowing it.

Here he was so relieved to elicit a response to do with winter that he rushed into a technical description of the playing without finding out if the children understood what he meant by the terms he used. Against a background of noise, disruption and children asking to go to the toilet, he continued to elicit responses about winter. He continued to be satisfied with any kind of response on the topic of winter and in return gave trite responses to the children:

Mark: Martin, sorry? A polar bear standing by the North Pole? Well, there's a thought to finish with. Yes, because it's very cold, isn't it, with the polar bears in the North Pole? An interesting thought to finish with there, Martin. Thank you. Those with packed lunches, go and get your packed lunches.

He dismissed the class as if the rudeness had never happened. His self-assessment of the lesson is an extraordinary example of ignoring the fact that this was a very weak lesson indeed, with the children barely under control, and very little learning going on. After the lesson he stated that he thought his purposes had been fulfilled to some extent, in that there had been some good ideas and nice images. He had not wanted to lose the children's interest by 'forcing work from them'; so he had little on which to assess them other than their responses. He would not change the lesson. He was fairly happy with it. He considered that the weakness of the lesson was discipline: the children did not yet view him as the teacher and played him up if the class teacher was out of the room.

The observer of this lesson considered that the purposes were not fulfilled: appreciating and interpreting the music had been hindered by unnecessary noise, movement and lack of attention from pupils. She commented that the pupils' level of understanding was reflected in their spoken responses to the music. They had not learnt any of the geographical, historical and social context of the music and composer as stated on the planning sheet. She considered that there had been *no* presentation to the lesson, which had lacked direction, depth and development from the student. Consequently the children's initial restlessness became harder to control as time progressed. There was very little feedback at the end of the lesson, which had ended abruptly because of discipline and noise problems. There was no conclusion, and no related work such as pictures or writing.

The observer's perceptions of the lesson stand in stark contrast to those of Mark. It is obvious that this is a very weak lesson indeed; yet Mark seemed to be inclined to assume that all had gone well. The only problem in his view had been discipline. This is a very revealing statement. He was having trouble admitting to himself that there was a problem in the lesson and until he had done that, he could not begin to admit the problems to anyone else. There are two major problems with Mark's lesson, which encapsulate all the minor ones, and are interconnected. The first one was the lack of pedagogical content knowledge, and within that the knowledge, skills and dispositions needed for successful management of order. Mark had musical knowledge to Grade 8; what he did not do was connect that knowledge with knowledge of learners, contexts and pedagogy, because these knowledge bases were almost non-existent. The lack of structure in the lesson is obvious: much of the time he was playing 'Guess what I'm thinking' with the children. They found it difficult to come up with the responses he expected about winter, because in the early part of the lesson at least he did not communicate his knowledge about the piece of music to them. Although he had specialist knowledge, he did not seem to want to share it with them, feeling that it was more about 'the reflection and communication of ideas' rather than the meaning or the structure of the music. Yet extracts from the lesson discourse showed how difficult it was to talk about the music without using some technical vocabulary, such as 'pizzicato'. This raises the question: Is it possible to communicate ideas about a piece of music without having recourse to some musical vocabulary? If this is the case, then the vocabulary and listening skills need to be taught first; otherwise children and teacher will not be able to move much beyond the rather trite and superficial observations recorded in this lesson. The listening skills and technical vocabulary act as a scaffolding to enable other learning to take place. Mark had not recognised here that the children needed access to the kinds of knowledge he possessed: without it the task was too vague and difficult. They responded by 'switching off'.

The crucial point about Mark's problems with order is his attitude to discipline. He seemed almost to ignore the discipline problems. In his evaluation of the lesson, he mentioned the discipline problem only towards the end. He had not wanted to reprimand them and had hoped that they would settle down on their own. As a reflection of the interrelatedness of Mark's problems, this shows an ignorance of learners. Children do not, as a rule, establish their own discipline unless their teacher has set up a powerful ethos whereby such behaviour is expected of them. Mark, by his own admission, did not have such a relationship with the class. He remarked that they did not see him as the teacher and played him up.

Instead, this was a disaster of a lesson, which may paradoxically have done more to prejudice the children against classical music than Mark with his evangelistic zeal could have anticipated. His planning was minimal: 'I try not to think about it too much beforehand and not make it seem forced.' His reluctance to operate even some procedures for order meant that he was constantly reprimanding the children: a sort of crisis management of order. A similar reluctance to ask the children to produce anything led to there being almost nothing on which he could assess them. Finally there is his failure to recognise or acknowledge that there was anything wrong in the way he planned and presented the lesson. In order to do so, Mark would have had to confront problems to do with himself: aspects of his character; weaknesses in planning; weaknesses in relationships with children; poor observational skills; lack of awareness of other people; and most importantly, a confused or hazy image of himself as teacher. At the start of his course he had seen himself as 'bringing children into new truth', perhaps as a guide or facilitator. This image of self as teacher must have sat uneasily with the need to be a firm disciplinarian. It seemed to be a part of teaching which did not accord with his personal beliefs of what teaching would be like; therefore he almost pushed it away from himself. In addition, Mark was used to succeeding academically: to have admitted there was anything wrong with his lesson or presentation would have been an admission of failure, and he was not used to failure. Until Mark confronted the problems in himself and his attitudes to discipline, he would not be able to move forward in developing his image of self as teacher. Thus this knowledge base too was scanty, and was a major cause of his failure to develop as a teacher. He could not reflect on his teaching because he could not admit there was anything wrong with it. Therefore he could not learn from his mistakes. A teacher reflecting honestly on this experience would have wanted to change the lesson, not to repeat the experience of children behaving so badly. He preferred to push aside the uncomfortable emotions, and blame the children for being badly behaved: an external factor beyond his control.

During Mark's second teaching practice, nothing happened to move him on. He was to an extent protected by his class teacher who planned in detail and asked him to work within her planning. Following the course, he was appointed on a two-year contract to a city middle school teaching a Year 6 class. Away from the protected context of teaching practice, he found it difficult to cope. His head teacher was less than impressed. She regarded the school as having to continue his training; it would take two years she thought. She thought that one of his problems was a surface appearance of confidence and ability to cope, while underneath he did have problems, but his natural pride and reticence made him reluctant to ask for help. Mark had a dreadful first year: discipline problems with the children; staff observing him and criticising him (which was constructive but which he found difficult to handle); and parents complaining. In an interview at the end of this year he said:

> Mark: At one point I found an awful lot of pressure on me from all different directions. I had parents coming in complaining, and I had comments from on high in the school, and everyone seemed to be getting at me at the same time, and I was feeling ill and actually taking two days off because of my mental insanity apart from anything else.

Amid all this, he was visting the university's teaching practice library and taking out videos of teachers to get some idea of what good teaching looked like; of what models of teaching might be. He was learning to observe, albeit somewhat belatedly, and generate some models of teaching and learning. This was in preparation for developing his own image as teacher; his own notion of what kind of teacher he wanted to be. It seemed that for Mark, the affective or emotional discomfort had to be enormous before he would start to do anything about it. In other words, a breakdown of some sort had to occur before he could recognise the need to change, and generate the will to change. However, it was a tough process, and he talked of losing his idealism, and of changing the kind of teacher he wanted to be. The steadily increasing knowledge of children, both empirical and cognitive, the knowledge of contexts, knowledge of models of teaching and learning, and above all the increased knowledge of self, were beginning to have an impact. In conclusion, he had both to improve his self-knowledge, and change himself in order to become a teacher.

Case study 13: Tom: Honesty in reflection

Tom's background and two of his other lessons (Case studies 2 and 3) have been given in Chapter 2. In this case study, we are concerned with his ability to evaluate teaching episodes and lessons honestly, not merely on the response of the children or his own performance, but on broader issues such as models of teaching and learning, and on setting versus mixed ability teaching. Even from his earliest days on the course, it was obvious that he thought deeply about what he was learning. In both reports from the school where he did his two block placements, the teachers commented on his problems with presenting ideas and information to the class, class management in general, and management of order in particular. However, by the end of his first year of teaching, he had overcome all these problems, was giving high quality lessons and running a complex system of class management with apparent ease. In short, he made huge progress. The interesting question is why did he develop so quickly in contrast to Mark, who was still floundering at the end of his first year of teaching? One possible answer lies in the quality and depth of Tom's reflections, in comparison with those of Mark. Like Mark he scored highly on the subject knowledge tests administered at the start of the course, apart from in music. He also valued the practical approaches and teaching ideas demonstrated especially in the science and maths courses. However, unlike Mark, he started to build connections straightaway between course input and school experience.

Tom began to learn how science could be taught at primary level, as well as thinking about the essential nature of science as a discipline:

Tom: An essential part of problem-solving is the collecting and sharing of ideas. You can always ask questions in science work and should not be afraid of finding the answers. Above all science is about exploration and should be fun.

He had encountered the term 'pedagogical content knowledge' in one of his education course readings, and he incorporated it into his thinking. He was aware of when he was extending his subject knowledge in science, and when he was acquiring pedagogical content knowledge, as for example in the session on paper parachutes, which later surfaced in his teaching (see Case study 3 Chapter 2):

Tom: Although I gained no subject knowledge, my pedagogical content knowledge improved enormously.

Despite his good degree in mechanical engineering, he further recognised that there were areas of subject knowledge where he needed to improve. Subject knowledge remained a concern for Tom: he did not assume that because of his good degree, he had adequate knowledge for the whole of the primary curriculum:

Tom: The maths sessions are good, as are most other sessions and lectures. However, I always get the feeling that we are just scratching at the surface of the subjects. To really get to grips with it an awful lot of reading must be necessary, far more than I am doing now, more even than is possible, given the demands of the course. This worries me. What am I going to do on teaching practice? Where are all the ideas going to come from, and upon what foundations of knowledge will my classroom knowledge rest?

This feeling is shown by his response to the music course. He was initially very enthusiastic, taking up the guitar and learning 'Wild Thing' and some Eddie Cochrane, but then he realised that he did not know much about music and that he had a great deal of work to do:

Tom: I can't help thinking that I would only be dabbling in this subject.

Unlike Mark, he acknowledged that subject knowledge was going to be a problem. Another central problem for him was how much structure or freedom to give the children in their science investigations. He saw that his school experience science had been over-directed, but he felt that it took a lot of confidence to give children so much apparent freedom. He was thinking seriously about the nature of science teaching:

Tom: Is it right to manipulate children into avenues that you have intended for them to go, or should they be allowed to explore freely?

His school experience further stimulated reflection on what sort of teacher he wanted to be and what kind of science teaching he considered was appropriate. The school in which he was placed was very formal and the children had little experience of investigations or group work of the kind promoted by the course:

Tom: We're taught lots of ideas about group work, open-ended, non-teacher-led lessons, etc., but how easy is it for someone totally inexperienced to try and practise these methods in a classroom. I think this is especially difficult when you are in someone else's classroom for one day a week. The situation is made worse by the fact that this school and my teacher are very formal and traditional. So when my fourth year children have only experienced this (formal) style of teaching, should I be surprised when my open-ended group work activities don't work out?

Tom was thinking about pedagogy, teaching approaches, class organisation and management, school and class contexts, and the nature of science teaching. He was also thinking about what kind of teacher he wanted to be. The notion of open-ended group investigations obviously appealed to him and resonated with his ideas of what science was about, but he recognised that he did not yet have the teaching skills to put these approaches into practice successfully, at least not in this formal context. The lessons went wrong, but he did not push away this fact; rather he considered the reasons why the lessons had gone badly. In addition, he was helped by the fact that he had his own rules and values, and a stronger self-image of what kind of teacher he wanted to be, as this comment on the education course reveals:

Tom: I am very aware of my own rules, which is perhaps why I am so worried at the moment about my school experience, where my values seem to clash greatly with those of the school. I can suffer my frustration in silence for one day a week for a term, but how could I swallow my values like this as a full-time teacher?

Thus, even at this early stage in the course, Tom was both learning from his mistakes and thinking deeply about subject knowledge, teaching approaches, contexts, values and his own image of himself as teacher. Another quality of Tom's reflections was that he was able to make connections between different areas of the course in maths, language and children's learning, particularly with regard to children's schemas. He was beginning to build up some models of children's learning and apply these to his teaching. Tom was a thoughtful student, constantly questioning his ideas and was prepared to extract the maximum possible from the course.

In the maths lesson from the end of the first year of teaching we see Tom much improved in pedagogical content knowledge and reflecting on wider issues of setting and streaming, social inclusion and children's learning. From the school where he had done his second teaching practice, he had taken the idea of running an integrated week. He had worked in such a context and found it successful for him. He organised a work schedule for his class each week. The Year 6 children worked in six groups of four on four, or five different subjects. However, there were also introductory whole-class lessons, lessons to build on and reinforce knowledge and skills, and whole-class plenaries at the end of the week, where the class came together for discussion and presentation of work. This lesson shows Tom working with the whole class, doing a tables test, then work to reinforce the concept of averages, finishing with a Bingo game based on the seven times table. Tom integrated the tables test, which was part of school policy, with the main thrust of the lesson. Once the children had marked each other's books, he praised those with ten out of ten and asked five of them to come to the front. He 'gave' each child a different amount of money for working so hard, and asked them to tell the class how much they had.

Tom: What can we say about the way I've shared out this prize money? What do you think, Emily? Remember, Emily got 1p. Are you happy with the way I've shared it out? She's not happy.

The class discussed how this 'gift' might be made fair. When a child supplied the answer, Tom asked him to explain how he had worked it out. He repeated the boy's explanation and moved on to another example with pieces of string. He involved another child to write on the board for him, and invited the class to estimate how long each piece of string was. The pieces were measured and the lengths were written on the board. Tom went on:

Tom: Right now – what I could do if I had the time and some sellotape is to stick these bits of string back together again to make it into one piece of string just like it was before I cut it up. Here's one I prepared earlier. It was the same length as this one before I cut it up into four pieces.

He invited the children to tell him how long it was. He received various incorrect answers, and he encouraged the boy doing the board work to calculate it for the class. Tom then folded the string in half and cut it. He asked the children how long the two halves were. He folded these in half and asked how long the quarters were. On receiving the right answer of $22\frac{1}{2}$, he monitored that the class could also write that number in decimals. He recapped what he had done to work out the average length of the pieces of string and further illustrated the concept of averages:

Tom: So this is the average length of a piece of string. This piece was longer. This piece of string here was also longer than the average. This piece of string was also longer than the average – no, it wasn't. It was shorter – no, longer. Can you see it's sticking out at the end here, and this little piece of string was what – longer or shorter?

Child: Shorter.

Tom: Shorter, Marcus. Right, so we can talk about averages of anything. We can talk about averages of pence, averages of pieces of string – we can talk about averages of time.

He did several problems using time, distance, weight and pulse rates.

Tom: I think after that we need to take our pulse rates and see how fit we are. All that exercise. So can you remember how to take your pulse? On your neck? Or can you find it on the side of your wrist – remember, we found it in PE? Who hasn't found it yet? Are you sure you're not dead yet, Johnathon?

He elicted various pulse rates from different children, maintaining their involvement with jokes, for example 'So Mark is practically in a state of hibernation over there.'

Tom brought in a new example of multiplying an average to find out how far he would cycle in a longer time, referring to his recent charity cycling trip from Land's End to John O'Groats, with which the class was familiar. He ensured again that one of the children explained how she had performed the calculation, and did another example with snails. He finished with a final problem about how much homework a child could do in a certain time: both of these problems required recall of tables.

The observer was impressed with this lesson, considering that the purposes were well fulfilled. He judged that most of the children had a good understanding of the concept of averages and of how to work out examples to get the average number from a set of numbers. There was no formal assessment in the lesson, but Tom had involved the children and had lots of feedback. The observer thought that the involvement of the children and the novelty of the presentation was excellent and effective. The money had been most appropriate, but the string example could have been improved, for the pieces had curled up, spoiling the visual effect. He felt that the whole-class organisation was very effective and well-handled. He had not seen anyone hesitant or shy to contribute. The strengths of the lesson had been: the children's high motivation and involvement; the very good relationship and easy atmosphere where children could express their understandings openly; and the use of everyday relevant examples. However, Tom had not catered for the whole ability range, for the high fliers were not stretched and the three low ability children were bewildered.

Tom thought he had fulfilled his purposes, in that he had been trying to reinforce the concept of an average, although the low attainers probably were still unsure of the concept, which he felt was quite difficult. For some of the class, he thought that the activities had been 'just adding some numbers and dividing them to get another number, and they don't associate the average with what they have at the start'. He could see that he had not catered for differing abilities, in that some had been left behind, even though he had tried to lighten the presentation with jokes. The more able could have raced away and gone on to much harder things. Half-way through the lesson he had become aware that maybe the children were not associating what they were doing with averages. Within the context of the whole-class lesson, the organisation had been suitable, but ideally it would have been better to present the work to cater for different levels of attainment. To do that he would have had to regroup them into ability sets from their existing random grouping, an idea which he disliked because of the stigma attached to ability groups. He had felt least competent at communicating the concept of an average. Next time he would make some of the questions more open-ended and give children the opportunity to generate their own problems.

There is evidence in this lesson that Tom had made major progress since his early days on teaching practice. He held the attention of the class for the whole hour. He had improved his lesson structure and task design. The lesson as planned fell into three segments: the test, the presentation of examples of averages, and the projected Bingo game. In the event he did not have time for the last item, and showing some flexibility, left it out. To teach (or reinforce) the concept of averages he had a whole range of examples, the money one being particularly successful. Some of the examples linked to previous work on time and distance travelled; some linked to work in PE; and some to the seven times table. Examples used also involved prior knowledge of estimation, fractions and decimals. It was a long presentation, but he leavened it with jokes, used many examples and involved the children as much as possible, in board work and in explaining their reasoning. This lesson took place before the introduction of the numeracy hour, but such a lesson would have fitted well into the framework, with plenty of mental examples. The response of the children showed how motivated they were: order was endemic to this classroom. However, having given a lesson which was good in many respects, Tom did not accept it as a perfect lesson, but was already thinking of how he might improve it. In particular, in thinking about how he might have to change his grouping in order to cater for all abilities, he was considering changing his practice, and reflecting on the dilemma of ability grouping versus mixed ability. To set the children into ability groups meant going against his values; yet he could see that the change in grouping could be beneficial in terms of task design and children's learning. In thinking about the ethical issues, his values, his materials and examples, and his practice, he was reflecting at the critical, the practical, and the technical levels described by McIntyre (1992).

Discussion

The case studies suggest that knowledge of self has some impact on beginning teachers' ability to deliberate on their practice. Some scholars, notably McIntyre (1992) have argued that reflection is a more central means for learning for experienced teachers than it can be or need be for beginners. This argument is superficially convincing, yet these case studies show that some beginning teachers are able to reflect or deliberate on their performance in ways that go beyond mere technical concerns. McIntyre proposed three levels of reflection: the technical, the practical and the critical. In the early days of teaching students reflect at the technical level on the attainment of such given goals as achieving and maintaining classroom order. They progress to the practical level where the emphasis is on articulating their own criteria, and developing their own practice. The final stage of critical reflection concerns wider political, ethical and social issues, and is, according to McIntyre, rarely practised even among experienced teachers.

Tom, in evaluating his maths lesson, was caught up in the dilemma of setting or mixed ability teaching in maths for academic, social, and ethical reasons. This would seem to me an example of critical reflection in McIntyre's terms. The case studies also suggest that before some beginning teachers are able to reach the first or technical level, there is an additional stage: that of rationalisation, where their concerns are to explain away poor or ineffective lessons by attributing them to external causes beyond their control. This was the case with Mark in his music lesson, who did not connect his lack of structure, his lack of attention to teaching musical concepts, or his poor presentation to the discipline problems he experienced. He was still at the stage of rationalisation, of not admitting how poor the lesson had been and ignoring the discipline problem, and because of this he was unable to acknowledge the impact of such a lesson on himself and his feelings about teaching. He could make no further progress in evaluation and reflection until he was honest with himself and about himself.

These two contrasting case studies show the importance of the role of reflection or metacognition, both in learning to teach and in improving one's practice. Tom and Mark started learning to teach on the same course at the same time. One clearly made huge progress in developing as a teacher; the other did not. Reflection, knowledge of self, and image of self as teacher were crucial factors in the relative speed of their development. It seems likely that in some cases there is a dysfunction in reflection: even with plenty of feedback, there are students who cannot engage in more than the most basic levels of reflection, as happened with Mark in his first year of teaching. The tendency to blame external factors for poor teaching or weak lesson may also be part of a student's whole orientation towards learnt to teach. The notions of internal and external orientations (Korthagen 1988) can be helpful in explaining why Tom was able to make so much progress as a teacher, and Mark so little, and may go some way towards explaining why students were able to utilise what they had learnt from the course to a greater or lesser degree in their first year of teaching. Korthagen (1988) suggested that not all student-teachers benefit from a teacher education based on the notion of reflective practice. Those with an external orientation towards learning to teach expected to be told how to teach, for others to evaluate and direct their practice. Those with an internal orientation towards learning to teach employed their own knowledge and values to examine their practice. One's orientation towards learning to teach is bound up with one's image of self as teacher: until beginning teachers resolve their self-images as teachers, they cannot turn their focus outward and concentrate on children's learning. Their ability to reflect may be effectively denied them until their self-image as a teacher is established. In order to resolve one's self image, one has to acknowledge aspects of oneself which one may not like, for example a monotonous voice or inadequate planning, and be determined to change them. One also has to acknowledge the effect of teaching on the self. This is the two-way process described in the first paragraph of this chapter. Thus knowledge of self, and honesty about oneself as a person and as a teacher, is an essential knowledge base, for without it, teachers cannot engage fully in the processes of reflection which can greatly aid teacher development. Knowledge of self, including the ability to engage in professional growth through reflection, means that one can learn so much more from all the teaching contexts and experiences one has.

These ideas about orientation towards learning to teach, and about levels of reflection are arranged in Figure 7.1. The levels of reflection are those proposed by McIntyre (1992), with the addition of a more primitive level: that of rationalisation, in which weak performance is explained in terms of external factors beyond the student's control. Parallel to these levels runs the continuum of orientation towards learning to teach, from external to internal orientation.

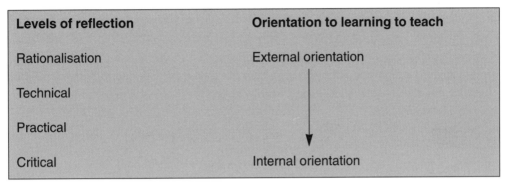

Levels of reflection	Orientation to learning to teach
Rationalisation	External orientation
Technical	
Practical	
Critical	Internal orientation

Figure 7.1 An assessment framework for reflection

Using such a framework, teacher educators could assess the levels of reflection reached by student-teachers, and tailor their own teaching to improve levels of reflection. In so doing, they would need to teach the processes of reflection, through modelling and demonstration. In addition, practising teachers might use this framework to examine their own evaluation and reflection: to analyse at what levels they might be operating, thus employing the framework as a tool for further development.

For example, two teachers' responses to the introduction of the literacy strategy might be very different. Teacher Y sighs with exasperation at the new initiative, duly does the training and implements it exactly as laid down in the framework. She moans in the staffroom that her children don't read whole books any more and that they are rushing through content without full understanding. Teacher Z does the same training, but one day a week provides extended writing and reading time, in line with her own beliefs about subject knowledge, children's learning in language and literature, and with her own values. She also abandons the 'clock': choosing instead to start lessons with text in the broadest possible interpretations, a picture, a told story or a TV news extract, and working the class as a whole, rather than always breaking into groups.

Expert teachers are like Teacher Z, who use all the knowledge bases of teaching; in other words their professional knowledge base, to evaluate government and other initiatives critically in the light of their own professional understanding. It is important not to accept blindly top-down initiatives, but to be able to reflect on them in the light of one's knowledge, values and experience. One's own self-image as teacher, and knowledge of self are crucial aspects of this process.

CHAPTER 8

Pedagogical content knowledge

Introduction

Pedagogical content knowledge is the special province of teachers: their own form of professsional knowledge and understanding. It was originally conceptualised by Shulman (1986a; 1986b; 1987a) as an amalgam of subject matter knowledge and general pedagogical knowledge. However in this model it is the blending of the knowledge bases, described in preceding chapters. All of these knowledge bases contribute towards the richest form of pedagogical content knowledge, which underpins expert teaching. It is possible to have a partially developed form of pedagogical content knowledge: indeed this is what most beginning teachers start with. Over the course of one's career, knowledge bases which are only partial or non-existent, grow and become fully developed as part of the amalgam. As a form of knowledge, it comprises facts, concepts, skills, processes, beliefs and attitudes in the same way that other disciplines do: the differences are that this is blending of many different kinds of knowledge; and it is the special province of the teacher. There are a number of key ideas which need to be grasped for a full understanding of pedagogical content knowledge. These are: the key notion of representation, which might be said to be the summation of all the knowledge bases in action; the idea of knowledge bases as interacting sets; the idea that sometimes only some of the knowledge bases work together; the idea that in an expert act of teaching, all of the knowledge bases are present in the amalgam; and the idea that the knowledge bases are the submerged 'nine-tenths of the iceberg'. These will be dealt with in turn.

Representation

A question of fundamental importance for teachers is how do they transfer or communicate their knowledge, understanding, skills, processes and attitudes within a subject to the children. How can learners come to know what teachers know? For this I would like to bring together two sets of ideas about the notion of representation, which is another way of talking about pedagogical content knowledge. The first set of ideas is from Shulman (1986b). He defined representation as ways of communicating concepts and processes of a subject discipline: the most powerful analogies, metaphors, examples, illustrations and activities. For Shulman, representation was part of transformation: the all-important process of turning subject knowledge into knowledge for teaching, which lies at the intersection of subject knowledge, pedagogy and knowledge of learners. In addition I would add that the kinds of activities done within a school subject can come to represent that subject in the minds of learners, as in the example of Helen's maths lesson (Chapter 3) or in history or science lessons which are purely comprehension. The examples of Jane and Jackie in Chapter 4, attempting to teach the notion of hierarchy, illustrate the power and value of good representations in teaching for understanding. Jane's class carried out a comprehension exercise: in planning for teaching this lesson, Jane did not consider that 'hierarchy' was a concept which needed teaching: thus she did not devise a suitable analogy or representation. On the other hand, Jackie realised that this was a difficult concept, and one which the children might well have trouble in understanding. She came up with the idea of a ladder as a suitable representation, and told the children that a hierarchy was like a ladder, thereby using an analogy. She further analysed the concept for sub-concepts and realised that they would also need to understand the idea of authority.

This brings me to the second set of ideas about representation: those of Bruner (1970). These are that there are three characteristic ways of representing the world: enactive representation, or understanding by activity, by doing something actively; iconic representation, or understanding by pictures, maps and diagrams; and symbolic representation, or understanding through the use of symbol systems such as spoken and written language, mathematical symbols or musical notation. Bruner considered that children first came to understand and represent the world enactively, then iconically and then through symbol systems, but he stressed that as adults, we use all three forms of representation and move back and forth through them as the occasion demands. Bruner's ideas can help teachers think about what kinds of representations they generate for particular age-ranges, and how to reinforce an idea through the use of different representations. Thus, in Jackie's lesson, she represented the concept of authority enactively, through a little bit of drama; then symbolically through spoken language. The concept of hierarchy was represented iconically through the ladder on the board; and then iconically and symbolically through the picture/writing matching activity. Finally the children represented their understanding enactively through their physical arrangement of the groups in Eygptian society and symbolically in the piece of writing for the tourist guide.

McDiarmid *et al.* (1989) highlighted the importance of generating appropriate representations across all subject knowledge:

> Over time teachers develop a repertoire of subject knowledge representations from outside sources and from their own ingenuity. As these representational repertoires develop, teachers have more options for connecting pupils with subject matter . . . This is an important part of learning to teach and it takes many years. We cannot provide beginning teachers with ready-made repertoires that will suit all the possible contexts in which they could teach.
>
> (McDiarmid *et al.* 1989, p. 196)

They add that teachers need to judge the pedagogical potential of a representation and determine how well it fits the learners and the context. Teachers might disagree on the appropriateness of a particular representation, such as the analogy of photosynthesis with eating food, or describing plants as factories. In addition to the competing considerations of what makes a good representation, there is the reality that teachers' reasoning takes place in concrete, dynamic situations, inherently fraught with dilemmas (Lampert 1985). Learning how to develop good representations is an important part of becoming an expert teacher, as is judging the power and appropriateness of particular representations, as the following example from maths demonstrates.

Case study 14: Sue: Selecting a representation

A teacher is faced with the task of teaching the concept of positive and negative numbers to her Year 4 class. There is a range of maths equipment available in her school, including numberlines for display and those small enough to fit on children's tables. She considers a number of possible representations with her class and their context in mind. As part of her recent MA course, she took a module in maths education, and is aware of a representation in a book, of a tall department store building with a lift travelling between three floors beneath gound level up to floor eight. The ground level is zero in this representation, the floors below ground are negative numbers, and those above ground are positive numbers. The children could be asked to imagine journeys in the lift which would involve shoppers heading from ladies' fashions on the second floor to household equipment on lower ground floor one. This would mean passing zero and would introduce them to sums such as two take away three. She likes this idea very much and also the idea from a display in another teacher's classroom, where the children have drawn sea scenes, with objects, birds, scenery, humans and sea-creatures at appropriate places above and below the water line, which represents zero. Underneath each picture in the display are the children's sums, using positive and negative numbers, the distance between the seagull and the basking shark, for example, or the lighthouse and the wreck. However, there is something about both of these representations which seems not quite right to the teacher. She is also aware of the 'digging a hole' analogy. You dig a hole in a pile of sand: the hole is the negative; the displaced heap of sand by the hole is the positive. If you add the two together, you get zero. This seems a good starting point as many of her children will have dug holes in the sand on the beach.

Thinking over all of this, she goes home and mentions it in passing to her husband, who is not a teacher. He laughs at the notion of negative numbers and suggests taking in one of their bank statements: 'Plenty of negative numbers on there.' If she had a class in secondary school she muses, this would not be a bad idea and would serve the subsiduary purpose of teaching about money management through a bad example in their case! However, it is through thinking of this last representation that she realises why she was not quite satisfied with any of the others that she has considered. The problem lies in the finiteness of all the representations apart from the bank statement. The lift, sea-scape and hole analogies all show a finite amount of numbers. The building has a basement and top-floor restaurant, there is the sea-bed in the ocean picture, and the digging a hole analogy has the same disadvantage as a representation. Her subject knowledge in maths makes her aware that this is not an accurate representation of numbers, for numbers stretch away into infinity on both sides of zero. Admittedly she would not be able to represent that within the confines of a classroom maybe, but she would like to touch on the idea. She remembers from several years ago when she taught reception, a five-year-old child asking her: 'What's the very last number?' and considers that if such young children can be thinking about such things, then her Year 4 class could be starting to think about infinity. The difficult concept of infinity needs to be visited and revisited several times over.

It is thus that she returns to the idea of using numberlines, which are part of the standard equipment. She likes the idea that they can be blank and numbers placed on them by children, to represent equal distances between numbers of the same size. She rejects the small desk-size ones for now and for her initial lesson makes a giant floor-size numberline, along which children may pace, and do sums enactively. There is a problem here in that she has too many children to use the numberline at once; so she divides the class into two mixed ability groups. She aims to work first with one group and then with the other. Knowing the rest of the class will be distracted, she invites them to watch, but instructs them that they can make notes of any answers the first group find difficult and give feedback at the end. She then swaps the groups and roles, using different numbers the second time. The children move from being able to walk 'two minus three', and similar examples, to being able to give answers mentally, to writing them down using maths symbols.

In this example, the teacher is working at the level of mastery, for she is able to consider and reject a number of representations for their appropriateness and power. She does not merely choose the first one she becomes aware of; instead she has the possibility of using several. She connects maths concepts, bearing in mind the under-lying concept of infinity. She is preparing for a particular group of learners in her classroom context. Later, she knows she will recycle these numberlines when working with the least able, or showing fractions and decimals on the numberlines. They will also come in useful for history in teaching about time BC and AD. In that all of the knowledge bases are present in this selection of a suitable representation, this is pedagogical content knowledge in its fullest form. She is using her substantive subject knowledge of positive and negative integers, and of infinity. She draws on syntactic knowledge of maths as a way of representing reality through symbols which can be manipulated. She believes that maths should demonstrate this, and that it should be investigational: hence the children 'explore' positive and negative numbers through their movements up and down the numberline. Her knowledge of curriculum materials is shown in her consideration of possible representations and the resources she would use to create or adapt these. She has considered the context and worked out the practicalities of organising the class for this lesson. Her models of teaching and learning include some knowledge of conceptual analysis and of Bruner's modes of representation.

She does not consider teaching as telling; instead, she understands the fundamental problem of transferring her knowledge and understanding to these children. She chooses an enactive representation for these children, believing that it will be the most memorable for them. She knows that these children enjoy lessons with much involvement and moving around; they will also enjoy observing each other and giving feedback. She considers that this is an appropriate moment to introduce this concept, as it has surfaced in some of the questions the most able groups have tackled recently. She knows it will be hard for some, but the enactive representation should aid understanding. Among her educational aims for this class, in a school served by two large council estates and a smattering of private houses, is to give them the best possible opportunities in life; therefore, she wants to share as much of her knowledge as possible. She has high expectations for this class. In terms of self-knowledge, she knows the enjoyment she and the children will all get from such a lively lesson, and the demands the organisation and control will make on her. All this affects her pedagogical strategies, and she makes it clear from the outset what her expectations of behaviour are. This example shows the richness, complexity and interconnectedness of the knowledge bases for teaching. It is not merely a matter of technical skills. In the next section, the model of knowledge bases is revisited in the light of this richness and interconnectedness.

Knowledge bases as interacting sets

The model of the knowledge bases was presented in Chapter 1 and is presented again here in Figure 8.1.

From the layout of the model, it can be seen that certain of the knowledge bases have been grouped together. This would seem reasonable in that there are obvious links between say substantive and syntactic subject knowledge, and beliefs about subject knowledge. One's beliefs about a subject are informed by one's grasp or otherwise of substantive and syntactic structures. Curriculum knowledge can be closely linked to these, for subject knowledge can be developed through curriculum knowledge, especially in areas of weakness; in addition, rich subject knowledge can inform and enhance curriculum knowledge in the selection and prioritisation of what to teach. Models of teaching and learning and general pedagogical knowledge would seem to be closely linked, for it is the understanding of models of learning and teaching which informs pedagogy. Contexts are an inevitable aspect of pedagogy and links can be made here, in that pedagogical strategies have to be shaped to the context in which one operates. Cognitive and empirical knowledge of learners have obvious links: teachers come to know their children both as social

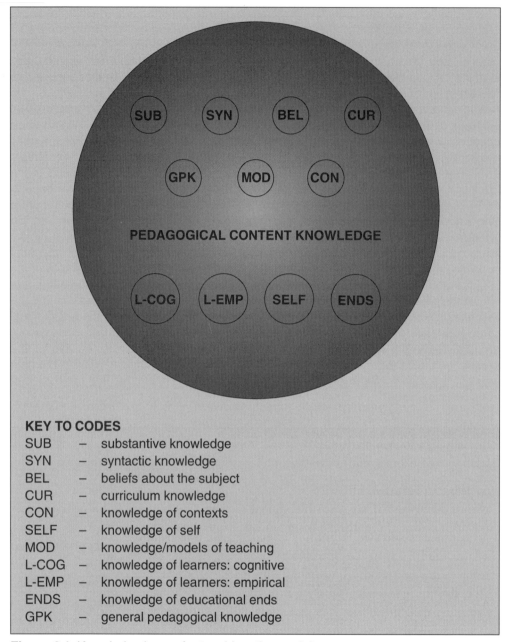

KEY TO CODES

SUB	–	substantive knowledge
SYN	–	syntactic knowledge
BEL	–	beliefs about the subject
CUR	–	curriculum knowledge
CON	–	knowledge of contexts
SELF	–	knowledge of self
MOD	–	knowledge/models of teaching
L-COG	–	knowledge of learners: cognitive
L-EMP	–	knowledge of learners: empirical
ENDS	–	knowledge of educational ends
GPK	–	general pedagogical knowledge

Figure 8.1 Knowledge bases for teaching: the model

beings and as learners. Knowledge of self can be linked to these in terms of understanding relationships with individuals, groups and whole classes. Finally knowledge of educational ends has particular links with knowledge of self, for one's motivation for teaching, but also with curriculum knowledge, as discussed in Chapter 3. In fact, all of these knowledge bases may be linked in other ways to form full or partial amalgams.

Partial amalgam

Case study 9 revisited: Melanie: Science in a complex context

This lesson on density given by Melanie is described in Chapter 6 (Case study 9). It did seem to be well-managed lesson and some investigative activity did take place. However, for Melanie this lesson was only a partial amalgam of pedagogical content knowledge. It was clear that Melanie herself did not have a full understanding of the concept of density. She told the children that it basically meant heaviness. A more accurate definition would have been that density is mass related to volume, but this would have necessitated Melanie (and her co-teachers) doing some analysis of the sub-concepts to be taught, and ensuring that the children understood these first. Thus her substantive subject knowledge was weak in this area: she was attempting to teach something of which she did not have full understanding. Her syntactic knowledge here is also weak, for there were no scientific questions generated by herself or by the children, no variables indentified, and no hypotheses tested. The children did investigate at one level: they made predictions and observed, but the entire actvitity was designed for them by the teachers, and laid out on a worksheet. This is in sharp contrast to the scientific investigation initiated in Tom's lesson on parachutes, described in Case study 3, Chapter 2.

Melanie, as observed elsewhere teaching English (Case study 6, Chapter 5), had good general pedagogical knowledge. She was able to engage and hold the interest of whole classes of children. She was able to break down material to be learnt into short sections, and vary the activities to maintain interest. In English she talked to children succinctly, challenged their thinking, and was able to draw understanding and ideas from them. She managed order with ease, setting up high expectations of work and behaviour. However, in this science lesson, the impression is of haste: of rushing the children through the practical activity without having time to investigate their own lines of thought or questions. The lesson discourse shows Melanie talking the children through the information provided on the worksheets: making sure the children had done what they were supposed to do. Thus the emphasis was on completion of activities and written work rather than learning. The model of teaching and learning implicit in this lesson was one of learning by doing; there is nothing wrong with this except that the children did not have time to engage with the idea of density or the processes of doing a scientific investigation. Without the essential element in the amalgam of full understanding of the scientific concept and sub-concepts, the end result was of activity without understanding: of going through the motions.

This is not to judge Melanie too harshly. She had good empirical knowledge of learners, as evidenced in her poetry lesson, and sufficient cognitive knowledge of learners to realise that the concept of density would be difficult for them. She also understood that she had to operate within this particular context, which meant organising and managing the children very closely within such a complex classroom system. She coped with the demands of the children doing other subjects, and recognised where she needed to have held back from beginning the lesson while the rest of the year base was still noisy. The lesson seemed to be well-managed: the children did the practical activity and wrote up the work in their science books. Melanie took care to show the liquids and objects to the children at the start of the lesson, although she did not feel she had the time to allow them to explore their own questions. She reflected on this afterwards and on the nature of the context which made her operate in this way: thus she showed some knowledge of self. She was not happy with the lesson, nor was she fully happy with the teaching context, and the approaches into which it forced her. These parts of the amalgam, were operating as well as they could without the other, essential elements.

In terms of curriculum knowledge, Melanie was following and attempting to teach the National Curriculum in science. However, the lesson activity might have come from some commercial scheme or book of last-minute ideas. Whatever its source, it was not fully evaluated by Melanie and her colleagues for its value in teaching either scientific concepts of processes or scientific investigation. Thus it was not so much selected from a range of representations which would teach the concept of density, as chosen as an interesting activity which held elements of the investigative process, and which would be practical and possible to do in a group. As a representation, there were problems, for there was no consideration of density as mass related to volume. There was also a problem concerning the activity as a representation of the syntactic structures of science: the children had no opportunity to generate questions; to design their own experiment; or to test one variable at a time.

Complete amalgam

Case study 6 revisited: Melanie: Composing a class poem

This lesson was described fully in Chapter 5 (Case study 6): the focus here is on the complete amalgam of pedagogical content knowledge and the representations which Melanie chose. In the preparation for the joint writing activity, Melanie chose two poems to represent the idea of poetry. These were likely to appeal to children: in their selection Melanie showed good empirical knowledge of learners and good curriculum knowledge of children's literature. One of these used rhythm and rhyme, the latter very cleverly in an appealing and funny poem; the other did not rhyme. Instead it employed devices such as repetition of the same phrase, and stark images to create a mood. This communicated to the children that not all poems are funny, and not all poems rhyme. Melanie also referred to earlier work: the game with the cat in the hexagons which was a representation of how poets play with language and use word association. The other game they had played in a previous lesson, of standing in two lines, and taking turns to complete a sentence starting with 'I love' (in one line) and 'I hate' (in the other line). This had acted as a representation of the idea that poetry is about feelings. The representation she chose for the class poem was of homelessness: she used news footage of people living in cardboard boxes and the character from the soap opera who had run away from home. Both of these were very familiar to the children and showed her good empirical knowledge of what children of this age would be interested in. Finally, the joint activity of composing and redrafting the poem was an accurate representation of the processes of writing poetry. This is what poets do. They cross things out and write additional words in, sometimes indicating where they will be placed in the poem by use of arrows. Melanie showed good syntactic knowledge of the processes of this kind of writing, and through the active representation, communicated this well, and vividly. In addition, the stress throughout was on liking and enjoying poetry: Melanie modelled this enjoyment of poetry and tried to create an ethos in which poetry was enjoyed and valued.

Case study 1 revisited: David: Creating a Roman galley

David, the teacher who gave the lesson in the Prologue of this book, was interviewed twice during the course of the research project: once immediately his 20-day course in history had finished; and again two years later, after the Roman galley lesson. Thus I had considerable access to his knowledge and thinking. His subject knowledge was deep and sophisticated. He had gained from his 20-day course in history a good understanding of the syntactic structures of the subject:

> David: . . . it's basically enquiry: asking questions; forming opinions about the past; and making statements about the past; and being prepared to change them in the light of new evidence of new resources. What I try to do with my children is to behave like historians in what historians do. From my understanding, they literally take an artefact or a document, read it, think about it, and make a statement about what this artefact is, and what it means, and what the past was like, and then re-evaluate it and argue with each other as well and have different opinions and statements. Yes, so they can behave like historians as I understand what historians are! I'm not saying I'm right, but that's my understanding.
>
> (Interview post-course)

This understanding had a major impact on his teaching. In talking about his Roman galley lesson, David demonstrated how the course had changed his syntactic knowledge, his thinking and his teaching:

> David: If I had not been on the course, I have a strong suspicion that all my teaching would be a comprehension exercise, and in the past it has been. I think I mentioned last time, it has been a case of finding the right textbook to copy from. I used to use stories a lot, but it's really made me think about how I use resources, what history really is. It's not about reading and writing in response to questions and things; it's about actually investigating and imagining and being there in time, in your mind. So that lesson is a complete result of the GEST course. So what you've witnessed is a sample of what normally happens, and that kind of enthusiasm is quite common in history.
>
> (Interview post-lesson)

David was honest about what his history lessons had been prior to the course, and was specific about how this new understanding of syntactic structures underpinned his teaching and even the language he used with the children:

David: I mean I was very careful in my quesioning to say: I *think* this is how big the ship was, and I *think* it could be this, and what do you think? It's not about having definite answers but this is what we think from the evidence that we have. Now I had a picture there and I was relying on the picture to be accurate, and I don't know if it is or not, but I don't know . . . But there's always that element of this could be what it was like. It's hard for them, because they want absolutes; they want to know this is what it was like, but I was saying to them that I wanted them to think, what *could* it be like. And I'll say to them: history is not about having definite answers; it's about what we think is the best possible answer to this problem, what is this, what is that? So that philosophy underpins the lesson; it's what we *think* would be the size of the ship based on the evidence we have and there are definite things – I mean we know that Caesar invaded Britain in 55 BC, but at the end of the day I want them to think about evidence, and how do we know this and how do we know that? Again, also making it fun is very important, bringing it alive, as I've already said, and really trying to get them inspired.

(Interview post-lesson)

Understanding how historians work had greatly increased his ability to acquire substantive content knowledge for teaching:

David: I feel now that given the information on the course, I could tackle any period of history in the curriculum. It's quite a statement to make, isn't it?

(Interview post-course)

He now knew where to find historical information. The understanding of syntactic knowledge, the skills and processes historians use, had equipped him to prepare to teach any period of history. Syntactic knowledge would seem to be crucial to one's ability to increase and develop substantive knowledge. Grossman *et al.* (1989) suggested that not only do novice teachers who lack knowledge of the syntactic structures of the subject matter fail to incorporate that aspect of the discipline in their curriculum, but a lack of syntactic knowledge may also seriously limit prospective teachers' abilities *to learn new information in their fields* (my italics). This can also be true of teachers with some or even many years of experience. David had been teaching several years before he attended the history course: on his own admission he had not built in any syntactic element in his history teaching prior to the course. His lessons had been purely comprehension and might as well have been English lessons. Post-course he demonstrated his confidence in his ability to acquire new substantive knowledge for teaching.

Not only had his syntactic and substantive knowledge of history improved, his beliefs about history had changed too. David described his experience of history teaching prior to the course, thus:

David: I did history to A Level and my history was horrendous based on the approach by the staff used. One master used to enter the room and on the blackboard went the information and you spent the lesson copying that out.

(Interview post-course)

It was very much the case that in the absence of any other images of teaching history, or any other notions of what history is, David fell back on doing what he had observed history teachers do when he was at school. It took the course to give him new insight and to change his beliefs:

David: The first five days blow you over. You think: 'Wow! I'm doing this wrong; I'm doing this right,' or 'I haven't thought about that one before.' You have time to reflect and then you can come back and discuss it further.

(Interview post-lesson)

David: In the first five days, it was an upheaval. Suddenly you've got a new approach and new ideas; you are told the curriculum is rubbish, which is like heresy, but it's brilliant! In the first five days you are just finding your feet really, and I needed the next 15 days, set out in weeks at a time, just to really get my head round it; to take on a new approach and be radical and learn from there. You need the time in between as well. You need the time to think about it and try it for yourself and to come back and say if it didn't work, and to ask why. You often go away and think of questions you want to ask next time you come. Whereas in five days you would not have time to reflect, I don't think.

(Interview post-course)

The process of change in his beliefs are set out very clearly here: it is apparent that the time to try out the new ideas and approaches, and then reflect on them, are an important part of the process. David also displayed sophisticated curriculum knowledge in his lesson on the Roman galley. He was dealing in depth with the Roman invasion of Britain. He had used a video about the invasion the previous day, to get the children familiar with the story. He also used an OHP, a black and white overhead transparency of an artist's impression of a galley from a child's book, some metre rules, a large lump of white chalk and a drum and drumstick. The video is a standard everyday sort of resource used for history, but David was inventive and creative with the other items. This kind of inventiveness and creativity came from the course, as David explained:

David: You saw the OHP, for instance. I never really thought of using that before. It sounds silly, but I've never thought of producing an acetate and putting pictures on it or text and to use it as a main focus for a lesson, or going away and photocopying one picture and using it as a focus, as a resource for the whole class over several weeks.

(Interview post-course)

He added that his attitude and approach to resources had changed:

David: Another approach which has changed is using one or two pictures to focus on one or two things. Before I would have more resources and get the children looking at them. But now I think if you have one or two they can focus on one or two objects. So where I come in is to make the approach different each time. Say you have a postcard of an Anglo-Saxon helmet: you may be able to keep the same postcard going for several weeks, but each time taking different themes from the postcard. In terms of resources I now know that I feel you don't need so many. You just need a few good ones you can fire a whole topic on, which really helps for as a coordinator you are under a lot of pressure to buy resources. Now I feel my role is not so much to provide resources as to provide ideas and approaches and ways of using resources. We have lots of stuff here that's just not used, and I'd rather have one or two things for each area with lots of ideas on how to use them, because I think it's more how you use a resource than having the resource itself.

(Interview post-course)

In thinking about how he used resources, David was drawing on a number of models of teaching and learning. As previously discussed, he recognised that his old model of teaching history had been a transmission model, based on his own experience of the subject, and of teaching and learning in his schooling. However, the course had given him other models of teaching and learning. An important model of learning, which informed his teaching, was learning through an enactive representation. In discussing how the children had learnt about Roman galleys and the invasion, he answered:

David: They learnt through role-play. Through actually going out on the playground with the boat already drawn, acting out being slaves and acting out being soldiers, and pretending to jump in . . . So the whole thing is role-play.

(Interview post-lesson)

This model of learning through acting out a situation from the past, or re-creating a house, town, market place or ship from the past had been gained from the course. David talked at length about this, and about another main model of teaching and learning from the course:

David: They had such a variety of approaches. I mean the two men were very different anyway. They actually got you as a group to try out for yourself the approaches they were discussing, rather than just sitting there and taking notes, and being lectured at for a whole day, which sometimes happens: you just sit there and make notes from an OHP. I've been to courses where you sat down all day and watched the screen and made notes from it. But the approach on this course was: 'Here's an approach: let's try it out, and let's do it.' 'So you think OK. Let's play at being a Roman; let's draw out a boat; let's make a model; let's do this.' So you actually, not as a child – you're on a different level – as teachers you're operating as children, but in the context of being teachers yourselves – and that worked really well. And there were times when we sat down, and one of the leaders would talk to us, and discuss things, but it was more of a dialogue rather than: 'I'm going to preach at you and you can make notes.' Those approaches worked really well. They were much more enjoyable and we learnt more; you come away remembering what you've learnt. By doing it at the time, it sticks in your mind.

(Interview post-lesson)

This active way of learning through engaging totally with the material to be learnt, particularly through the exercise of the imagination, made a major impression on David. Because the learning operated on two levels, with David as teacher and in role as a child, he was able to assimilate fully what this way of learning could do for himself and for his children. If he came away remembering the material, skills and processes, the likelihood was that the children would remember through the same model of teaching. In passing, David mentioned the dialogue model of teaching which one of the leaders used. This was a form of Socratic dialogue, in which the course leader, though clearly an expert, encouraged the members to raise ideas and points that had arisen in their practice and in their reflections in trying out some of the course ideas in school. It was essentially a collaborative teaching activity, in which learners could proffer viewpoints and ideas, and have them discussed critically, even challenged by the course leader and by other members of the group. It is noteworthy that David's initial discourse, using the overhead transparency picture of a galley, was in this Socratic tradition:

> David: So it was very much me at the front, talking. But I asked them to think. I wouldn't call it chalk and talk. It was more like a dialogue really. It was a conversation about: what do we think this was, and how big do you think this is. That is how I would say it was organised really. And then we went out in the playground, which was different again.
>
> (Interview post-lesson)

David and the children were exploring ideas about the ship together, with David asking leading questions to steer the lesson to his purposes, in the form of a conversation.

Another model of teaching used in the lesson was storytelling. The use of stories to communicate meaning, morals, aspects of humanity, truths, and dilemmas, and to set imaginations working is another very ancient model of teaching. Humans seem to be almost programmed to pay attention to stories, such is their appeal and power. There is a wealth of literature which deals with the whole business of storytelling and its value in teaching and learning (see for example, Rosen 1990; Fines and Nichol 1997; Bage 1999). David was clear about the use of this model in his lesson, where he used dialogue, and where he switched to role-play:

> David: Storytelling is very important. The idea of storytelling is very important. So running through the whole lesson there was a story about the invasion. So I use storytelling as a very important key. And really capturing their imagination is very important as well. If you can get them thinking for themselves, rather than relying on you to give all the answers, and the evidence, they get their imaginations going. That's really it.
>
> (Interview post-lesson)

Some of the quality and richness of this lesson in terms of teaching and learning lay in the way David switched from one underlying model to another, from one teaching approach to another, more-or-less seamlessly. He also did not teach this lesson in isolation, but was thinking where he might take the children next. This lesson had built on the previous one with the video, and indeed David used 'building' as a metaphor for the way he ensured continuity and progession, using his knowledge of children's learning to construct a meaningful scheme of work:

> David: Next time we come to another history lesson, I always tend to, like building blocks, have one lesson building on the other; so the next lesson, which could be, you know, invading the land and setting up camps on the British mainland. I'll always build on what they've learnt already.
>
> (Interview post-lesson)

Some of this understanding may have been acquired from his teaching experience to date, but also from the course, where he appreciated the time to reflect upon new ideas and return to them:

David: The first five days you were really challenged about how you taught history. And you needed time to go away and really reflect on what you'd learnt, so that you could come back the next five days, you know – we worked through some of the issues . . . You need that chance to have dialogue with people . . . You could come back and engage with more different ways of doing history.

(Interview post-lesson)

This way of learning has something in common with Norman's (1978) theory of complex learning, which happens over a period of time. David and the children, in their own contexts, went through phases of accretion, restructuring and tuning. The children were introduced to the notion of the invasion via the video in the accretion phase; they restructured their knowledge through the picture of the galley, the story, the creation of the galley in the playground and the role-play. They would then move on to combined accretion and tuning in the invasion proper and the settlement in camps, towns and villas. Thus David's teaching was underpinned by a number of models of teaching and learning, which opened up the possibilties for designing teaching activities from which the children would learn and remember. For this, David employed a whole range of approaches from his teaching repertoire. This has already been dealt with in some detail in Chapter 4 in the section on pedagogical repertoires. David made it clear that his role in the lesson was a 'multi-various one'. He listed these roles: he was a guide; he asked the right questions to get them thinking; he kept order; he inspired them; he steered the lesson and 'kept it on course', getting them thinking and motivated; leading the role-play; and telling a story. Of these, he saw the story running through the entire lesson as very important. These different roles and actions were, if you like, his approaches and strategies. As well as that he used the 'top tray' tools (Tauber and Mester 1995) of voice, vocal animation, body language and use of classroom space. His presence in the classroom was absorbing: the children focused fully on him. He also used humour and suspense, and props such as the metre rule and the drum. The combined effect of all these approaches, strategies and tools was to generate interest and enthusiasm. This ability to inspire and enthuse will be discussed fully in the final part of this section, in pedagogical content knowledge.

One final aspect of David's general pedagogical knowledge deserves attention. He talked at length about whole-class teaching as his preferred organisational strategy. He stated that he found it very effective, and particularly in the school context in which he found himself working:

David: The idea of having a kind of mixed ability grouping of children all doing something different at the same time works in some schools, but doesn't work here, because inevitably, while working in one group, another group has a fight or a child leaves. That's the nature of the children here: they are not very good at working independently. I find the whole-class approach for me personally is, in this area, in this school, the only effective way of communicating with the children, knowing they are responding to me and taking it in. In general, even if I wasn't here, I'd still use the whole-class approach. You have to, I think because of things you do, activities involved, means moving around and role-play, and you can't really do it in groups. I'd rather do whole-class teaching anyway. One group works on something and wonders what the other group is doing. If I move away from the group, they stop working. Human nature I think, but I always teach history now with a whole-class approach. Not all things though: in English, maths and science you can set up different tasks, but history is always a whole-class approach. I just find it easier to work that way, especially when you focus on one or two resources. I find the whole class working at the same time can fire off each other. I just find it easier that way. So very effective and it works.

(Interview post-course)

There are several knowledge bases entwined in this explanation of why he used a whole-class teaching approach and organisational strategy. He shows a deep understanding of the children and of the community: knowledge of contexts, and empirical and cognitive knowledge inform his teaching approaches. He was aware of group work strategies, but found that they did not work so well in this context with these children. So his knowledge of pedagogy entwined with his knowledge of children and contexts meant that he selected different teaching strategies and forms of organisation for particular subjects. David talked further about the particular problems of teaching in this school context, with these children:

David: In this school they have a problem reading anyway. Very few can actually go to a textbook and read it. I used to think you had to read everything first and then research it; so before it was very much teacher-led and teacher-directed, because I thought that you had to do that. In the past I knew there was no way they could read textbooks; so I thought: how can they cope with a manuscript from years ago? But now I feel confident, and I would give them manuscripts and we would literally read them together.

(Interview post-course)

The new teaching approaches from the course had shown him how to use historical documents with children. Before he knew they would not be able to read topic books independently, and had dismissed the idea that they would be able to tackle the primary sources of documents. However, he now knew that by working on the documents together, they could read some parts of them, enough to get their meaning. Thus his expectations of these children had been raised also. He had also this to say about the value of storytelling as a teaching approach, rather than giving them facts in topic books:

David: Storytelling is very important. If I had done the lesson through facts: this happened, that happened, this happened, they would have switched off. By doing a story, something about stories just locks children on to you. I tell a story any time and the children are right there; they want to hear stories. As soon as you say: I'm going to tell a story today – Bang! They're there! So the idea of storytelling is very important.

(Interview post-lesson)

Lists of qualities or skills in effective teachers often include the ability to attract the interest of children and maintain it. David here gives some insight into how this is done, with the storytelling and one of the other teaching approaches he used in this lesson:

David: I used the overhead projector. I use that a lot, because as soon as I put it on, you saw what happened, like: Oh, wow! They've got a picture to look at. And I like to provide some kind of focus, be it a picture, or an artefact or something; so it's one thing that grabs their imagination and grabs their attention, and that was the OHP.

(Interview post-lesson)

He knows that if he is to engage the interest of these children so that they will learn something, he has to use this variety of approaches. The only knowledge base which David did not make explicit in the interviews and in his teaching, was that of educational ends. Nonethethless, in his concern that the children actually engaged with the material he was trying to teach them, rather than copied out of books without understanding or undertook busy work, he is showing his educational aims implicitly. These children had been brought up in poverty in a very deprived area. Through his teaching, David gave them enthusiasm and excitement about learning. Maths and English were both incorporated into this lesson and the writing task, at the end, would provide him with evidence of their learning (although their oral responses gave him some knowledge of their understanding).

It is clear from what has been written so far in analysis of David's knowledge bases, that the course had a considerable influence on him as a teacher. He was also explicit about the impact of the course on himself as teacher, on his practice, and on the kind of teacher he now knew himself to be. In discussing the resolution of the course, he saw the sort of teacher and coordinator he had become as the culmination and outcome of the course:

David: The resolution is me. Is that OK? . . . Each of us carried something away with us, something from the course, whether it is ideas or a basic enthusiasm for history at last, or 'I feel competent'.

(Interview post-course)

He felt equipped to be a good coordinator, not merely providing resources for the staff, but ideas and teaching approaches as well. This had not always been the case, as the following extract illustrates:

David: So when I became coordinator of humanities, my interest was geography and history was tagged on to it and I had to do it. I had no ideas on anything really, what to resource, how to tackle an area, or where to begin really. The course has helped in a way. It's made me feel a competent historian. It's made me feel anyone can be a historian in ways that historians use: it's open to all of us. Here am I, a 'geography expert' doing history and loving it, and enjoying it and feeling competent enough as coordinator as well. So it's given me enthusiasm. I'm full of praise for the course: it is brilliant. It's made me feel competent at teaching history, and being able to pass on the knowledge to others in the school. I'm the historian now! It's changed completely.

(Interview post-course)

Enthusiasm in teachers is essential for generating enthusiasm in children. David now had that enthusiam and he knew how he had acquired it:

David: The course leaders generated the enthusiam. Because they're so enthusiastic, it kind of lifts you up. We all came in, not sceptical . . . I know there were teachers there who thought: 'I can't teach history; I don't want to teach history; it's boring; I don't get anything out of it.' . . . but in the past courses have been a drag. Here was one that was different. It was refreshing . . . You went away thinking: 'Right! I feel I can do this now. I'm enthusiastic to do it!'

(Interview post-lesson)

David was fully cognisant of his enthusiasm and its importance in children's learning, but he also related this quality to being able to express himself in the classroom:

David: One thing the course leaders said is that teachers are there to be creative in the classroom. Teachers often are and it hits a chord with you. And you think 'Yes, they often are.' You say be creative in your classroom. It's an expression of who you are . . . Yes, it's important to me really and so's the freedom to experiment and create. The pressure still exists and you still have the study units. But now I feel I can justify to walk into my class and say: 'You've covered this, this and this, but you haven't covered these other areas. 'I now feel in a position to justify why I haven't done that. They inspire you really. It's good to know that there are people out there, who are professionals, who are arguing for you, and fighting your case, because we've just been pushed from pillar to post, and told: 'You must do this, this and this.' Suddenly there are people there saying: 'This is wrong: you shouldn't be doing it.'

(Interview post-course)

David was empowered by the course, and reskilled as a teacher and as a professional. From the preceding extended discussion, it is clear that for this subject, David was employing the full amalgam of pedagogical content knowledge. He chose powerful representations of the Roman invasion, and the Roman galley. For the galley, he used the enlarged overhead transparency of the galley from a children's history book. This iconic representation focused their attention and held their interest. It was as accurate a representation as he could acquire, but he used appropriate language to convey the idea that it was what he thought the ship might have looked like. He representated the space between the oarsmen by using children, and the whole ship by drawing its outline in the playground. These were enactive representations, with the children role-playing the people in the ship. The invasion itself was also represented enactively: the drum evoking the rowing rhythms required to propel such a ship. These were creative uses of simple curriculum materials. David felt free to operate in this way, to be creative and select such representations as a result of the course he had attended. He saw himself now as the creative professional, not merely the servant of the state delivering the curriculum, but as the professional teacher, able to choose what subject content and processes he would teach to his children, and how he would teach it.

Conclusion

The difference between competent teaching and expert teaching is the usage of the fullest form of pedagogical content knowledge. The knowledge bases underpin acts of expert teaching: they are the submerged bulk of the iceberg and the observable qualities and teaching skills are the visible portions. In this chapter the difference is illustrated in the three case studies of David's history lesson and Melanie's science and poetry lessons. David's history lesson is an example of expert teaching. Melanie's colleagues and head teacher were very pleased with her classroom performance, but as we have seen, in the science lesson she was operating an incomplete amalgam in her lesson, lacking scientific subject knowledge, and having her usual good pedagogical knowledge, and beliefs about teaching and learning science suppressed by the complexities of the context. However, we have seen Melanie able to employ a range of representations in her poetry lesson, to teach what poetry is and how to write it. From this it is clear that pedagogical content knowledge is subject specific: a teacher may be expert in one subject and merely competent in another. For primary teaching, where the prevailing norm is for one teacher to teach all of the subjects up to the end of Key Stage 2, this clearly has implications, which will be explored in the last two chapters.

CHAPTER 9

Suggestions for development of practice

In subject disciplines, different conceptions of the nature of the subject or different paradigms can affect the way one perceives that area of human activity. This is true of teaching. If one conceives of teaching as a list of skills, qualities, aptitudes and dispositions, as in some of the examples given in Chapter 1, or in the DfEE standards, then the focus in improving one's teaching is achieving that particular skill or acquiring a quality. However, this says nothing about how one does so. For example, one might wish to develop Standard 4ki:

> Use teaching methods which sustain the momentum of pupils' work and keep all pupils engaged through: stimulating intellectual curiosity, communicating enthusiasm for the subject being taught, fostering pupils' enthusiasm and maintaining pupils' motivation.

> (DfEE 1998a)

The fundamental question is: how is this done? The answer is complex, and not merely a matter of practising being enthusiastic and ticking a box when this has been demonstrated the requisite number of times. In the model of teaching knowledge bases, there is material for thought and reflection, to inform one's experimentation and practice. If one just applies the model briefly to this one standard, we can see which knowledge bases are implicit in its wording; and therefore which ones need development.

'Use teaching methods which sustain the momentum of pupils' work' clearly refers to general pedagogical knowledge and models of teaching and learning. There is also implicit reference to empirical and cognitive knowledge of learners: just how does one keep five-year-olds, eight-year-olds or ten-year-olds interested? If we add in the next bit: *'and keep all pupils engaged through: stimulating intellectual curiosity, communicating enthusiasm for the subject being taught, fostering pupils' enthusiasm and maintaining pupils' motivation'*, the need to understand both learners and

learning is even clearer. At the same time, there is a strong suggestion of deep knowledge of and passion for a subject. The deep knowledge, as we have seen, must comprise knowledge of substantive and syntactic structures, and beliefs about the subject. In addition, the phrase 'stimulating intellectual curiosity' implies that teachers must possess this quality in themselves. Thus the description in the standard tends to refer to the observable parts of teaching: one must reflect upon what knowledge, understanding and qualities are implicit in the wording. The standard is like the visible tenth of the iceberg above the waterline: the knowledge is the nine-tenths which lies beneath. To become expert in teaching, one must have the full range of knowledge, as outlined in the model of knowledge bases, which underpins the visible skills, aptitudes and qualities.

This model suggests an alternative way of thinking about teaching and reflecting on practice. The value of this alternative way lies in the possibility it presents for looking below the surface aspects of teaching to the deep knowledge and understanding which lie beneath. The knowledge bases can first be considered separately and then as part of the whole professional knowledge base of pedagogical content knowledge. Linked to them all is the key notion of representation. What follows is a brief consideration of each knowledge base as a way of considering teaching: preparing for teaching and reflecting on episodes of teaching.

Subject knowledge: substantive and syntactic structures

For each subject taught, it is worth examining the substantive and syntactic structures of that subject. It is quite possible to study a subject to degree level, or teach it for several years in school, without becoming fully aware of what these are. This is no-one's fault, exactly, it is just that so much is taken for granted in advanced and degree level subject study. A further problem with not understanding the structures of the disciplines lies in the resulting tendency to treat the fruits of the subject discipline as if they are uncontested facts or literal truths, instead of interpretations of facts. We have tended to simplify what scientific, mathematical or historical enquiry had revealed to us to the point where such knowledge could be correctly understood without reference to the structures which had produced them (Schwab 1978). This was done in the interest of effective teaching, because we did not think that what was taught would be affected by presenting knowledge in this way. If these ideas seem difficult, we only have to think back to the example given by David in Chapter 8, of the history teaching he experienced at school: of a master entering the room, writing down facts and information on the board, and the class copying it, without reference to the methods of enquiry which had produced this information. This is not an uncommon experience of school history.

Schwab argued that the process of change to include the structures of the disciplines in school subjects would be difficult and painful. This may be overstating the problem, but the two attendant problems he suggests certainly need to be considered by teachers. He argued that teachers would need to find appropriate ways of including structure as a facet of curriculum content. A far more complex second problem is that:

> we will no longer be free to choose teaching methods, textbook organisation and classroom structuring on the basis of psychological and social considerations alone. Rather, we will need to face the fact that methods are rarely if ever neutral. On the contrary, the means we use colour and modify the ends we actually achieve through them. *How* we teach will determine *what* our students learn. If a structure of teaching and learning is alien to the structure of what we propose to teach, the outcome will inevitably be a corruption of that content. And we will know that it is.

(Schwab 1978, p. 243)
(emphasis as in the original)

A full understanding of the shifting and dominant paradigms in each subject, and the modes of enquiry or creation, are necessary in order to devise lessons which accurately reflect the parent discipline of the subject taught in school. This is demonstrated in the case studies of Tom's science and poetry lessons, Melanie's science and poetry lessons, and David's history lesson.

What does this mean for teachers? As part of subject knowledge, they must come to know the structures of the subjects they teach. This might mean some sort of mapping exercise of each subject they teach: a tall order for primary teachers in present school organisation, for in the class teacher system, they have to teach all the subjects of the National Curriculum. The implications of this for the profession are examined in Chapter 10. Ideally this mapping should be done as part of initial teacher education, but inevitably, some may not happen until teachers experience some substantial in-service training. However, teachers may begin to do this for themselves. A slight difficulty is that disciplines are of different types: some are pure forms of enquiry about the universe in which we find ourselves; and some are what might be termed practical or productive disciplines, in that their purpose is to make or create objects, devices, pictures, works of art, drama, literature or music or aesthetic experiences to be used and appreciated by others. However, it is still possible to map out the key or first-order concepts of each discipline, examples of second- and third-order concepts, and ways in which these concepts might be related to each other.

As far as syntactic structures are concerned, one would need to map out which skills and processes are fundamental to a particular subject: for example in art, an understanding of the processes of producing a piece of art, would lead a teacher to give very different kinds of art lessons to the sort in which all the children in the class draw pictures of Viking boats to go in folders. I am not suggesting this kind of analysis is easy. However, the mere process of engaging in consideration of the essential substance of a subject, its organising paradigms and key concepts, and in the syntactic structures of how knowledge, understanding or art are produced within the subject, may force one to look at the subject differently, and to comprehend it in ways which might have been hidden before.

Beliefs and attitudes about subjects

Before undertaking such a mapping exercise as described in the previous section, it is worth writing down what one considers a subject to be. I have tried this with successive cohorts of specialist and non-specialist students training to be primary teachers (Turner-Bisset 1999b; 2000c). Interestingly, it makes little difference whether students have a degree in history or A Level history: the answers are very similar. Very few students have any conception of it as an enquiry-based subject. The enquiry element has often been absent from their own experience; it has not been made explicit during the teaching of it. As Schwab (1978) pointed out, the kinds of lessons they received were likely to have been a corruption of the discipline as it really is. Likewise with maths: children and teachers can learn that it is about procedures and tricks without fully coming to understand that the symbols are a representation of reality, or that maths involves investigation and proof. Similarly in science, a reliance by teachers on notes, recipe investigations and tests can lead children, and hence future teachers to assume science is about mastering lots of factual information, difficult ideas and formulae, without any notion of the full set of processes of scientific enquiry or the organising frameworks which guide enquiry.

One's beliefs about a subject can influence one's attitudes towards it. Attitudes are complex things for they are shaped by perception and experiences, but beliefs do play a part. If children or teachers believe that a subject is about much rote learning of factual information for tests, then it is unlikely that the enjoyable parts of subjects will make much impact on them. In the productive disciplines, one's attitudes can be coloured by negative feedback from family or teachers. It is commonplace in art for example to hear from children, students or teachers that they 'cannot draw' and are therefore 'no good at art'. This is a pity, for there are many ways of making art without drawing, and many ways of appreciating art or using it for a career in art history or working with photographic images. The same refrain occurs in music. One hears the saying: 'I am not musical.' In the light of the obviously huge part music plays in most people's lives, even if it is through listening rather than playing, the idea that people have no musical leanings or ability seems unlikely. It is often undeveloped through lack of time, money or appropriate influences. Lack of confidence in one's musical abilities can lead people to dislike it as a school subject; the same is true of maths, where negative attitudes, dislike and lack of confidence abound (e.g. Schuck 1997). Negative attitudes can be hard to shift in any subject, however, it is extremely important to change them, for it is hard to imagine any teachers communicating enthusiasm for a subject which they do not understand or dislike. Enthusiasm as we have seen is a key element in pedagogy: hence it is of crucial importance to understand the nature of the subjects in the primary curriculum, and to like, enjoy and value them. Probably the best ways of changing beliefs and attitudes towards subjects is by attending extended in-service courses, which enable one to have time to be exposed to what may be new ideas and conceptions of a subject, to reflect on the new ideas, to carry out action research and to reflect further on one's own research (Askew *et al.* 1997; Medwell *et al.* 1998; Turner-Bisset and Nichol 1999). This has implications for the design and duration of continuing professional development.

Attitudes again can be altered through quality in-service training: the kind which gives adequate time to developing teachers' own abilities in writing poetry or prose (for example, Arvon Foundation courses) or art, drama, design technology or music; or courses which develop deep subject knowledge and understanding. This knowledge base of beliefs and attitudes about subject knowledge is closely bound up with knowledge of self. What is required is some kind of reflection on self, whether stimulated by a course, or by oneself: as to why one has positive or negative attitudes towards certain subjects. What is it about maths or music or writing poetry which makes me think I cannot do it, or that it is a waste of time? What is it in my own personality or experience, which makes this subject difficult or unattractive to me? Sometimes negative attitudes can be traced back to a particular teacher or school. They might also be engendered by enculturation or peer pressure: for example that dance is a sissy subject only for girls. A useful exercise is to examine one's attitudes towards a subject as a first step towards changing them; if one becomes aware of what makes maths seem hard, one can tackle that aspect of it. It is recognised that none of this is easy, however, it is well worth doing in the pursuit of mastery with awareness, or being an expert teacher.

Curriculum knowledge

It has been stated in Chapter 3 that curriculum knowledge has several dimensions: curriculum knowledge related to subject knowledge for teaching; knowledge of the curriculum as differentiated subjects and integrated subjects; and critical understanding of the curriculum. Expert teachers need knowledge and understanding of all of these, which will be dealt with in turn.

Obviously as a starting point (and this is what is required of newly qualified teachers) one needs knowledge of the current National Curriculum, the literacy and numeracy strategies, and the local agreed syllabus for religious education. To these may be added knowledge of the QCA exemplar schemes of work (with the proviso that they must be treated critically as examples only, and not strict guidelines), knowledge of local authority and commercial schemes of work, teaching programmes, teaching packs, topic books, children's literature and all the commercially available resources such as TV programmes, videos, internet resources, pictures, artefacts and so on. In addition to this must be added knowledge of how to use all these schemes and resources. Furthermore, there are the curricular materials which arise from oneself as an individual. These might include stories from one's own childhood to spark off memories from children for creative writing; or gifts such as the voluptuous lady figurine described in Chapter 3, an unwanted gift used for art lesson,

It is of crucial importance that one examines all curriculum materials with a knowledgeable, informed and critical understanding, for if one does not do so, one is in danger of merely selecting teaching ideas and activities because they seem to work, or planning schemes of work around content only, without incorporating the syntactic elements of a subject. Deep subject knowledge of the kind described in this book, is essential for the critical assessment of curriculum materials. Without this deep subject knowledge, one cannot judge the appropriateness and teaching power of particular representations of concepts, skills and processes, and one is in danger of providing the kind of corrupted image of a subject which Schwab (1978) described and warned against. However as well as this, knowledge bases such as knowledge of learners and contexts, also have a role to play in the development of curriculum knowledge, for one develops representations and learning activities for particular contexts and groups of learners. Developing good or excellent curriculum knowledge means that one must be well-informed about the wealth of material which is available. Attaining this state is partly a matter of individual preparation, as one works with curriculum documents and packs to prepare lessons. However, in-service training on non-pupil days could incorporate development of these knowledge bases. Groups of teachers could examine a selection of government and commercially prepared materials and judge them against a range of criteria. The importance of this activity lies in the critical analysis and informed debate of the teachers undertaking it. It is appropriate to select from a range of curriculum materials to find the best ways of teaching the concepts, skills, processes, attitudes and values embedded within each subject. This kind of in-service activity is also valuable for making the implicit, explicit: the kind of awareness and informed understanding which is important for expertise.

The second dimension, that of knowledge of curriculum as differentiated subjects and integrated subjects is important for developing an understanding of the whole curriculum, and how the different subjects relate to each other. This was discussed more fully in Chapter 3: teachers need to be aware of the difference between a non-differentiated curriculum and a genuinely integrated one. Knowledge of the key concepts, skills and processes of each subject can help one to understand where genuine links can be made between two subjects. These ideas are further discussed in Turner-Bisset (2000a). Knowledge of the whole curriculum, of the subjects, areas of study and cross-curricular links could be developed through in-service activities similar to those described for understanding of curriculum materials.

The third dimension of curriculum knowledge, critical understanding of the curriculum is not so easily acquired. History of education is a somewhat unfashionable and discredited area of study, seen as belonging to the applied science paradigm of teaching, and to the 'raiding the disciplines' approach to teacher education popular in the 1960s and 1970s. However, it is important to understand not only where our present system of education came from, but to have some sense of the varying aims and purposes of primary education down the years. In addition to this, it is necessary to have some understanding of change and continuity in the primary curriculum; to know that the present curriculum is only one of many possible curricula for primary children; and to be able to treat the present curriculum documents with this critical awareness, looking beyond the glossy packaging to the meaning beneath. Some teachers will have experienced the pre- and post-Plowden forms of primary curriculum, as well as more recent developments; others will only know what is currently presented. For those without this type of curriculum knowledge, there is no substitute for reading, discussion and writing on these topics, perhaps as part of a master's or doctoral programme. Such study is important as we have seen, and should be encouraged by those who design, implement and fund both initial and in-service training.

Models of learning and teaching

Learning

Knowledge and understanding of how children learn comes from two main sources: private theory, or one's own experience of learning, and of observing and teaching children; and public theory, or reading and ideas from courses. In Chapter 4, several theories of learning were presented and explored, with the belief that it is better to have knowledge of a number of theories of learning, rather than subscribe to one particular theory. The advantages of this are that one increases one's options for enabling children to learn; and that the different theories offer a framework by which one can analyse one's own practice. Any experience of learning can be analysed using the theories of learning presented in Chapter 4: it is not an exhaustive list, but a useful one. A summary of the theories of learning is given in Figure 9.1 and can be applied to reflection on learning and teaching.

Theories of learning

- Stones' psychopedagogical analysis: rote learning; conceptual learning; motor learning; psychomotor learning; problem-solving (Stones 1992);
- Schema theory: assimilation and adaptation; Piaget (1959);
- Bruner's enactive, iconic and symbolic representation (Bruner 1970);
- Assisted performance: Vygotsky's zone of proximal development (Vygotsky 1978);
- Behaviour modification; Skinner and the behaviourists (Skinner 1938);
- Norman's theory of complex learning (Norman 1978).

Figure 9.1 Summary of learning theories

Two approaches are suggested for development of the models of learning part of this knowledge base. The first involves some reflection on one's own experiences of learning anything at all: it might be learning to drive a car, to swing a golf club, salsa dancing or cookery, as much as learning done in school. It is worth applying each of these theories to an episode of learning, to examine it from different angles, so to speak. Thus, to take the example of swinging a golf club. I recently had my first experience of this at a kind of electronic golf centre, similar in concept to tenpin bowling. This looked at first glance like motor learning, but it soon became clear to me that this was psychomotor in nature. I had to learn about the grip, the stance, the backswing, the swing itself, the follow-through, as well as addressing the ball and focusing on where I wished it to go. I began to assimilate some of these ideas through my early success of hitting the ball accurately on my first four swings. There followed a period of cognitive dissonance whereby I walloped the tee or the playing surface, and either missed the ball completely or sent it dribbling a few inches. This was accompanied by some affective dissonance as I squirmed inwardly at the thought of making an idiot of myself in front of my more experienced companions. Fortunately, they had all been through the same process, and offered support and comfort during this phase. I began to get an idea, from watching the others, of what a swing should look like, and thus used an enactive representation of the conceptual-motor learning I was trying to undertake. Later, the club professional analysed my swing on video: this was another useful enactive representation, especially when compared with Tiger Woods' swing, on a split screen. My companions offered various useful bits of advice and feedback, and suggested ways in which I could improve, thereby assisting my performance, through the zone of proximal development. Thus far I had engaged in quite a lot of accretion, as I tried to learn something new. I had restructured some of my thinking about the task ('any fool can hit a golf ball' gave way to a more sophisticated understanding) and some of my actions in experimenting with different grips, stances and movements. I only began to engage in a little tuning towards the end of the game, when

I started to be rather more consistent in hitting the ball and aiming it at a particular hole. If I were to return to the game, there would be much more of this. I will not say that I reached the stage of accommodation, except in understanding some of the inherent difficulties and fascination of the game. It is important to analyse one's own learning in this way, for through this kind of analysis, one can begin to understand what children might be experiencing when trying to learn how to hit a rounders ball, bake a cake or write a poem. The attachment of examples to theories by way of illustration assists the process of understanding and applying the theories.

Having analysed one's own learning in this way, one could apply some or all of these theories to episodes of children's learning. This is the second approach with regard to reflecting on models of learning. A list of questions to ask about an episode of learning is suggested in Figure 9.2; the list is underpinned by the theories of learning in Figure 9.1.

Questions to ask

- What kind of learning is this: rote, conceptual, motor, psychomotor, problem-solving?
- What kind of mental representations are being used: enactive, iconic, symbolic?
- How do the tasks and activities contribute to assimilation and accommodation of new ideas, concepts, information, skills, processes and attitudes?
- What is the zone of proximal development for a sample of the children engaged in this learning?
- What assistance is given to the children in moving them through this zone?
- Are the learning tasks examples of accretion, restructuring, enrichment, practice or revision?
- How is engagement or motivation maintained: through encouragement and positive feedback, or constructive criticism?

Figure 9.2 Questions for analysis of children's learning experiences

This kind of analysis may be carried out for any lesson: it may be that in some lessons where learning does not occur, there is less on which to comment. The suggestion is made that the lessons in this book are analysed in the same way, as well as one's own lessons. The framework having been used for reflection, can then be used for planning, in order to answer the crucial question: How will the children learn what I want them to learn? Answers to this question can shape task design, along with the need to represent the discipline accurately, and can help one avoid time-filling activities.

Teaching

In Chapter 4, I introduced the notion of the pedagogical repertoire, having distinguished between pedagogical and organisational strategies. The repertoire is summarised and presented in Figure 9.3.

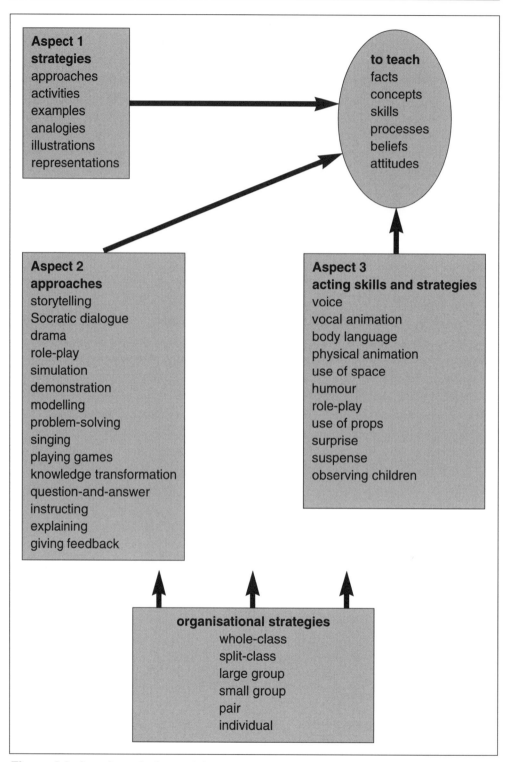

Figure 9.3 A pedagogical repertoire

Again lessons can be analysed using this model of the pedagogical repertoire, as well as planned using it. Humans like variety: the kind of teaching in which the pedagogical or organisational strategy is the same day after day, week after week, can easily generate boredom and disaffection. It is possible, for example to devise a planning grid for a scheme of work which includes a column for teaching approach. Using this one can avoid the kind of scheme which I have witnessed myself of, for example, watching a video and answering questions on a worksheet for the same subject each week. Teachers must, using their professional judgement, use their own pedagogical or organisational strategies in the literacy and numeracy hours, and their own timings, in accordance with the approach chosen.

General pedagogical knowledge:

This is the broad knowledge of classroom management, management of resources, of pupils, and of helpers and assistants, which is common to all subjects. It is often the minutiae of teaching: decisions have to made, often on the spot, for example, as to whether to hand out materials for a task right at the beginning or part way through an explanation, to avoid having the children fiddling with them. It is also the pedagogical tactics and relationship-building from knowledge of learners, self and context, which can pre-empt such problems in the first place. It encompasses all the many and varied tactics for getting children involved and motivated, such as those Kirsty described in Case study 8 (Chapter 5). Here the material for reflection might be the extent and variety of one's strategies, their clarity, efficacy, and enjoyabilty.

Knowledge of learners: empirical and cognitive

To develop these knowledge bases, there is no substitute for spending time with children, talking to them, observing them, playing with them and working with them. It is further developed through contact with parents and other colleagues in the school, although information from the grapevine needs to be treated with caution if one is not to label a child wrongly or stereotypically. For empirical knowledge of learners, one might reflect on how one came to know what one knows about six-year-olds, or ten-year-olds. One might consider teaching activities or representations one has chosen for particular children, and examine why those ones were chosen: What knowledge of learners fed into that selection of teaching approaches? As regards cognitive knowledge of learners, one needs to treat with similar caution the various fruits of assessment, for it is an inexact science: tests only measure certain things, and information from other teachers can sometimes lower expectations of certain children. As previously remarked, assessment information is best treated as ongoing and provisional, to be revised as children learn and develop.

Here one might reflect on several different aspects of cognitive knowledge of learners. One might consider how knowledge of child development has informed one's teaching: for example, have notions of readiness, helped or hindered in developing appropriate learning activities for children? In thinking about all the different methods of assessment, their uses and value in different contexts, one needs to bear in mind their provisional nature, and the fact that assessments might be coloured by other knowledge of these children. Awareness of tendencies to make fixed judgements of children, might be the first stage in developing a more flexible understanding. An example to reflect on here is the opportunity to flourish given to special needs children Aaron and Sophie in Case study 10 (Chapter 6), whereby being able to express their understandings of a historical situation orally through drama, revealed previously unseen aspects of these children. Thus one might also consider how one's teaching strategies have an impact on the kinds of assessment we do, and the information gathered.

Knowledge of educational contexts

In Chapter 6 it was noted that teachers need knowledge of eduational contexts at the levels of classroom, school, community and society. There is some difficulty here, for we have all known excellent teachers who have taught in the same school, or even the same year group for many years. However, I would argue that expert teachers need to have had experience of a number of classroom contexts, preferably in several schools. The reason for this is that because knowledge of contexts is so crucial in teaching, moving from one context to another can be initially deskilling. It can be a very different matter to teach Reception or Year 1, having just taught Years 5 and 6. This is partly a matter also of knowledge of learners, which was dealt with in the previous section. The value of knowledge of a range of contexts lies in the understanding of what it is possible to achieve by experimenting with the physical organisation of the classroom, the organisation of children, classroom management, the use of adult helpers and the uses of display. The classroom context should be designed with the emphasis on creating conditions for learning and teaching. Classroom contexts can be the focus of reflection, as in the case study on Melanie's science lesson, or Fines' (1994) unorthodox classroom design. The foci for reflection are suggested in Figure 9.4.

The next level of context, that of school community, is of equally crucial importance. The point has already been made about the necessity of 'fitting in' in terms of relationships with people, working in teams, impression management and the introduction of change or new ideas. Again the value of knowledge of a number of different schools is the understanding of what is possible; just because a school is organised in one way does not mean that that is the only way in which it can function effectively. Some might argue that this is an issue for heads and managers,

Points for reflection

- the impact of classroom contexts on teaching and learning;
- the uses and misuses of group organisation;
- the value of a variety of forms of organisation;
- the relationship between self-as-teacher and context;
- the roles of significant others such as teachers in the same team, classroom assistants and parent helpers;
- the issue of whether a classroom is organised with regard to one's own understandings of learning and teaching, or with regard to fitting in with the school community.

Figure 9.4 Points for reflection on classroom contexts

but in the kind of predominantly 'flat' management structure of primary schools, all can have their say over for example the timing of assemblies or the use of the hall. In David's school, the main use of the OHP prior to his using it for teaching had been for the display of hymn words on the wall for assemblies: his new use of it sparked off ideas in other teachers. Knowledge of local communities is a deeper enrichment to the knowledge base of contexts: the community is both a rich potential resource and the daily reality of the children. At the level of society, teachers need to be aware of the historical contexts of primary education; the consistent underfunding; and the tensions between the needs of society and the needs of the individual.

Knowledge of all of these gives a sense of perspective to teachers, and they can be aware of how political initiatives can impact on their daily classroom practice. To be informed gives one the possibility of subverting some unsuitable initiatives or exercising one's professional judgement on others.

Knowledge of self

The twin aspects of this knowledge base need to be considered. These are the investment of self, of one's own personality in teaching; and the impact of teaching on the self. For the first of these aspects, teachers might reflect on what sort of people they are; which aspects of their personality they utilise most in teaching; and how their personal interests and passions feed into their teaching. All teachers are people before they are teachers, and it is worth reflecting on the character traits, dispositions, qualities and passions which feed into the job. For the second of these aspects, one could examine the kinds of emotions that teaching has engendered in oneself on a variety of occasions. These might cover the whole gamut from euphoria to despair. It is worth thinking about what provoked these and what response they brought about in oneself in terms of teaching. Kirsty in Case study 8

(Chapter 5) spoke of how the children's response to the quick fun activities had spurred her on, had in fact driven her to do better for the children to engage them in maths and to make it more fun. They provided her motivation. At the opposite end of the scale, Mark in Case study 12 (Chapter 7) had been in the depths of despair when he felt he was doing badly. Teaching is also character-building: one needs courage, determination, stamina and staying-power, among other qualities. One has to develop organisational and management skills or one would go under. So the second source for reflection is thinking about how teaching has impacted on the self, to change the self in the two-way process which is described here.

Knowledge of educational ends

Three sets of educational ends merit study by teachers and reflection on their manifestations in the classroom and the broad educational context: the educational ends of society, the educational ends of schools and the educational ends of self as teacher. For the first of these, the framework developed by Alexander (1995) of the various competing traditions in primary education, is a useful tool for framework and analysis. This was described in Chapter 3. Part of its usefulness is in provoking consideration of the purposes of primary education and the ways in which these have changed over the years. The next layer of analysis is at the level of school aims: these again should be examined and analysed to discover which of the competing traditions might underpin them, whether explicitly or tacitly, and to match them against the the third layer of educational ends: one's own. One needs to be aware of one's own perceptions of primary education and its purposes; and aware of one's own values. A useful starting-point might be considering why one entered teaching. Other points for analysis are key or critical incidents which illuminate one's values, the ethos which one tries to create in the classroom, the values, skills and abilities one tries to promote in children, and the intrinsic rewards of the job. I would suggest re-examining Kirsty's lesson (Case study 8, Chapter 5) and David's lesson (Case study 1, Prologue and Chapters 3, 4 and 8) to consider some of these points, as well as episodes from one's own teaching.

Pedagogical content knowledge

Finally offered as material for reflection and development are the twin aspects of the amalgamation of all these knowledge bases: pedagogical content knowledge, and representations for teaching. Having considered a lesson (be it one of one's own, one of the case studies in this book, or an example observed of another teacher) for the knowledge bases which underpin it, one can begin to identify gaps in one's knowledge. These gaps can then be remedied. For example, an advisory teacher may have excellent subject and curriculum knowledge, but in teaching unfamiliar classes as part of his or her job, often does not have much knowledge of particular learners: this has to be remedied quickly, and often in action, as it were. A teacher may have excellent knowledge of learners, a variety of models of teaching and learning on which to draw, and good pedagogical content knowledge, but lack the knowledge of substantive and syntactic structures of maths or science which would make for expert teaching. With a full amalgam of pedagogical content knowledge, one can judge the appropriateness, worth and teaching potential of a whole range of representations, analogies, illustrations and activities. For example, to teach a 'walking bass line' in music, there is the possibility of a very appealing enactive representation of literally jumping from a card marked with one note, to other cards similarly marked, when one hears the movement from one note to another in the music. I have observed this representation being used very success-fully and enjoyed by teacher and children. However, it is only really suitable for small groups of children at a time; thus its worth must be judged against the organisational tactics one would have to employ to occupy other children while each group did the bass line activity.

Conclusion

In this chapter I have tried to indicate briefly the possibilities for conceptualising teaching using the model of knowledge bases as a framework for reflection. Through thinking of teaching in this way one can become aware of the knowledge bases which underpin acts of expert teaching. The many and varied skills, processes and qualities listed as effective teaching characteristics in published sets of teaching competences become part of the different knowledge bases. Teaching is thus a highly complex, knowledge-based profession in which the rich bodies of knowledge interact and blend to produce teaching of quality.

CHAPTER 10

Implications

Summary

This book has introduced a new paradigm of teaching: that of teaching as a knowledge-based profession. It is based on the model of knowledge bases and on a broad interpretation of the term 'knowledge', which encompasses concepts, facts, processes, skills, beliefs, attitiudes and values. It is important to understand that the model does not present a static view of knowledge for teaching, but the vision of knowledge as interacting sets implies that teaching knowledge is constantly being revised. In addition, the model of teaching knowledge illustrated in the case studies in this book shows that one's pedagogical content knowledge varies in the exact composition of the sets of knowledge bases according to the subject being taught. This notion has considerable implications for primary teachers in particular, which will be explored in this chapter.

In Chapter 1, I discussed seven different paradigms of teaching and argued that they were all in some ways partial models of teaching. Teaching as a common-sense activity is unsatisfactory for its dismissal of the complexities of teaching knowledge; what may appear to be a pragmatic and intuitive way of working is in fact informed by a range of knowledge bases. Teaching as a craft has its emphasis on the skills of teaching, whereas I would argue that while complex craft knowledge is essential for expert teaching, it is only part of what is required, and only one of several knowledge bases. Teaching as an applied science is also partial in that knowledge from the four 'foundation' disciplines of history, philosophy, psychology and sociology are only part of the knowledge base for expert teaching; in addition teaching is not so simple as applying theory to practice, for theory and practice operate together in a symbiotic relationship. Teaching as a system is an equally unsatisfactory paradigm. Its rationality has an appeal in the emphasis on specifying objectives clearly in order to recognise if we have achieved them: the paradigm is apparent in the current vogue for target-setting and evaluation. However, it ignores the complexities of teaching, and particularly the often multi-layered nature of one's goals and approaches in teaching, which this book has sought to illustrate. Teaching as reflective practice is clearly an important paradigm: the need for honest reflection at the highest levels in order to develop as a teacher is shown in the chapter on knowledge of self (Chapter 7), but knowledge of self, and the ability to reflect are only part of the knowledge bases for teaching.

Teaching as competence has emerged as a powerful paradigm, in that it seems logical and practical to break down teaching into a number of different skills, qualities and abilities, but as a paradigm of teaching it has serious weaknesses. Teaching is such a complex job that typically one is using a number of skills simultaneously, for example, choosing words carefully, listening to what children say, scanning the class to pre-empt order problems, and making mental notes for future action. The standards in Circular 4/98 (DfEE 1998a) by which all new entrants to teaching are trained and judged, are a messy conception of teaching. There are serious weaknesses in these standards. They are representative of a technicist conception of teaching: master all of these and one will be a good teacher. Teaching of quality is not merely a matter of acquiring skills; it is based on a number of interacting knowledge bases, which underpin the skills, qualities and abilities outlined in the standards. The standards are poorly organised, with a division between subject knowledge and teaching. Such a division is inappropriate, once one has an understanding of peda-gogical content knowledge. There is an overemphasis on teaching rather than children's learning. There are no gradations in the standards: they are either there or not there in a teaching performance. In reality, teachers are likely to be better at some aspects or skills of teaching than at others, and a scale with gradations might be an improvement. This has now been suggested in the *Hay McBer Report* (DfEE 2000). A more serious criticism is the fact that they lend themselves to a tick-box mentality in training and assessing teachers. There are far too many of them, and they atomise teaching inappropriately. I would argue that a more holistic and multi-layered approach is necessary. The competence paradigm in general and the standards in particular, are only a partial representation of what it means to teach.

Readers will note that I have left until the end any comment on the paradigm of teaching as an art. This is because the new paradigm of teaching as a knowledge-based profession, has perhaps more in common with teaching as an art than with any other paradigm. Teaching is a deeply complex intellectual and practical activity. I have conceptualised it as a creative act (Turner-Bisset 1999a). As shown in some of the case studies and examples given in this book, teachers select from the store of experience, pedagogical repertoire and wealth of possible representations, the most appropriate teaching approaches and representations for specific learners in particular contexts. Expert teaching is a synthesis of knowledge, skills and understanding from all of the knowledge bases; in deciding which elements to use and fusing them in the act of teaching, teachers are immersed in a creative activity.

This understanding of creativity is based on an idea of it being about synthesis, not so much of original ideas, but of existing ideas and knowledge put together in new and sometimes unexpected ways. Also expert teachers, by verbal and non-verbal channels of communication, create the kind of ethos, in which there is mutual respect, children can speak out and take risks, and in which there is created in children a thirst for learning and an enthusiasm for whatever subject is being taught, as in the example of Kirsty's maths lesson. In this sense the teaching as an art paradigm is present in the new model. However, I would argue that teaching as an art is not innate; it can be taught and learnt. Just as artists may master craft skills in order to create works of art, teachers master a whole range of skills, knowledge and processes, in order to create lessons which engage children and which communicate concepts, facts, skills and attitudes to them.

Thus the new paradigm of teaching as a knowledge-based profession has elements in it of the other paradigms, but I would argue it is a more complete model, because it addresses all of the subjective and syntactic knowledge for teaching. It also has some advantages over the itemised standards and the lists of qualities, skills and dispositions which dominate the findings from research into effective teaching, because the model is underpinned by the knowledge bases described in this book. I offer this conceptualisation of teaching as a source for reflection and professional development. It is useful for beginning teachers in comprehending what they need to know in order to becomes teachers. It is also potentially useful as a framework for professional development. Finally, it might be of use to policy-makers in understanding the complexities of teaching, and the rich and varied knowledge bases which comprise the teacher's expertise. It must be said however, that the model has implications, in particular for primary teachers.

The examples given in this book in the case studies are subject-specific. Teachers have been shown to be teaching well in one subject, and only just adequately or inadequately in others. The case studies have been chosen deliberately to illustrate this point. This happens for a number of reasons. It might be partly because of needing to develop the subject knowledge base in an area of the curriculum, or needing to develop knowledge of particular learners, or one's pedagogical repertoire, or because of contextual factors. Kirsty, who was happy to be labelled an expert teacher of maths, was less happy with English, and with history, because she did not consider she had the pedagogical content knowledge for those subjects. She stated that she did not really know how to go about these subjects in the same way in which she did maths. To be an expert teacher in the primary phase is a massive undertaking. It would be necessary to have subject specific pedagogical content knowledge in all subjects of the primary curriculum. This understanding has implications for the recruitment, training and professional development of primary teachers.

Conclusions

Historically primary teaching, perhaps because of its traditions of altruism and humility, has not attracted the brightest and best candidates for training. It seems to me that we need to seek to attract the most able and talented people we possibly can into the profession, for there is so much knowledge, in the broadest sense of the word, to master across the range of subjects and knowledge bases. The kind of person needed to be an expert primary teacher is the good all-rounder, performing well in all areas of the curriculum and with outside interests and abilties in a wide range of areas such as science, literature, sport, the arts, and drama. In short, we need the most able people, with a passion for learning, rather than those who struggle to write coherently or to pass maths exams. To attract such people, teaching needs to move from being one of the 'minor' professions to being one of the major ones such as medicine or the law. The learning and development of young minds is at least as important as treating illness or handling legal problems. Salaries should reflect the difficult task of developing the highly complex range of knowledge bases needed to be expert teachers in primary schools. The task of initial teacher education is huge, and a key consideration is how to use the time, particularly on one year post-graduate courses, to develop pedagogical content knowledge across a range of subjects.

It is also important to consider that one may not be able to develop all the subject knowledge for primary teaching during initial training. In the reports on both the effective teachers of numeracy (Askew *et al.* 1997) and of literacy (Medwell *et al.* 1998), the influence on the most effective teachers of extended and substantial periods of in-service training was evident. There is also the evidence from the case study of David (Case study 1), with which this book began. He stated that the extended 20-day course in history had not only had a major impact on his history teaching, but in other areas of the curriculum also. To him it was important that the course was extended over a year, that he and his fellow course members had time to reflect on new and sometimes revolutionary ideas, to trial them in their classrooms, to reflect and discuss their experience with their peers and course leaders. To develop deep subject knowledge and pedagogical content knowledge in all areas of the primary curriculum is likely to take years and be an essential part of professional development. In addition, in-service training needs to be substantial and well-supported financially. A day here and there is not really adequate for the kind of professional development under consideration. Thus policy-makers need to understand the kinds of initial and in-service training required by a knowledge-based profession.

There are further implications also. Expert teaching is demanding professionally and personally. It can make huge demands on the self, which may encroach on time outside the job (what there is of it) and on personal and family life. It is important to understand that in conceptualising teaching as a creative act, rather than a series of technical skills, that some consideration needs to be given to renewal. Teachers are not an inexhaustible resource; they need time to recharge their batteries, to pursue their interests which are part of their selves-as-teachers and above all to maintain enthusiasm and passion for teaching and learning. In expert teaching, such as that of David or Kirsty, there is enthusiasm, energy, laughter, joy and fun. These are part of the ethos which expert teachers create; they can only communicate these feelings if they themselves experience them while teaching. They need both the confidence and sense of empowerment which the knowledge bases give them. In addition, they need freshness and energy, which they are unlikely to have if they are worn down by unnecessary bureaucracy and inspection. Teaching is a creative activity and because of this it is hard to do it well when one is exhausted.

Expert teaching

Perhaps some of the final words in this book should come from one of the teachers. Kirsty was remarkable for the positive ethos she created in her classroom: an atmosphere in which it was not only acceptable to speak up and take risks, but one in which it was expected. She talked of teachers operating at the cusp of the children's understanding: taking them to where they were just pushing forward the boundaries of their knowledge and understanding. At the same time she was actively generating a positive attitude towards maths. She had this to say about the nature of teaching:

> Kirsty: Teaching is not common sense; it is not intuitive. Not just anyone can do it – definitely not. I know that because I am a musician, and when I started, I was given music to coordinate. I knew how to play the violin, but I didn't know how to get the steps up to it. I knew then that it wasn't intuitive.

The problem for her as a beginning teacher was in not having developed the pedagogical content knowledge for music, although she was a music specialist. She recognised that this knowledge had to be developed. She had clear ideas about what made an expert teacher:

> Kirsty: I think it's good subject knowledge, and having excellent relationships with the children. Expert teachers are those that have good pace, and they assess and their assessment informs planning, like a continuous cycle all the time; and it's moving forward, not standing still. They evaluate their lessons and then improve and build on them. I think it's teachers who are jackdaws and are very open to good practice around them. I'm like a jackdaw: I pick up and use that, and apply that and

modify that. It's just always moving forward and never standing still: thinking I can learn, and there's more to learn out there. It's just having a hunger to improve all the time.

The notion of teachers as jackdaws resonates with the understanding of curriculum knowledge and a pedagogical repertoire. Teachers constantly borrow and adapt ideas from elsewhere and from other teachers, but in making them their own they are engaging in the creative synthesis of knowledge bases. Expert teaching was for Kirsty characterised by drive and movement: she spoke of the response of the children driving her on, driving her teaching. She saw it as constantly improving and constantly moving forward. For this one needs both energy and enthusiasm, as well as a long-term commitment to the development and learning of the children one teaches. She further understood the need for metacognition in teachers and used the analogy of children becoming experts to explain her understanding:

Kirsty: I think to be an expert teacher, you have to be able to articulate your thought processes clearly, and that should extend to being able to talk about your subject just as well as your thinking. It's like my children today. Some of them could give me the answer, but couldn't say how they had worked it out. So that's the next step on really, to be able to apply it to different situations, and it's like that with a teacher. You think: 'Oh this worked in this situation, and it worked really well. Can I modify it, change it, so I can apply it to another area of the curriculum, or a different class, or a different child?'

Expert teachers analyse and develop their understanding of teaching and all the knowledge bases which underpin it. Their understanding of their work is not tacit. To be expert, as Kirsty stated, one needs to be articulate about the knowledge, thought processes, skills and attitudes needed for high-quality teaching. In understanding that knowledge bases mesh together in different combinations, and that pedagogical content knowledge is organic, constantly changing and developing, expert teachers realise that their knowledge needs revisiting and reconstructing through the daily acts of teaching, and through having time to reflect on their teaching. They have energy, drive, a passion for learning and for the subjects they teach and they communicate enthusiasm and joy in learning. They also, as Kirsty stated, create a thirst for learning in the children they teach. It is my personal belief, based on the case studies and evidence from the research projects from which they come, that one cannot generate such enthusiasm or passion, or thirst for knowledge, in a conception of the job which might as well be teaching by numbers. Expert teachers are self-empowered professionals: it is for them to spell out to policy-makers the nature of teaching. The model of knowledge bases can help teachers to be articulate about the job, and to empower them as professionals.

References

Abell, S. K. and Smith, D. C. (1994) 'What is science? Preservice elementary teachers' conceptions of the nature of science', *International Journal of Science Education* **16**(4), 475–87.

Alexander, R. J. (1984) *Primary Teaching*. London: Holt, Rinehart and Winston.

Alexander, R. J. (1992) *Policy and Practice in Primary Education*. London: Routledge.

Alexander, R. J. (1995) *Versions of Primary Education*. London: Open University/ Routledge.

Alexander, *et al.* (1992) *Curriculum Organisation and Classroom Practice in Primary Schools: A discussion paper*. London: DES.

Askew, M. *et al.* (1997) *Effective Teachers of Numeracy*. Final report of a study carried out for the Teacher Training Agency, 1995–96 by the School of Education, King's College, London.

Bage, G. (1999) *Narrative Matters: Teaching and learning history through story*. London: Falmer.

Ball, D. (1988a) *Knowledge and Reasoning in Mathematical Pedagogy: Examining what prospective teachers bring to teacher education*. Unpublished doctoral dissertation, Michigan State University, East Lancing.

Ball, D. (1988b) 'Prospective teachers' understandings of mathematics: What do they bring with them to teacher education?' paper presented at the annual meeting of the American Educational Research Association, New Orleans.

Ball, D. (1990a) 'With an eye on the mathematical horizon: dilemmas in teaching elementary school mathematics', paper given at the annual meeting of the American Educational Research Association, Boston.

Ball, D. (1990b) 'The mathematical understandings that prospective teachers bring to teacher education', *The Elementary School Journal* **90**(4) 449–66.

Banks, F. *et al.* (1996) 'Knowledge, school knowledge and pedagogy: reconceptualising curricula and defining a research agenda', paper presented at the European Conference for Education Research, Seville, Spain.

Bassey, M. (1977) *Nine Hundred Primary School Teachers*. Nottingham Primary Research Project. Nottingham: Trent Polytechnic.

Bennett, S. N. (1976) *Teaching Styles and Pupil Progress*. London: Open Books.

Bennett, S. N. (1982) 'Time to teach: teaching processes in primary schools', *Aspects of Education* 27.

Bennett, S. N. (1987) 'The search for the effective primary teacher', in Delamont, S. (ed.) *The Primary School Teacher*. London: The Falmer Press, Taylor and Francis.

Bennett, S. N. (1995) 'Managing learning through group work', in Desforges, C. (ed.) *An Introduction to Teaching: Psychological Perspectives*. Oxford: Blackwell.

Bennett, S. N. and Carre, C. G. (eds) (1993) *Learning to Teach*. London: Routledge.

Bennett, S. N. and Dunne, E. (1992) *Managing Classroom Groups*. Hemel Hempstead: Simon and Schuster.

Bennett, S. N. and Turner-Bisset, R. A. (1993a) 'Knowledge bases and teaching performance', in Bennett, S. N. and Carre, C. G. (eds) *Learning to Teach*, 149–64. London: Routledge.

Bennett, S. N. and Turner-Bisset, R. A. (1993b) 'Case studies in learning to teach', in Bennett, S. N. and Carre, C. G. (eds) *Learning to Teach*, 165–90. London: Routledge.

Bennett, S. N. *et al.* (1984) *The Quality of Pupil Learning Experiences*. London: Erlbaum Associates.

Bennett, S. N. *et al.* (1991) 'The impact of training on the quality of social interaction in co-operative groups', paper presented at the European Association for Research on Learning and Instruction conference, Turku, Finland.

Bennett, S. N. *et al.* (1992) 'A longitudinal study of primary teachers' perceived competence in, and concerns about National Curriculum implementation', *Research Papers in Education* 7(1), 53–78.

Blyth, W. A. L. (1965) *English Primary Education: A sociological description: Volume 1: Schools*. London: Routledge and Kegan Paul.

Blyth, W. A. L. *et al.* (1976) *Place, Time and Society 8–13: Curriculum planning in history, geography and social science*. Glasgow: Collins/ESL.

Brown, G. (1995) 'What is involved in learning', in Desforges, C. (ed.) *An Introduction to Teaching: Psychological perspectives*. Oxford: Blackwell.

Brown, M. *et al.* (1998) 'Is the National Numeracy Strategy research-based?', *British Journal of Educational Studies* 46(4), 362–85.

Brown, S. and McIntyre, D. (1993) *Making Sense of Teaching*. Buckingham: Open University Press.

Bruner, J. (1966a) *The Process of Education*. Cambridge, Mass: Harvard University Press.

Bruner, J. (1966b) *Towards a Theory of Instruction*. Cambridge, Mass: Harvard University Press.

Bruner, J. (1970) 'The course of cognitive growth', in Klintz, B. L. and Brunig, J. (eds) *Research in Psychology*, 289–96. New York: Scott, Foresman and Co.

Bruner, J. (1971) *The Relevance of Education*. New York: W. W. Norton and Co.

Buchmann, M. (1987) 'Teaching knowledge: the lights that teachers live by', *Oxford Review of Education* 13(2), 151–64.

Burns, H. W. and Brauner, C. J. (1962) *Philosophy of Education, Essays and Commentaries*. New York: The Ronald Press Company.

Calderhead, J. (ed.) (1988) *Teachers' Professional Learning*. Lewes: Falmer Press.

Calderhead, J. (1989) 'Reflective teaching and teacher education', *Teaching and Teacher Education* 5(1), 43–51.

Calderhead, J. (1992) ' The nature and growth of knowledge in student teaching', *Teaching and Teacher Education* 7(5/6), 531–35.

Calderhead, J. and Robson, M. (1991) 'Images of teaching: student teachers' early conceptions of classroom practice', *Teaching and Teacher Education* 7, 1–8.

Carey, T. (ed.) (1995) *The Faber Book of Science*. London: Faber and Faber.

Carpenter, T. P. *et al.* (1988) 'Teachers' pedagogical content knowledge of students' problem solving in elementary arithmetic', *Journal for Research in Mathematics Education* 19, 385–401.

Carr, E. H. (1964) *What is History?* Harmonsdworth: Penguin.

Carre, C. G. (1993) 'Knowledge bases for science', in Bennett, S. N. and Carre, C. G. (eds) *Learning to Teach*. London: Routledge.

Carre, C. G. (1995) 'What is to be learned in school', in Desforges, C. (ed.) *An Introduction to Teaching: Psychological perspectives*. Oxford: Blackwell.

Central Advisory Council for Education (CACE) (England) (1967) *Children and their Primary Schools*. (The Plowden Report.) London: HMSO.

Cobb, P. *et al.* (1988) 'Curriculum and teacher development, psychological and anthropological perspectives', in Fennema, E. *et al.* (eds) *Integrating Research on Teaching and Learning Mathematics*. Madison: Wisconsin Centre for Education Research.

Cochran, K. F. *et al.* (1993) 'Pedagogical content knowing: an integrative model for teacher preparation', *Journal of Teacher Education* 44(4), 263–72.

Cockburn, A. D. (1995) 'Learning in classrooms', in Desforges, C. (ed.) *An Introduction to Teaching: Psychological perspectives*. Oxford: Blackwell.

Collins, A. *et al.* (1989) 'Cognitive apprenticeship: teaching the crafts of reading, writing, and mathematics', in Resnick, L. B. (ed.) *Knowing, Learning and Instruction: Essays in honour of Robert Glaser*, 453–94. Hillsdale, NJ: Erlbaum.

Cooper, P. and McIntyre, D. (1996) *Effective Teaching and Learning*. Milton Keynes: Open University Press.

Crawford, K. (1996) 'Packaging the past: the primary history curriculum and how to teach it', *Curriculum Studies* 4(3), 401–16.

Cullingford, C. (1995) *The Effective Teacher*. London: Cassell.

DES (1967) Children and Their Primary Schools. A Report of Central Advisory Council for Education (England) (The Plowden Report) Chairman Lady B. Plowden. London: HMSO.

DES (1972) *Teacher Education and Training*. A report by a committee of enquiry appointed by the Secretary of State for Education and Science, under the chairmanship of Lord James of Rusholme. HMSO: London.

DES (1983) *Teaching Quality*. London: HMSO.

DES (1984) *Initial Teacher Training: Approval of Courses*. Circular 3/84. London: HMSO.

DES (1989a) *Education Reform Act (1988): The School Curriculum and Assessment*. Circular 5/89. London: DES.

DES (1989b) *Initial Teacher Training: Approval of Courses*. Circular 24/89. London, DES.

Desforges, C. and Cockburn, A. (1987) *Understanding the Mathematics Teacher*. Lewes: Falmer Press.

Desforges, C. and McNamara, D. (1979) 'Theory and practice: methodological procedures of the objectification of craft knowledge', *British Journal of Teacher Education* 5(2), 139–52.

DFE (1992) *Initial Teacher Training (Primary Phase)*. Circular 9/92. London: DFE.

DFE (1993a) *The Initial Training of Primary School Teachers: New Criteria for Courses*. Circular 14/93. London: DFE.

DFE (1993b) *The National Curriculum and its Assessment* (The Dearing Report). London: SCAA.

DfEE (1998a) *Teaching: High Status; High Standards: Requirements for courses of initial teacher training*. Circular 4/98. London: DfEE

DfEE (1998b) *The National Literacy Strategy: Framework for teaching*. London: DfEE.

DfEE (1999a) *All Our Futures: Creativity, culture and education*. National Advisory Committee on Creative and Cultural Education. Sudbury: DfEE.

DfEE (1999b) *The National Numeracy Strategy: Framework for teaching mathematics from Reception to Year 6*. London: DfEE.

DfEE (1999c) *The National Curriculum*. London: QCA/DfEE/HMSO.

DfEE (2000) *Hay McBer Report*. London: DfEE.

Dickens, C. (1854) *Hard Times*. Harmondsworth, Middlesex, England: Penguin Edition (1969).

Donaldson, M. (1978) *Children's Minds*. London: Fontana.

Eisner, E. W. (1985) *The Educational Imagination: On the design and evaluation of school programmes*, 2nd edn. New York: Macmillan.

Elbaz, F. (1983) *Teacher Thinking: A study of practical knowledge*. New York: Nicholls Publishing.

Elton, G. R. (1969) *The Practice of History*. London: Fontana.

Eraut, M. (1989) 'What is learned in in-service education and how?' *British Journal of In-Service Education* 9(1), 6–14.

Eraut, M. (1994) *Developing Professional Knowledge and Competence*. London: The Falmer Press.

Ernest, P. (1988) 'The attitudes and practices of student teachers of primary school mathematics', *Proceedings of the XIIth International Psychology of Mathematics Education Conference, Volume 1*. Veszprem, Hungary: OOK.

Ernest, P. (1989) 'The knowledge, beliefs and attitudes of the mathematics teacher: A Model', *Journal of Education for Teaching* 15(1), 13–33.

Ernest, P. (1991) *The Philosophy of Mathematics Education*. London: Falmer Press.

Evans, R. W. (1994) 'Educational ideologies and the teaching of history', in Leinhardt, G. *et al.* (eds) *Teaching and Learning in History*. New Jersey: Laurence Erlbaum Associates.

Evans, R. (1997) *In Defence of History*. London: Granta Books.

Feiman-Nemser, S. and Buchmann, M. (1989) 'Describing teacher education: a framework and illustrative findings from a longitudinal study of six students', *Elementary School Journal* 89, 365–77.

Feldman, D. H. (1980) *Beyond Universals in Cognitive Development*. Norwood, NJ: Ablex.

Fines, J. (1994) 'Creating a classroom for learning', *Nuffield Primary History Project, Newsletter No. 2*. Exeter: University of Exeter.

Fines, J. and Nichol, J. (1997) *Teaching Primary History*. Oxford: Heinmann.

Flanders, N. A. (1970) *Analyzing Teaching Behavior*. Reading, Mass: Addison-Wesley.

Foss, D. H. and Kleinsasser, R. C. (1996) 'Preservice elementary teachers' views of pedagogical and mathematical content knowledge', *Teaching and Teacher Education* 12(4), 429–42.

Fox, R. (1995) 'Development and learning', in Desforges, C. (ed.) *An Introduction to Teaching: Psychological perspectives*. Oxford: Blackwell.

Galileo, G. (1610) 'The starry messenger (Siderius Nuncius)', in Carey, J. (ed.) (1995) *The Faber Book of Science*. London: Faber and Faber.

Galton, M. (1987) 'An ORACLE chronicle: a decade of classroom research', *Teaching and Teacher Education* 3(4).

Galton, M. and Simon, B. (eds) (1980) *Progress and Performance in the Primary Classroom*. London: Routledge and Kegan Paul.

Galton, M. *et al.* (1980) *Inside the Primary Classroom*. London: Routledge and Kegan Paul.

Gardner, P. (1993) 'The early history of school-based teacher training', in McIntyre, D. *et al.* (eds) *Mentoring: Perspectives on school-based teacher education*. London: Kogan Page.

Gipps, C. (1992) 'What we know about effective primary teaching', in *The London File: Papers from the Institute of Education*. London: The Tufnell Press.

Graves, D. (1983) *Writing: Children and teachers at work*. Exeter, NH: Heinemann.

Grossman, P. L. (1987) 'A tale of two teachers: the role of subject matter orientation in teaching', paper presented at the Annual Meeting of the American Educational Research Association. Washington, DC.

Grossman, P. L. (1988) *A Study in Contrast: Sources of pedagogical content knowledge for secondary English*. Unpublished doctoral dissertation, Stanford University, Stanford, CA.

Grossman, P. L. (1989) 'Learning to teach without teacher education,' *Teachers College Record* 91, 192–208.

Grossman, P. L. *et al.* (1989) 'Teachers of substance: subject matter knowledge for teaching', in Reynolds, M. C. (ed.) *Knowledge Base for the Beginning Teacher*. New York: Pergamon.

Gudmundsdottir, S. and Shulman, L. S. (1987) 'Pedagogical content knowledge in social studies', *Scandinavian Journal of Educational Studies* 31, 59–70.

Hargreaves, D. (1993) 'A common-sense model of the professional development of teachers', in Elliott, J. (ed.) *Reconstructing Teacher Education*, 86–92. Lewes: Falmer Press.

Hauslein, P. L. and Good, R. (1989) 'Biology content cognitive structure of biology majors, biology teachers and scientists', paper presented at the 62nd annual meeting of the National Association for Research in Science Teaching, San Francisco.

Highet, G. (1963) *The Art of Teaching*. London: Methuen.

Hirst, P. H. and Peters, R. S. (1970) *The Logic of Education*. London: Routledge and Kegan Paul.

HMI (1978) *Primary Education in England: A survey by HM Inspectors of Schools*. London: HMSO.

HMI (1983) *9–13 Middle Schools: An alternative survey*. London: HMSO.

HMI (1992) *The New Teacher in School*. London: HMSO.

Jackson, P. W. (1968) *Life in Classrooms*. New York: Holt, Rinehart and Winston.

Kagan, D. M. (1992) 'Professional growth among preservice and beginning teachers', *Review of Educational Research* 62(2), 129–69.

King, R. (1978) *All Things Bright and Beautiful? A Sociological Study of Infant Classrooms*. Chichester: Wiley.

Korthagen, F. A. J. (1988) 'The influence of learning orientations on the development of reflective teaching', in Calderhead, J. (ed.) *Teachers' Professional Learning*, 35–50. Lewes: Falmer Press.

Kounin, J. S. (1970) *Discipline and Group Management in Classrooms*. London: Holt, Rinehart and Winston.

Kounin, J. S. (1983) 'Classrooms: individuals or behaviour settings', *Monographs in Teaching and Learning, No. 2*. Bloomington, IN University School of Education.

Kyriacou, C. (1997) *Effective Teaching in Schools: Theory and practice*. Cheltenham: Stanley Thornes.

Lampert, M. (1981) 'How teachers manage to teach: perspectives on the unsolvable dilemmas on teaching practice', *Dissertation Abstracts International* 42, 3122A. (University Microfilms No. 81–126, 203).

Lampert, M. (1984) 'Teaching about thinking and thinking about teaching', *Journal of Curriculum Studies* 16, 1–18.

Lampert, M. (1985) 'How do teachers manage to teach? Perspectives on problems in practice', *Harvard Educational Review* 5(5), 178–94.

Lawlor, S. (1990) *Teachers Mistaught: Training in theories or education in subjects?* London: Centre for Policy Studies.

Leinhardt, G. (1988) 'Situated knowledge and expertise in teaching', in Calderhead, J. (ed.) *Teachers' Professional Learning*, 35–51. London: Falmer Press.

Leith, G. O. M. (1964) 'A handbook of programmed learning, Birmingham England', *Birmingham University, Educational Review Occasional Publications No. 1*.

Lerman, S. (1990) 'Alternative perspectives of the nature of mathematics and their influence on the teaching of mathematics', *British Educational Research Journal* 16(1), 53–61.

Lewis, M. and Wray, D. (1995) *Developing Children's Non-fiction Writing: Working with writing frames*. Leamington Spa: Scholastic.

Lortie, D. C. (1975) *Schoolteachers: A sociological study*. Chicago: University of Chicago Press.

McDiarmid, G. W. and Wilson, S. (1991) 'An exploration of the subject matter knowledge of alternative route teachers: can we assume they know their subject?' *Journal of Teacher Education* 42(4), 93–103.

McDiarmid, G. W. *et al.* (1989) 'Why staying one chapter ahead doesn't really work: subject specific pedagogy', in Reynolds, M. C. (ed.) *Knowledge Base for the Beginning Teacher*. New York: Pergamon.

McEwan, H. and Bull, B. (1991) 'The pedagogic nature of subject matter knowledge', *American Educational Research Journal* 28(2), 316–34.

McIntyre, D. (1992) 'Theory, theorising and reflection in initial teacher education', in

Calderhead, J. (ed.) *Conceptualising Reflection in Teacher Development*. London: Falmer.

McNamara, D. (1991) 'Subject knowledge and its application: problems and possibilites for teacher educators', *Journal of Education for Teaching* 17(2), 113–28.

McNamara, D. and Desforges, C. (1979) 'Professional studies as a source of theory', in Alexander, R. and Wormald, E. (eds) *Professional Studies for Teaching*. Teacher Education Study Group, Society for Research into Higher Education, University of Surrey: Guildford.

Marks, R. (1990) 'Pedagogical content knowledge: from a mathematical case to a modified conception', *Journal of Teacher Education* 41(3), 3–11.

Masterman, M. (1972) 'The nature of a paradigm', in Lakatos, I. and Musgrave, A, (eds) *Criticism and the Growth of Knowledge*, 59–89. Cambridge: Cambridge University Press.

Medwell, J. *et al.* (1998) *Effective Teachers of Literacy*. A report of a research project commissioned by the Teacher Training Agency. Exeter: University of Exeter.

Meloth, M. S. *et al.* (1989) 'Teachers' concepts of reading, reading instruction, and students' concepts of reading', *Journal of Teacher Education* 30(5), 33–9.

Meredith, A. (1995) 'Terry's learning: some limitations of Shulman's pedagogical content knowledge', *Cambridge Journal of Education* 25(2), 176–87.

Mortimore, P. *et al.* (1988) *School Matters: The junior years*. London: Open Book Publishers.

Munby, H. and Russell, T. (1989) 'Educating the reflective teacher: an essay review of two books by Donald Schon', *Journal of Curriculum Studies* 21(7), 71–80.

Namier, L. B. (1927) *The Structure of Politics at the Accession of George III*. London: Routledge and Kegan Paul.

NCC (1993) *The National Curriculum at Key Stages 1 and 2*. York: National Curriculum Council.

Newton, D. P. and Newton, H. D. (1998) 'Knowing what counts in history: historical understanding and the non-specialist teacher', *Teaching History* August 92, 42–5.

Nias, J. (1989) *Primary Teachers Talking: A study of teaching as work*. London: Routledge.

Norman, D. A. (1978) 'Notes towards a complex theory of learning', in Lesgold, A. M. *et al.* (eds) *Cognitive Psychology and Instruction*. New York: Plenum.

OECD (Centre for Educational Research and Innovation) (1994) *Making Education Count: Developing and using international indicators*. London: Organisation for Economic Co-operation and Development.

OFSTED (1993a) *Curriculum Organisation and Classroom Practice in Primary Schools: A follow-up report*. London: DFE.

OFSTED (1993b) *Primary Matters: A discussion on teaching and learning in primary schools*. London: DFE.

Opie, I. and P. (1969) *Children's Games in Street and Playground*. Oxford: Oxford University Press.

Ormrod, J. E and Cole, D. B. (1996) 'Teaching content knowledge and pedagogical content knowledge: a model from geographic education', *Journal of Teacher Education* 47(1), 37–42.

Perrott, E. (1982) *Effective Teaching: A practical guide to improving your teaching*. London: Longman.

Peters, R. S. (1965) 'Education as initiation', in Archambault, R. D. (ed.) *Philosophical Analysis and Education*. London: Routledge and Kegan Paul.

Peterson *et al.* (1989) 'Teachers' pedagogical content beliefs in mathematics', *Cognition and Instruction* 6(1), 1–40.

Phillips, R. (1998) *History Teaching, Nationhood and the State*. London: Continuum Publishing Group.

Piaget, J. (1959) *The Language and Thought of the Child*, 3rd edn. London: Routledge.

Popper. K. (1961) *The Poverty of Historicism*. London: Routledge and Kegan Paul.

Pring, R. (1976) *Knowledge and Schooling*. London: Open Books.

Pungo, L. (ed.) *The Structure of Knowledge and the Curriculum*. Chicago: Rand McNally.

QCA (1998) *Maintaining Breadth and Balance at Key Stages 1 and 2*. London: QCA.

Rosen, B. (1990) *And None of it was Nonsense: The power of storytelling in school*. London: Mary Glasgow Publications.

Rosenshine, B. and Furst, A. F. (1973) 'The use of direct observation to study teaching', in Travers, R. M. (ed.) *Second Handbook of Research on Teaching*. Chicago: Rand McNally.

Roth, K. J. (1989) 'Subject matter knowledge for teaching science', paper presented at the annual meeting of the American Education Research Association, San Francisco 1989.

Rovegno, I. C. (1992) 'Learning to teach in a field-based methods course: the development of pedagogical content knowledge', *Teaching and Teacher Education* 8(1), 69–82.

Ryan, D. (1960) *Characteristics of Teachers*. Washington DC: American Council on Education.

Ryle, G. (1949) *The Concept of Mind*. London: Hutchinson.

Schon, D. A. (1983) *The Reflective Practitioner: How professionals think in action*. New York: Basic Books.

Schon, D. A. (1987) *Educating the Reflective Practitioner*. San Francisco: Jossey-Bass.

Schuck, S. (1997) 'Using a research simulation to challenge prospective teachers' beliefs about mathematics', *Teaching and Teacher Education* 13(5), 529–39.

Schwab, J. J. (1964) 'The structure of the disciplines: meanings and significances', in Ford, G. and Purgo, L. (eds) *The Structure of Knowledge and the Curriculum*. Chicago: Rand McNally.

Schwab, J. (1978) 'Education and the structure of the disciplines', in Westbury, I. and Wilkof, N. J. (eds) *Science, Curriculum and Liberal Education*, 229–72. Chicago: University of Chicago Press.

Shulman, L. S. (1986a) 'Paradigms and research programmes in the study of teaching: a contemporary perspective', in Wittrock, M. C. (ed.) *Handbook of Research On Teaching*, 3rd edn, 505–26. New York: Macmillan.

Shulman, L. S. (1986b) 'Those who understand: knowledge growth in teaching', *Educational Researcher* 15(2), 4–14.

Shulman, L. S. (1987a) 'Knowledge and teaching: foundations of the new reform', *Harvard Educational Review* 57(1), 1–22.

Shulman, L. S. (1987b) 'Sounding an alarm: a reply to Sockett', *Harvard Educational Review* 57(2), 473–82.

Silberstein, M and Tamir, P. (1991) 'The expert case study model: an alternative approach to the development of teacher education modules', *Journal of Education for Teaching* 17(2), 165–79.

Simon, B. (1981) 'Why no pedagogy in England?' in Simon, B. and Taylor, W. (eds) *Education in the Eighties: The central issues*. London: Batsford Educational.

Simon, B. and Wilcocks, J. (eds) (1981) *Research and Practice in the Primary Classroom*. London: Routledge and Kegan Paul.

Skinner, B. F. (1938) *The Behaviour of Organisms: An experimental analysis*. New York: Appleton-Century-Crofts.

Smith, D. C. and Neale, D. C. (1989) 'The construction of subject matter knowledge in primary science teaching', *Teaching and Teacher Education* 5(1), 1–20.

Sockett, H. (1987) 'Has Shulman Got the Strategy Right?' *Harvard Educational Review* 57(2), 208–19.

Squires, G. (1999) *Teaching as a Professional Discipline*. London: Falmer.

Stein, M. K. *et al*. (1990) 'Subject matter knowledge and elementary instruction: a case from functions and graphing', *American Educational Research Journal* 27(4), 639–63.

Steinem, G. (1992) *Revolution From Within: A Book of self-esteem*. London: Bloomsbury.

Stone, L. (1981) 'History and the social sciences in the twenty-first century', in Stone, L. (ed.) *Past and Present*. London.

Stones, E. (1992) *Quality Teaching: A sample of cases*. London: Routledge.

Sulzby, E. (1988) 'A study of children's early reading development', in Pellegrini, A. (ed.) *Psychological Bases for Early Education*. Chichester: Wiley.

Tauber, R. T. and Mester, C. S. (1995) *Acting Lessons for Teachers: Using performance skills in the Classroom*. Pennsylvania: Greenwood Publishing Group.

Tharp, R. and Gallimore, R. (1988) 'A theory of teaching as assisted performance', in Tharp, R. and Gallimore, R. (eds) *Rousing Minds to Life: Teaching, learning and schooling in social context*. New York: Cambridge University Press.

Thompson, I. (1984) 'The relationship of teachers' conceptions of mathematics and mathematics teaching to instructional practice', *Educational Studies in Mathematics* 15, 105–27.

Tom, A. R. (1984) *Teaching as a Moral Craft*. London: Longman.

Trevelyan, G. M. (1913) '*Clio: A muse, and other essays*', London: Longmans, Green and Company.

Turner-Bisset, R. A. (1997) *Subject Matter Knowledge and Teaching Competence*. Unpublished doctoral thesis, University of Exeter.

Turner-Bisset, R. A. (1999a) 'The knowledge bases of the expert teacher', *British Educational Research Journal* 25(1), 39–55.

Turner-Bisset, R. A. (1999b) 'History is boring and all about dead people: challenging non-specialist primary teachers' beliefs about history', in Phillips, R. and Easedown, G. (eds) *History Education: Subject knowledge, pedagogy and practice*, 65–83. Standing Conference of History Teacher Educators in the United Kingdom.

Turner-Bisset, R. A. (2000a) 'Reconstructing the primary curriculum: integration revisited', *Education 3–13* 28(1), 3–8.

Turner-Bisset, R. A. (2000b) 'Meaningful history with young children', in Drury, R. *et al*. (eds) *Looking at Early Years Education and Care*. London: David Fulton Publishers.

Turner-Bisset, R. A. (2000c) 'Beliefs and practice in teaching primary History', paper presented at the British Educational Research Conference, Cardiff.

Turner-Bisset, R. A. and Nichol, J. (1999) 'A sense of professionalism: the impact of twenty-day courses in subject knowledge on the professional development of teachers', *Teacher Development* 2(3), 433–54.

Van De Groot, A. D. (1965) *Thought and Choice in Chess.* The Hague: Mouton.

Vygotsky, L. S. (1962) *Thought and Language.* Cambridge, MA: MI Press.

Vygotsky, L. S. (1978) *Mind and Society.* Cambridge, MA: Harvard University Press.

Wilson, S. M. (1989) *A Case Concerning Content: Using case studies to teach subject matter.* East Lancing, MI: National Centre for Research on Teacher Education, Michigan State University.

Wilson, S. M. and Wineburg, S. S. (1988) 'Peering at history with different lenses: the role of disciplinary perspectives in teaching history', *Teachers' College Record* 89, 525–39.

Wilson, S. M. *et al.* (1987) '150 different ways of knowing: representations of knowledge in teaching', in Calderhead, J. (ed.) *Exploring Teachers' Thinking*, 104–25. London: Cassell.

Wolfe, J. M. and Murray, C. K. (1990) 'Negotiating a stance toward subject matter: the acquisition of pedagogical knowledge in student teaching', paper presented at the annual meeting of the American Education Research Conference, Boston.

Wood, D. (1988) *How Children Think and Learn.* Oxford: Blackwell.

Woodhead, C. (1996) 'Hard lines', *Panorama*, BBC1, broadcast on 7 June.

Woods, P. and Jeffrey, B. (1996) *Teachable Moments: The art of teaching in primary schools.* Buckingham: Open University Press.

Wragg, E. C. (1984) *Classroom Teaching Skills: The research findings of the Teacher Education Project.* Beckenham, Kent: Croom Helm.

Wragg, E. C. (1993) *Class Management.* London: Routledge.

Wragg, E. C. (1997) *The Cubic Curriculum.* London: Routledge.

Wragg, E. C. *et al.* (1989) 'Primary teachers and the National Curriculum', *Research Papers in Education* 4, 17–37.

Wray, D. and Lewis, M. (1997) *Extending Literacy: Children reading and writing non-fiction.* London: Routledge.

Young, M. F. D. (ed.) (1971) *Knowledge and Control: New directions for the sociology of education* [Durham Conference of the British Sociological Association of April 1970] London: Collier-Macmillan.

Young, M. F. D. (1998) *The Curriculum of the Future: From the 'new sociology of education' to a critical theory of Learning.* Basingstoke: Falmer Press.

Zeichner, K. M. *et al.* (1987) 'Individual, institutional, and cultural influences on the development of teachers' craft knowledge', in Calderhead, J. (ed.) *Exploring Teachers' Thinking*, 21–59. London: Cassell.

Index